healing that extends throughout their marriage and deep into their family life. Ultimately, their story is of grace, where we can cease striving and rest in our identity as beloved children of Jesus.

—STEVE SHACKELFORD, Chief Executive Officer,
Redeemer City to City

How to review *Savage Marriage*? It's HOT! Read this book, and put it into practice! It's one couple's story but much more. It's amazing truth that can help set you free and strengthen and encourage individuals and couples. Phil, Priscilla, and family share their stories of how Jesus redeems and sets free (from sexual addiction) husbands, wives, and families to be the image-bearers He created us to be for His glory and our good. I could not put this book down. My wife and I are working together through the helpful study questions at the end of each chapter. *Best* book I have read in a long, long time!

—LEE WOOD, Founder, 1Body Church,
Global Catalyst and Movement Leader

Phil Fretwell has been my friend for over forty-five years. I've known him before, during, and after this journey through darkness, pain, healing, and now fruitfulness. Phil and Priscilla were willing to seek God not just about their problems but to find the roots of their problems. In the process, they discovered that fear and ego blocked them but that God alone could free them and heal them. Their story is raw and real, but their bravery in sharing their savage marriage will inspire bravery for others to find beauty for ashes and discover for themselves that truth indeed sets us free and keeps us free.

—TIM GILLIGAN, DMin, Lead Pastor, Meadowbrook Church

Real, raw, and wise—*Savage Marriage* is the book the Christian community has needed for years. We must move away from saying we feel *good* or *blessed* and learn to speak truth to the depth of our suffering and then seek to experience the fullness of life. *Savage Marriage* is a resource for all Christians when we're ready to be honest about our sin.

—JOHN CROSSMAN, CEO, Crossman Career Builders, Author of
Career Killers/Career Builders: The Book Every Millennial Should Read

We have known Phil and Priscilla for eighteen years. We've camped with them, raised kids together, and even served at our local church together. When Phil came clean, it was the first time I (Doug) could see clearly the path to freedom in my own life. The day I confessed to similar territory in front of Priscilla was the first time I experienced Jesus's hope in my life and hope for my marriage and family. We have watched, from a front-row seat, Phil and Priscilla choose freedom over bondage, with boldness. Their humility encourages others to become vulnerable, and allows the Holy Spirit to minister in ways we've never seen before. Our hope is that the song of freedom from bondage in the pages of *Savage Marriage* will be heard and received by many.

—DOUG & WENDY GOHN

There are rare times when we come to both greatly admire a book *and* recognize that the story we read was something we desperately needed. *Savage Marriage* is that combination. Phil and Priscilla shockingly tear down the facade that barely concealed the pretense of a "good Christian marriage" to reveal what each of us fears while at the same time longs for—healing and restoration. My experience in the pages of this book was anxiety and awe, compelling me to say: read this book!

—TIM GREGORY, LMFT

Over the last few years, Phil and Priscilla have amazed me with their humility and candor as they've walked out their deliverance from sexual sin. God has used their story to set many others free, and it will do that for you too.

—JEFF WIELAND

Savage Marriage is a gripping true story of hope and how God can help you overcome and navigate seemingly insurmountable obstacles in your marriage.

—STAN MILLER, Founder, Storicate

Savage Marriage gives hope to the hopeless by providing a proven path to God's power that breaks the chains of sexual addiction and releases his grace to restore broken marriages.

—DOMINIC SPUTO, Founder, Alliance for Persecuted Christians,
Author of *Heirloom Love: Authentic Christianity in This Age of Persecution*

I've worked with countless couples searching for answers on how to save their marriages. *Savage Marriage* unlocks secrets that can get you to the other side of all "the junk" accumulated in your life and marriage. Phil and Priscilla's story is riveting but, more importantly, transparent as they allow you into their lives. There are so many books written on marriage that are good, but few are as needed and necessary as this book.

—NORM DUBOIS, Lead Pastor,
East Coast Believers Church

You've heard many stories of marriages failing because of betrayal or sexual addiction, but not like this one. What would happen if a husband and wife came together to heal? Then what would happen if they found the courage to share their pain with their children and closest friends? "What would happen?" is answered in this book. In these pages, a broken man and a shattered woman tell their story that reflects God's heart for restoration. Marriage doesn't have to end because of secrets and shame, but it does have to change. *Savage Marriage* shows you how.

—DWIGHT BAIN, Nationally Certified Counselor,
Executive Coach, Author

This book is unlike most Christian marriage books. It gets to some of the primary root issues that have sabotaged marital relationships for decades and are rarely discussed in the church world. So many marriage books begin with the "ideal" and talk about how to avoid the broken places, and they're authored by those who either haven't been restored from significant brokenness or haven't yet faced their own. This book, however, begins with the broken places that often go unspoken in Christian circles and then moves us toward more holistic, realistic, and sustainable practices. Phil and Priscilla have become wounded healers in this space. I love this book. I'm very hopeful that *Savage Marriage* will be read far and wide by couples who need resurrection and introduced as a significant part of real, authentic marriage groups in the church.

—DAVID LOVELESS, Executive Director
of Campuses & Leadership Development,
First Baptist Church of Orlando, Author of *Nothing to Prove*

Savage Marriage is a lifeline of hope and encouragement for all couples who want to enjoy more spiritual, emotional, and physical intimacy. Phil and Priscilla's vulnerability will captivate your emotions, allowing you to feel and experience healing and restoration that's typically confined to the offices of pastors and counselors. Whether you've been married for just a few years or decades, their journey of triumph over betrayal and sexual addiction will give you hope that God can help you overcome your past and fight for your future.

—HOWARD DAYTON, Founder & Chairman, Compass—
Finances God's Way, Author of *Money and Marriage God's Way*

Behind the masks of polite society, many of us are hiding hurts and secrets we hope will never see the light of day. As long as the secrets remain hidden, they exert a growing, toxic influence over our lives and relationships. Phil and Priscilla's personal story, *Savage Marriage*, offers us the golden keys, not only to full restoration but to a liberated life that most people can't even imagine. Get ready for an unnerving journey into the power promise of Jesus: "The truth will set you free" (John 8:32 NIV).

—STEVE RICHARDSON, President, Pioneers USA

Phil and Priscilla turn their pain into power as they transparently share how God freed and healed them from betrayal and sexual addiction. Their story will not only move you emotionally but encourage you to connect with your spouse spiritually. *Savage Marriage* will help struggling marriages and also be a valuable resource for marriage counselors and pastors who want to share with troubled couples an authentic example of how God can resurrect marriages on the brink of destruction.

—MARK MERRILL, President, Family First,
Author of *Lists to Love By for Busy Husbands*

Through *Savage Marriage*, Phil and Priscilla take the reader on an incredible journey into their valley of brokenness and the still waters of redemption. Phil's "double life" and the thickness of Priscilla's own idols are unmasked and left impotent through the hope of the gospel. Their story is of restoration and the power of confession, forgiveness, and

SAVAGE
MARRIAGE

SAVAGE MARRIAGE

TRIUMPH OVER BETRAYAL AND SEXUAL ADDICTION

PHIL AND PRISCILLA FRETWELL

Content Editing by Jen R. Miller at wordswithjen@writersroot.com
Cover Design by Faceout Studio, Jeff Miller
Authors' photo by Shane Valentine
Interior design and typeset by Katherine Lloyd, The DESK

ISBN: 979-8-9855402-0-8 (Print)
ISBN: 979-8-9855402-1-5 (eBook)
ISBN: 979-8-9855402-2-2 (Audio)

Printed in the United States of America

10 9 8 7 6 5 4 3 2 1

To our children, daughters-in-law, and son-in-law—
Tim and Johanna, Sarah and Shawn,
Michael and Chelsea, Anna Hope, and Becca:
You have embraced our savage adventure with God
and come out stronger than when it began.
We are so thankful for your ministry in our lives.

CONTENTS

FOREWORD

I met Phil through a brief phone call while he was on a plane to the Middle East for a business trip. Although our call wasn't lengthy, I knew there was something unique about Phil. With other men, I'd often spend a lot of time trying to convince them about the path forward of humility and transparency that I believed would help them. Not with Phil. He was like a sponge, soaking up every word. This man was broken and needed only a little nudging in the right direction. Phil's heart was wide open, and he had already decided he was willing to do "whatever it takes" to save his marriage.

Stories like Phil's and Priscilla's are not pleasant to experience. However, allowing God to use our failures to bring hope and healing to others is part of His eternal purpose. Phil and Priscilla were diligent to the process, allowing God to work in both of their lives individually so their marriage could be reconciled. They were both faithful to do "whatever it takes" to find God in the midst of their great pain.

It wasn't long before God allowed Phil and Priscilla to help others who were in the same broken state they were in. Because of their willingness, I've seen Phil and Priscilla impact hundreds of couples in their local area and many more nationally through our ministry.

In 2005, I founded Whatever It Takes Ministries with my wife, Jenny. She and I had the privilege to travel around the globe to share and teach others how to find freedom in their lives and move forward on the path to reconciliation in their marriages. Whatever It Takes Ministries hosts weekend intensives for couples and for men-only and women-only groups to help them find healing for some of life's toughest challenges. It's been my privilege to serve with Phil and Priscilla on such weekends.

Over and over, I've seen Phil and Priscilla allow God to use their story as a message of hope for others. God has gifted them to share with precision and passion. Their impact on couples and individuals is astonishing.

Besides serving with Phil and Priscilla, I consider them my closest friends; they have been instrumental in my life in many ways. I'm thrilled and grateful they have captured their story in book form for the world to read.

Most would agree that the subject matter is extremely difficult to discuss, let alone publish a book about. I'm proud of their courage to share boldly so others may benefit from their pain.

I'm most excited that through this book they have clearly articulated the steps God took them through on their journey of hope, freedom, and restoration. You will not only be captured by their story but gain wisdom and understanding of the principles and truths they went through and adopted as the foundations for their renewed relationship.

I encourage you to read this book slowly while asking God to illuminate in you His methods. Take time to reflect on the probing questions at the end of each chapter. As you do so, my prayer is that you, too, will discover true freedom, hope, and healing in your life and relationships.

Whatever It Takes!

—Paul Speed, Cofounder, Whatever It Takes Ministries Inc.

ACKNOWLEDGMENTS

God used many people to help us write *Savage Marriage*. Although space doesn't allow us to mention everyone by name, there are a few people who were particularly instrumental to our rescue, healing, and reliving of our story through *Savage Marriage*.

Paul and Jenny Speed, founders of Whatever It Takes Ministries Inc., were instrumental in helping us find healing and restoration. God used their testimonies of humility, openness, and brokenness to place us on a journey of freedom and healing. It's marvelous for us to serve as volunteers with Whatever It Takes Ministries in their conferences and events, and some of Savage Marriage Ministries has been developed from things we learned from Paul and Jenny. Jenny passed away in 2019, but she lives on in eternity with our Lord Jesus and through our memories and the words in this book. We're grateful to Paul and Jenny for their leadership, mentorship, and friendship.

We thank Doug and Wendy Gohn, dear friends of many years. Their encouragement and insights into *Savage Marriage* have helped shape this book.

Thank you to our editor, Jen R. Miller, who provided countless hours of advice, encouragement, and guidance. We couldn't have done it without her.

We thank our five children and Phil's sister, Cindy, for writing recollections of our journey from their perspectives, included herein. Their voices lend intimacy and realism to what happened in our marriage and remind us of the amazing grace God demonstrated in our lives.

There's also been a number of people who've provided advice and encouragement as we've written this book, including Pastor Norm Dubois from East Coast Believers Church, Dr. Dwight Bain from The LifeWorks Group, Jay Fechtel, Dominic Sputo, Tim Gregory, and Jeff Wieland. They provided treasured words of life to us as we pushed through difficult parts of our story.

Finally, we are so blessed by our children and three children-in-law: Anna Hope, Becca, Tim and Johanna, Shawn and Sarah, and Michael and Chelsea. Their forgiveness for the pain we caused them was instrumental in our healing. It's wonderful to see how they have each turned their pain into insight, maturity, and victory over their own challenges. We are so appreciative of their encouragement in our lives. Our journey with them has truly been a time of revelation for us all.

—Phil and Priscilla Fretwell

A NOTE FROM THE AUTHORS

This book is about how God rescued our marriage from betrayal, sexual addiction, and the wounds of our pasts. We've described what we went through in detail so you can see the full beauty that emerged when we revealed our hearts and thoughts as the individuals we truly were. Although your marriage is different from ours, couples share one common truth: we each have a past that affects our marriage. We hope that by reading our story, *Savage Marriage*, you will see bits and pieces of your own journey and that God will lead you to embrace hope for your savage adventure to begin.

We realize that some parts of our story are very frank and may even feel offensive to some. Our objective isn't to shock but to help readers who are buried in shame, thinking they are the only ones with similar problems. When we share our story with groups, some listeners ask, "How can you stand up there and say all that?" The answer is easy: the grace of God has taken away all our shame, and there's no reason to hide in the shadows.

Working for years with other couples struggling in marriage, we've seen that many people have been in circumstances similar to ours, and we've experienced and witnessed how helpful it is to have someone come alongside to truthfully say, "We understand because we've been there."

If you are struggling in your marriage, we hope that you will feel us walking alongside you because of our transparency in this book.

We are not pastors, theologians, or licensed marriage counselors but a couple who love and delight in the Word of God and by experience believe in marriage, healing, and transformation. All we have is our story and the desire for God to use it as He sees fit. If you are reading this book, our prayer is that God will use our story to rescue, redeem, and invigorate your marriage. We've seen Him do supernatural things in our marriage, and we believe He can work the same miracles in your marriage if you are open to receiving His transformative grace, love, forgiveness, and counsel.

Thank you, Father, for your incredible gift of our story.

—Phil and Priscilla Fretwell

Chapter 1

TWO CROOKED STICKS

This people honors me with their lips, but their heart is far from me.

—Matthew 15:8 (ESV)

Wearing a mask wears you out. Faking it is fatiguing. The most exhausting activity is pretending to be what you know you aren't.

—Rick Warren

PRISCILLA

"Hello?" I answered.

"Hi, this is 16,000 Movies calling about some videos that were rented this past weekend. It looks like they weren't returned."

"What videos? I didn't rent any videos." I had been out of town with some girlfriends. The clerk quickly rattled off strange, unfamiliar titles. I was a movie buff and read *People* magazine cover to cover but didn't recognize any of these movies. "I've never heard of them. What are they rated?"

The clerk replied bluntly, "They're triple X, for adults only."

I paused. We had an account at 16,000 Movies, but I didn't like going there because the adults-only section wasn't completely closed off, and it was hard to keep track of my kids as they ran through the store, eagerly picking up movies and begging to rent them. "We don't rent movies like that," I replied curtly, embarrassed that someone had our name and number associated with a list of people who watched X-rated videos. After all, we were good churchgoers and certainly didn't watch filth like that.

"Well, ma'am, we have a camera that records everyone who rents videos. If you'd like to come to our store, we can show you the footage and figure out who's renting on your account."

This has to be a mistake. Phil and I had been married for ten years, and I trusted him completely. "No, that's okay. I'll call my husband."

I'd never suspected Phil could be watching porn. For the first four years of our marriage, we hadn't even had a television. *Phil's going to say, "No, I didn't rent any videos," and I'll call the store and tell them their system is messed up. I didn't rent the videos, and Phil didn't either.*

I quickly dialed Phil's number. "Hey, it's me. I got a call from 16,000 Movies. They said two movies were not returned from last weekend. Did you rent any movies?"

PHIL

Priscilla's simple question sent me reeling, and images from the previous weekend flooded my mind. My breathing turned rapid and shallow as my thoughts swirled, momentarily disabling my usual calm and logical thinking. I wanted to run and hide.

The weekend Priscilla had spent away with some girlfriends, I had stayed home with our three children, ages eight, seven, and five. That Friday after work, I'd stopped by 16,000 Movies because it had an adults-only section, unlike the video store we usually frequented. Since age ten, I had struggled with porn and masturbation, but I'd never shared this with Priscilla. Porn was a constant noose around my neck, something I'd learned to live with, reasoning that all men dealt with a "normal" level of lust. I had occasionally gone inside adult video stores and gazed at the covers, wanting to see more, but had never been brave enough to buy anything. It was too risky.

With Priscilla out of town, it had been a perfect opportunity to indulge myself. I'd strolled back and forth in the adult section, then eventually picked two tempting titles and sheepishly carried them to the checkout counter.

"Did you find everything okay?" the clerk asked without looking at me.

"Yes," I stammered, wondering if her question was some kind of humiliating joke she liked to play on men who rented adult videos. *Hurry up, lady. I just want to get out of here.* The thought of someone seeing me with those videos made me nervous. I was well known in the community and a leader in my church in Orlando. I couldn't imagine explaining the videos to anyone. I was accustomed to watching porn on the internet or TV in the solitude of hotel rooms while away on business trips, but this was the first time I'd risked bringing porn videos into our home.

After leaving the store, I breathed a bit easier, got into my car, and turned toward home. *No one will ever know. Priscilla's out of town, and after the kids go to bed, I can immerse myself in the videos. It won't hurt anybody.*

On Sunday night, I'd made a point to return the videos to the after-hours drop box so I wouldn't have to see anyone. As I'd slid the videos through the slot, I'd wondered, *What happens if a clerk doesn't check in these videos?* Thinking about someone calling our house had caused a sudden pang of fear. Then I'd reasoned that such a scenario couldn't happen. *They must have procedures in place for checking in videos—certainly adult videos. They wouldn't risk talking with somebody's wife about unreturned X-rated videos.*

"Phil, are you there?" Priscilla's question cut through my thoughts, her voice ending in a higher pitch. Like a chess game, I considered all combinations and permutations of answers. Each response created another path that required more answers. I needed time to think and figure out how to feign ignorance of the videos and fix this problem. I didn't want to hurt Priscilla. More importantly, I wanted to protect myself. Not knowing how to answer, I managed a weak "I'll be home in a few minutes."

I'd been caught. I was in one of my worst nightmares.

I had worked for years to keep my porn use secret. Occasionally, I had talked with close friends about it, but porn was the kind of discussion Christian guys kept vague. One person would say something like, "I struggled a bit last week with some things on the internet."

All the other men would nod knowingly, and a few would volunteer that they also had. Then everyone would agree to do better next week and ask, "What's for lunch?" This well-worn pattern for my "accountability groups" had allowed me to release a little guilt while keeping secrets from Priscilla.

This time was different because I'd been caught, and unlike a men's accountability group, Priscilla wouldn't be so quick to nod knowingly and let it go. I needed a better story. The fifteen-minute drive home would give me time to figure out what to say.

PRISCILLA

My heart was gripped with uncertainty, and fear was starting to creep in, kindling my anger. Phil had paused too long. He'd deflected my question and simply said he was coming home. My chest felt like it was going to explode. I had hoped for his easy explanation, a denial—anything that would have indicated a crazy mistake by the video store. But no, he'd said he was coming home, and my heart had instantly been crushed and hurled into the pit of my stomach. *Why would he do this? How could he bring porn into our home?* My imagination was running wild and stoking my outrage. *He's betrayed me! He's gone against every vow he's ever made to me. I'm supposed to be the only one in his eyes and life.*

Then the realization of what had just happened hit me: Our perfect marriage was no longer perfect. It was now blemished, scarred, and tainted, and I was injured and hurting. What I had thought was solid ground was actually sinking sand. I could feel the foundation of our marriage shifting and crumbling beneath my feet. I slumped onto a chair at the kitchen table, unable to bear the weight of my broken heart.

Although I knew that porn was considered mainstream entertainment by many and that even some Christians watched porn occasionally in the privacy of their bedrooms, it wasn't something my Christian upbringing could let slide. I'd grown up in a conservative Christian home, and my parents had been rule followers, missionaries in Brazil for most of my life, which had set the framework for my thinking. One of their warnings had been to hold on to my prized virginity or else no one would marry me. So I had been very careful in my dating life, hearing my dad's voice every time a guy had begun to get a little too close. But some dates had gotten out of hand and gone a little too far. I'd felt dirty, used, unworthy, and racked with shame. Exactly how I felt sitting at our kitchen table, waiting for Phil's arrival and explanation. And I felt betrayed, sinned against, and angry.

How can this be happening? I've been a good Christian girl; I've followed all the rules and married my Jesus-loving knight. Phil's a confident leader and strong in his faith. He teaches weekly Bible studies! In fact, a Bible study for our church's singles group, meeting at Phil's place, was where our dating relationship had blossomed. He was a solid Christian! This man knew a lot of Scripture, and others looked to him as a well-versed Bible teacher. He hadn't even kissed me until we were engaged! Most of all, he regularly professed his commitment and love to me.

After ten years of marriage, suddenly discovering I wasn't desirable enough to keep Phil's attention was a fierce blow to everything I thought I knew—about Phil, our marriage, and especially myself. *There must be something wrong with me. Am I not sexy enough? Does my lack of self-confidence in bed turn him off? What's the matter with me that he'd turn to porn?*

PHIL

I walked in the door and met Priscilla's tense face. Her lips were tight, and so were her folded arms. No smile, no warm welcome, and certainly no kiss hello. *I'm in a serious predicament.* I tried to temper my anxiety. I was usually good at easing a tense situation, but in this case, my heart was beating fast, and my words felt stuck in my throat.

I joined Priscilla at our familiar kitchen table, which now seemed like a cold judge's bench separating us rather than bringing us together as it had for so many years.

"Did you rent the movies?" she asked squarely.

"Yes, I did." I stared into her eyes, then quickly dropped my gaze in shame. I had always admired Priscilla's regard for purity, so I had hidden everything from her, thinking she would not be able to handle my porn use. *How can I recover our relationship without doing more damage?* She was silent, waiting, and I glanced up to see her looking at me, searching for truth.

PRISCILLA

Phil's face was completely drained, white as a ghost. His eyes were wide, alert, and full of regret, darting around the room like his mind was spinning in search of a plausible answer. Phil always had the answer to every question—part of his field of expertise as a consultant. He appeared desperate for words to appease my hot anger, anything to avoid a massive blowup.

PHIL

Priscilla was cold and measured outwardly, but I could tell she was a volcano of hot lava. "Where did you watch them?" she demanded.

I mumbled, "In the family room—after the kids went to bed."

"In the family room!" she erupted. "You brought those videos into our *house*? What about the kids?" Priscilla jumped from her seat and began to pace, throwing her hands into the air as her voice rose with anger and boiled over. "They always get up in the middle of the night, wanting water or having a bloody nose! How do you know they didn't see you?"

PRISCILLA

My words were dipped in venom, angry as fire and fueled by my disgust. I sat back down and stared intently into Phil's eyes, waiting for his answer or an acknowledgment or *something* to tell me how he was going to make this right. Although I was deeply offended that he would do this to me, I was even more upset that he would risk exposing our children to porn. I had given our entire marriage and family life, all my time and effort, to caring for and protecting our treasured babies. *How could he be so reckless?*

PHIL

Priscilla's question was a good one. What if one of our kids had seen me? The truth was I hadn't been thinking much about our children at the time, other than getting them quickly to bed. My mind had disengaged as it always did when lust took over. I realized she was right. The kids could have walked in, and I would have hurried them back to bed and rationalized that they were too young to understand what they had seen. But the fact was they hadn't walked in or seen anything.

I finally responded, trying to diffuse Priscilla's wrath with logic. "I waited until I was sure they were asleep. They didn't get up; no one saw anything." I watched with hope for her to breathe a sigh of relief. Instead, her eyebrows scrunched together as her face flushed red.

She fired back, "Are you kidding me? Just because they didn't see anything makes it okay? Why did you even *want* to watch that crap?"

I had never shared with Priscilla anything about my exposure to porn as a child. *Maybe I should. Maybe she'll feel sorry for me if she knows the truth that I'm a victim. She might even show me a little grace.* My only question was how much to share.

In the heat of Priscilla's demanding glare, I decided to pull back the curtain to my childhood, just a little. I needed to appear sorrowful and repentant to be convincing. That wouldn't fully be an act. I was, in fact, very sorry—that I'd been caught. "Priscilla, I've had a problem with pornography from my childhood," I shared with an air of resignation, as though I was finally letting her in on a big, painful secret. "When I was ten or eleven, I found some magazines in a neighbor's trash and got hooked on them. But after I became a Christian, I knew it wasn't right, and I threw them all away. When you were away, I got pulled back into my old temptations. I'm so sorry." I dropped my eyes as my voice trailed off. I hadn't told her the whole story about my porn use, but I hoped she'd sense my despair and I wouldn't need to tell her more. After all, she was a very caring wife and mom. I was counting on her nurturing instincts to kick in.

PRISCILLA

"Phil, frankly, I couldn't care less about your childhood porn viewing. I care about my kids! I care about having a good marriage—like we had yesterday. These are the things that matter to me. You should have cared about these too and thought about our family and marriage before you decided to rent those movies. You should have cared for *us* instead of yourself! Your past should have remained in the past." I had seen right through him and was livid that he thought he could manipulate me into feeling sorry for him.

Phil didn't know I had also been exposed to porn as a teen. Down the street from my childhood home, I had babysat for a couple with two little kids. Being a snoopy fifteen-year-old, I'd looked through all the rooms of their home while the kids napped. In the master bedroom, I discovered porn magazines and books stacked neatly on a bedside table. I sat on the edge of the bed and quietly flipped through the magazines. I knew I wasn't supposed to look at such pictures, but I couldn't put them down. Sex was not discussed in our home, so what I saw, which my eyes should never have seen, was all new to me. Seeing something so private made me feel ashamed, guilty, and dirty.

My sister and I rented an apartment in our early twenties and decided to add cable TV. Watching HBO became a norm for us. When our parents visited us from Brazil, my dad asked, "What is this smut you have on your TV?"

"It's cable TV, Dad." I rolled my eyes.

"You're going to disconnect it right now," he demanded. There was no debating with my dad. We did what he said, even though we were paying for the cable.

As time passed, I remembered only a little of the smutty movies, but the magazine pictures had been engraved in my psyche. Although I had struggled to forget them, to keep them hidden in the recesses of my mind, they had become a source of guilt years later as I had thought about them during intimacy with Phil.

I'd stopped looking at such things years ago, disgusted with the mere thought, so why couldn't Phil stop looking at them? It was that simple. Just say no, right? It had worked for me. I didn't understand why this was so hard for him.

Although his porn revelation released memories of my shame, I decided to keep my past to myself. I didn't have a problem staying away from porn. It was Phil's problem that had created a sudden, unexpected deluge between us. He had done wrong, not me. Mr. Fix It needed to shift into high gear.

Minutes passed between us in silence. I had no more questions for him, and apparently, he had nothing else to offer me. I was done! All I knew was that he needed to repair this problem he'd created in our marriage. I stood and snapped, "Get this fixed because I will *not* live like this!"

PHIL

"I'm going to find a good Christian counselor to help me," I assured Priscilla. "I've needed this all along, and I'm glad it came out. I hate myself for looking at those videos, and I don't want to live with this guilt and temptation. I don't want to ever do it again."

Everything I said was true. I hated the way I felt after my repeated failures. Priscilla didn't need to know how many failures. One was enough. Further disclosure would hurt her all the more, and I'd already hurt her enough. *A counselor can help me and provide a safe, confidential place for me to get honest.* I felt relieved.

Trying my best to appear contrite and conciliatory, I searched Priscilla's face, still hoping for some sign of mercy and grace.

PRISCILLA

Even though I was fuming, I recognized that Phil admitting he had a problem was out of character for him and an unexpected surprise to me. He always had everything together. Mr. Perfect. You could ask Phil anything because he knew everything. Even though I had demanded he fix the problem, him admitting he needed help took the razor edge from my anger and resentment.

I wanted our life to return to what it had been before Phil's confession about 16,000 Movies. *A good Christian counselor will surely fix his porn issue. That's what counselors do—help people get their lives together.* A counselor was certainly someone I could trust to correct his problem.

I started to leave the house for school pickup, and Phil took a step toward me, wanting a hug like all was forgiven. I put a hand on his chest to stop him and shook my head. "No, I don't think so. All is not forgiven. All is not well. The last thing I want to do is be that close to you." I stepped around him and left through the kitchen door.

PHIL

In the wake of Priscilla's departure, I slowly began to breathe again. Alone at the kitchen table, I wasted no time searching for a Christian counselor. I recognized Brian's name from the radio. His credentials looked great and included many years of experience. I immediately called and set an appointment for the following week, vague with the receptionist about the reason for my visit. Brian's website had assured me that everything would remain confidential, which was exactly what I wanted. I was an elder at church and taught weekly Bible studies. If this got out, it would ruin my reputation and cause needless additional pain for Priscilla.

PRISCILLA

For days after Phil's confession, I spiraled and didn't have anywhere to turn. *I can't tell my friends, especially my church friends. My family? No way—not them.* I knew that God's Word could be a source of comfort, but as an adult, I'd always been too busy to read the Bible. God knew how full my hands were as a mom of three young kids. Besides, my life had been going pretty well until that call from 16,000 Movies. Also, reading my Bible stirred up resentment toward my dad. In fifth and sixth grades, all I had wanted to do after school was watch my favorite sitcoms. But my dad had made me read my Bible every day and write a summary of what I'd read before I could watch TV. He'd made reading the Bible a chore rather than a delight.

Having nowhere else to go, I picked up my Bible. It felt foreign in my hands. With my thumb on the edge, I slowly feathered the pages. The flow stopped in the book of Psalms, with my finger pointing at Psalm 147:3. My eyes scanned the words, and there, in my despair, loneliness, and isolation, I saw God. He was there, talking to me. Desperate, I put my faith in His Word as the truth: "He heals the brokenhearted and binds up their wounds" (NIV).

His assurance burst the dam I'd built inside me, and a flood of tears streamed down my face. I wept until all my hurt was released.

In the margin of the passage, beside the verse, I wrote:

My heart is broken, when will it be restored? 3/98.

I didn't know it then, but it would take eighteen years for my question to be answered.

PHIL

In my first session with Brian, I quickly told him about my porn problem. He nodded knowingly like he'd heard my story a thousand times. "So, Phil, it sounds like you're ready to get to business." Brian was straightforward, and it felt good to share with trust that no one else would learn about my problems. He provided encouragement and advice on how to control my unwanted behaviors.

I developed a good relationship with Brian and learned how to navigate the counseling sessions to appear that I was doing well and have something positive to report to Priscilla without lying if she asked (which she usually didn't).

A typical session began with pleasantries; then Brian would turn serious. "Phil, part of our meeting is about accountability. So how has this week gone for you?"

"Better," I would start, "but not perfect."

"Well, if it had been perfect, you would be Jesus!" We'd both laugh, and I'd feel relieved. I didn't lie and didn't feel like I had to say too much.

Sometimes he asked detailed questions about my week, and I would try to answer while minimizing my failures. On days when I felt guilty about a fresh failure, I'd confess with more contriteness, wanting to feel Brian's compassion and assurance of forgiveness. If my failure had occurred more than a week prior, I typically had read my Bible and prayed enough to feel better about myself before my next counseling meeting, and I'd try to be vague with my answers. Regardless, I always felt better after meeting with Brian. Sort of like going to the dentist to get a cavity filled, I'd approach the meeting full of anxiety but feel great when it was over.

My basic issue was that I was not HOT with Brian—honest, open, and transparent. I was simply honest, sparingly. My goal was to answer his questions truthfully, without providing embarrassing information I felt was unnecessary to share. When he asked a question, I answered like a lawyer, with carefully crafted responses. If I had been truly open, I would have provided details beyond the questions he asked. If I had been truly transparent, I would have provided pertinent information without his prompting questions. The truth is I was merely honest without being open or transparent. All liars and cheaters learned this lawyerly skill of being honest only, and I was no different.

It would be eighteen years before I'd realize I had to be HOT to be healed.

PRISCILLA

We didn't talk much about Phil's sessions with Brian. He'd only say, "I'm going to see Brian today." I was hesitant to ask questions, but occasionally I'd hint at one. Phil would say, "You know, I don't think Brian wants us to talk about it. It's supposed to be confidential. If you're going to ask me after every session what we discussed, I'm probably not going to share much with him out of fear that I'll have to also share it with you." Phil's explanation left me in the dark about the details shared between him and Brian that would have given me insight into Phil's progress. Not knowing details made me feel disconnected, but I felt I had little choice. I needed to trust that Brian and Phil's new accountability partner were helping him control his temptations. From what I knew, this was how most men's accountability groups worked. Men needed a "safe place" to share, and I would just have to live with that.

As a means of accountability for Phil's business trips, he suggested I look at his hotel receipts so he wouldn't be tempted to watch movies. I did. But after a few trips, I realized his offering was bogus. He could change receipts with Wite-Out or pay cash. I had wised up and told him, "I'm not going to be your Holy Spirit and check these receipts anymore. I'm done with this."

He also put filters on the computers and his phone and asked me to examine the reports. An old proverb came to mind: "Where there's a will, there's a way"—around everything. I didn't want to be Phil's police, checking to see if he kept all the rules. It was all too stressful and overwhelming for me. I told him I was off the police force and that he was on his own with his recently acquired accountability partner and Brian.

PHIL

I met with Brian for five years after getting caught renting the porn videos. Even though I continued to struggle with the cycle of porn and religious good works, I felt I at least understood more about my struggle. With the additional help of computer and phone filters and meetings with Jeff, my accountability partner, the length of time between failures had increased. I broached with Brian the subject of no longer meeting. "Brian, do men continue to meet with you for the rest of their lives?"

"Well, honestly, Phil, most men meet until they feel like their sin activity is down to a level they can successfully manage on their own, and then they stop coming."

"I think I'm there. I'm not perfect—because if I was, I'd be Jesus!" Brian laughed and agreed. "But I'm doing much better."

That's when my professional counseling with Brian ended.

Over the eighteen years following Priscilla's discovery of the porn videos, we convinced ourselves that every issue in our marriage had been resolved.

But we were two crooked sticks pretending to be straight.

> I had settled for an explanation of God rather than an encounter with Him that could have changed my life.

Looking back on what happened when my sin was first exposed, I see that I had no idea God was throwing me a lifeline. He was pursuing me, wanting my attention. As we were writing this book with thirty years of marriage behind us, Priscilla and I reflected on what we wished we could have communicated to the younger versions of ourselves many years ago. We wrote the following letters to ourselves.

Dear Thirty-Seven-Year-Old Me,

God threw you a lifeline ten years into your marriage, but you were more interested in protecting your image than being healed. Sure, you wanted healing, but you wanted pain-free healing. You didn't really want to be honest, open, and transparent with anyone, and you manipulated Priscilla into believing you were fixed.

Your real goal was to look good and be somebody at work and in church. If you knew the future would get much worse, would you have taken a different course?

Your basic issue was pride. Though you knew Scripture, you settled for an explanation of God rather than an encounter with Him that could have changed your life. You didn't act on the truth that God resists the proud and gives grace to the humble. So, while you were praying for God to help you, He was actually resisting you in your arrogance. If you had humbled yourself, your situation would have been much different, and you would have saved yourself and your family so much pain through the years.

Wishing it had been different,

Sixty-Year-Old Me

PRISCILLA

Dear Thirty-Six-Year-Old Me,

I wish you had a restart button to change the choices you made for so many years. Why did you let fear influence your decisions? Why did you let your anger and pride be your guide? You let the million little pieces of this puzzle become overwhelming as you wondered how you'd piece together a path to healing. Instead of being a solo act, you should have asked God to join you—the One who knows how to solve every puzzle. You should have trusted in Him and Him alone. You repeated the same mistake for many years: putting your trust in a man. Growing up, you placed your trust in your dad. When you married, you placed your trust in Phil. When he failed you, you put your trust in a counselor. You believed your dad, Phil, and Brian would all fix your problems. But real healing only comes from God. He alone is worthy of your trust.

Rather than go through hard discussions, you wanted everything to go away. You believed if you looked good, you were good. You traded real healing for the appearance of a perfect marriage and family. In the process, you lost your soul to anger, fear, and unforgiveness. Pride has a way of doing that. You put yourself in a prison of your own making, and it took you eighteen years to find freedom.

> *Hurting for the choices you made,*
> *Fifty-Nine-Year-Old Me*

PHIL

I recently opened Priscilla's Bible and saw the verse she'd circled years earlier. I was surprised, realizing for the first time how deeply she must have felt my betrayal. Back then, I had been pleased to protect her from the worst of who I was and thought my actions preserved the image and reputation I'd designed for myself and my family. I hadn't realized that the full impact of my pride and my refusal to be HOT had not yet been revealed. It was awaiting us further down the road, and the little bit of pain I'd felt from that weekend of porn was only a drop in the bucket. The hurricane was still eighteen years ahead.

| Savage Questions for Reflection |

1. What resonates in your life about the "Dear Me" letters? How do they apply to your marriage?

2. How well do you and your spouse share the deepest thoughts and intentions of your hearts? How can your spouse know the real you better? Describe an event that took you to a new level of being HOT with your spouse.

3. On a scale of 1–5, with five being *very important* and one *not important*, how important is it for you to be admired by others and seen as a success? Describe an example of how this has impacted your ability to confess your weaknesses and failures.

Chapter 2

WHAT'S BEEN PLANTED GROWS

Do not be deceived, God is not mocked; for whatever a person sows, this he will also reap.

—Galatians 6:7

Sooner or later, everyone sits down to a banquet of consequences.

—Robert Louis Stevenson

PHIL

It was a small hard bump. I hadn't noticed it before, and it immediately got my attention as I finished my shower.

"Phil, are you coming to bed?" Priscilla called from our bedroom.

"Just a minute—I'm doing something." I grabbed my phone and launched a frenzied internet search for pictures of genital warts. While the images weren't conclusive, they also didn't calm my fear. *Could I have a sexually transmitted disease?*

Eighteen years had passed since 16,000 Movies called Priscilla about the porn videos, unraveling what she had thought was a lily-white marriage. In the five years that had followed, I'd worked on my issues but without Priscilla knowing much about what was going on inside me. From her standpoint, she thought I was "cured." She wasn't aware that the seeds of pornography planted in my childhood had continued to grow and had not been completely uprooted during my years of counseling.

After I had stopped meeting with Brian, I had gradually—not all at once but a little at a time—resumed viewing porn on the internet and on TV in my hotel rooms during business trips. Because lust is never satisfied, my appetite had increased to include occasional outings to strip clubs. I had first crossed that line when I was sixteen and visited Club Juana. I knew I was doing wrong and that the Bible said, "Be sure that your sin will find you out" (Num. 32:23). However, intellectual knowledge held no power to keep me on the straight and narrow road because I believed my actions were exceptions to the rule.

> My next failure was always just a clock tick away—inevitable.

I continued repeating the cycle of failure followed by religious good works (praying, reading my Bible, going to church, etc.) and inevitably another failure. It was the same cycle I'd experienced right after becoming a Christian, but now I felt more shame because I was teaching weekly Bible studies and serving as an elder at our church. I felt that my next failure was always just a clock tick away—inevitable. The only unknown was how many ticks would pass before I failed again.

Early in our marriage, we knew of a pastor who had resigned from his church after having an adulterous affair. In conversation with a friend, I'd asked, "How could a pastor do that to his wife and kids?"

Introspectively, he had replied, "That's also what I initially thought. Then I recognized the pride in my heart. If adultery can happen to a pastor, it can happen to me." I shook my head in disbelief that a pastor—of all people—had broken his marriage vows.

After that conversation, I had prided myself on having never been with another "real" woman while Priscilla and I were married. My failures were isolated to my thought life and masturbation, both fueled by porn. I considered both as victimless crimes that no one needed to know about. Masturbating when I traveled helped me stay "true to Priscilla."

That was about to change.

I traveled alone to Peru for a weeklong business trip. I arrived a day early with nothing to do and thought it would be nice to enjoy a massage at the hotel spa. But there was more to my thinking than just a massage. Since Priscilla's discovery of the porn videos, my appetite for porn had grown, fed by the free and ample availability of sexually explicit material I could view in secret on the internet. While traveling, I would spend hours on the internet looking at porn, always searching for something new and more exciting. As those images and thoughts fertilized my brain, I desired real-life experiences. That desire led me to visit hotel spas regularly, with the hope that maybe the masseuse would offer something more than a massage. I had seen some seedy massage parlors that appeared to call out, "Come see what I have to offer!" But I had been too scared to visit them, not knowing what might happen or who might see me. Instead, I confined myself to hotel spas in international locations, believing this was the best way to stay safe in my hiding.

Nothing out of the ordinary happened to me at those spa visits, except in my mind, as I let sexual fantasies run roughshod over my Christian values.

I set up a massage appointment at the hotel spa in Peru. It was a very nice luxury spa and didn't appear to be the kind of place to offer anything extra. As the massage progressed, I began to read hints in the masseuse's every move. My adrenaline increased, and my heart began to pound as my mind imagined where this experience could go. The lust coursing through me was overwhelming as I tried to appear nonchalant and unaware of her unspoken suggestions. Near the end of my hour, she offered a "happy ending." By that time, my mind was already primed by numerous sexual fantasies of what could happen. Mentally, I was in no shape to refuse. I accepted and paid her fifty dollars extra, then left.

Within hours, the high of that new experience had worn off, and guilt and shame ushered me into despair. A glaring fact confronted me: I had engaged in a sex act with another woman, a *real* woman. In the loneliness of my hotel room, I opened the Gideon's Bible to words of forgiveness and comfort. Although using Scripture in the past had effectively assuaged my guilt about routine internet porn and masturbation, this was different. I wasn't so certain my feelings of guilt would go away as easily.

I found the topical index in the Bible and read every verse that seemed to apply to me. I prayed, confessed my sin, and asked God to forgive me. I promised Him I would never again break my marriage vow to "keep myself only for Priscilla."

Repentance was my typical routine after every failure. But this time, my conviction and confession were more earnest because I felt like the bar of forgiveness had risen substantially. This time, guilt plagued me.

Over the next several days, I rationalized my sin. *It was only a massage with an orgasm. I didn't have a relationship with her and certainly had no affection. It was purely physical, and no one will ever know. Harmless. The spa is in a known-brand hotel, so lots of people must do this!*

Over the next few weeks, in my effort to cope with my guilt, I began to tell myself I was actually a victim of an unscrupulous masseuse who preyed on helpless men like me, putting us in inviting situations where it was impossible to say no. It was entrapment!

But it wasn't long before I did it again.

And again.

My familiar cycle of sin and shame now included real women. I hated myself afterward, but I couldn't stop.

Weeks before I left on a trip, a battle would begin to form in my mind against a struggling resolve to remain true to Priscilla. My good intentions would slowly erode as the time to leave for the airport grew near. The more I tried not to think about going to a massage parlor, the more it dominated my thoughts, true to addiction.

Once the plane landed and I was in a taxi to the hotel, I was already searching the passing stores, wondering if a massage parlor was close by.

During this time, intimacy with Priscilla was perfunctory, and it didn't seem like she really enjoyed sex. I pushed her to try new things that would provide me with more passion and excitement, but porn was my sex tutor, setting a high bar, impossible for any woman to reach. I settled for sex in the dark with my wife while allowing my mind to fantasize about women in massage parlors and porn scenes, imagining myself a participant with them. Intimacy with Priscilla had become group sex in my thoughts—her, me, and the images in my mind.

"Phil, what are you doing in there?" Priscilla's voice jarred me from examining all my years of sin against her and what I'd just discovered about genital warts. "Are you coming to bed?" she called out.

"Just a second! I'm on my phone returning a few emails. Be there in a minute!" I worried whether the tone of my voice had belied the desperation consuming my soul. I had quickly learned that the painful warts could be transmitted to a partner—and there was no cure.

No cure.

Those words wrecked my mind.

Although I had been willing to sacrifice Priscilla's emotional intimacy, there was no way I could sacrifice her health. *I need to tell her.*

My thoughts leaped to the explosive weekend eighteen years earlier when I'd confessed to renting the porn videos. The revelation to Priscilla that I had occasionally struggled with porn had been devastating and had taken five years to put behind us. Now I had something new to deal with—an STD. What I had thought was just "normal lust" that wouldn't hurt anyone had grown into a monster.

I quaked at the thought of how unleashing this monster to Priscilla would affect her and our marriage, and the monster grew larger in my mind, now threatening to destroy my family. *My kids might disown me! I could lose everything . . .*

Yearning for deep sleep to remove the emotional pain, I fumbled with the sleeping pills I used for overnight plane trips and swallowed one. I slipped into bed and gave Priscilla a few brief kisses, not wanting to do anything to further expose her to contracting the disease.

The next day, I woke early and began to strategize how to get out of this predicament. I researched preventive medicines I could slip into Priscilla's coffee unnoticed. *Or maybe I can just tell her I don't know how I got an STD. "There are lots of strange things in other countries, and somehow I must have caught it by mistake."*

Nothing I came up with was believable. Every avenue of thinking brought me back to my initial conclusion: I had to tell Priscilla.

Fear gripped my heart, and I could hardly breathe. I wondered if I should drive off a bridge. Priscilla would collect life insurance and probably be better off without me. But those thoughts were short lived, and I began to work on a confession plan. I would be heading to the Middle East on Saturday and couldn't drop this bomb on her and then leave. *I need to take this business trip and tell her when I return.*

The night before I left was a departure from our ritual. I'd always pushed Priscilla to have sex, especially the night before a business trip, telling her sex helped me with self-control. But this night was different. I wasn't sure if I had already passed the disease to her unknowingly and didn't want to consciously do anything to jeopardize her health. Instead of the typical routine, I worked on emails later than normal, then slid into bed. "I'm tired," I mumbled and kissed her good night. With the help of my sleeping pills, I drifted off.

PRISCILLA

Phil leaving for a trip to the Middle East was not new. He had averaged one trip every month for the past ten years, covering the Middle East, Africa, India, and Latin America. His absence put a strain on our family life, but we had gotten used to it. After all, I'd reasoned, he didn't have a choice; this was his job, and I knew it was important to him. Phil's travel had become our norm, but this trip felt different. Out of the ordinary. There had been no departure sex. We always had sex before Phil left for a trip, and sex was a must when he returned.

The night before he'd left, I had taken a shower and waited in bed while he'd worked on emails, which had seemed to take longer than usual. After a while, I called out to him, "Hey, babe, are you coming?"—a suggestive invitation to our expected time of intimacy. He replied that he'd be there in a minute. When he finally came to bed, there was very little conversation. He simply gave me five little kisses, the last part of our nightly routine before dozing off, and rolled over and turned off the light. *That's it? Does he want to go to sleep? No departure sex? Weird; no departure sex . . .* I'd been okay with that—not at all disappointed.

I had always been unsure about sexual intimacy. When Phil and I had married, I'd been a twenty-seven-year-old virgin. I had no idea how to navigate sexual intimacy with him. I'd received all my insight in the girls' locker room and from HBO movies, and I was super inhibited, shy, and extremely awkward. We occasionally laughed at memories of our honeymoon.

Shortly after we married, I had a gnawing feeling there was a third person in bed with us. While having sex, I sometimes saw a disconnected look in Phil's eyes, as if he were looking straight through me. *Am I not here? How strange. I'm right here but not being seen.* I wanted to ask Phil, "What are you seeing?" or "What are you thinking about? Why aren't your eyes connecting with mine?"

Insecure younger me was very uncertain with my sexuality. *Dare I question him? Maybe this is how it's supposed to be.* Images from porn magazines, planted when I was fifteen years old, had remained in my head. With no one I could talk to—no friend, mom, or sister—I accepted the images were here to stay. Even though I desperately wanted to be "one" with Phil during our lovemaking, my secret thoughts of others, planted by those images, were robbing my passion and true intimacy with him. It never occurred to me that porn planted in my youth could be the same problem planted in Phil's youth. I didn't want to ask him, for fear I would have to reveal my struggle with sexual images. It was better to just keep the past in the past.

About five years before the ominous call from 16,000 Movies, I began having recurring dreams of Phil in infidelity, though I had no reason to believe he was unfaithful. I'd wake up super angry and agitated at him. Our conversations almost always went like this: "Ugh! I had another dream last night."

"What happened?" he'd ask. At that time, I believed the concern and care in his voice were real.

"We were at a party. Everyone was talking, and we were standing together, but you were flirting with a woman, coming on to her, and ignoring me. I was standing right beside you, and you didn't even care about me. It was as if you didn't see me or know I was there. I woke up so mad I could be spitting bullets at you."

Phil would conjure up tenderness. "Honey, you know I love you. I only have eyes for you. I enjoy seeing only your breasts—no one else's."

To a certain extent, I believed him. At all the work and church gatherings we had attended, I'd never witnessed Phil in a circumstance similar to my dreams. He was not a flirty guy. It wasn't his style, at least outwardly. What I didn't realize was that the dreams disclosed to me what was going on in his mind.

After a dream, I'd feel angry all day and have a short fuse with our kids and everyone else who crossed my path. Other stressors also contributed to the cord of anger I'd been carrying since childhood. Phil was so focused on needing to manage his reputation that he would constantly remind me to look good so he could look good, which meant I had to play the agreeable corporate wife. Having grown up in rural Brazil as a missionary kid, I found this act to be a real stretch.

When I was eight, our family had moved from Brazil to the United States, then had moved almost every year after as my dad had switched jobs. It had been a struggle for my parents to put food on the table. The economic crisis of the eighties hadn't helped. We were stuck living in government-subsidized apartments and scrapping for food. There was a Pak 'N Save grocery store next door, and my dad watched the dumpster. When he saw food thrown away, we went dumpster diving. It was so humiliating. I was fearful classmates would see me. I felt like I wasn't good enough—disregarded like the food in the trash. Although we'd never gone hungry, pulling food out of the garbage had always reminded me that I was on the bottom rung of the social ladder and would amount to nothing. That's how I had seen myself. I had questioned God, "Is this how You see me?"

When I married Phil, Mr. Corporate Executive, I hobnobbed to look regal in front of a whole bunch of people I didn't know or even care about. I felt totally displaced, the stepchild playing Cinderella. Phil would say, "Just smile, and you'll do fine."

As I learned how to handle myself, corporate dinners and events got easier over the years. Some of Phil's confidence in such settings rubbed off on me. But the pressure to look my best, dress the part, remember names, and always smile never diminished. This role and the pressure bled into other groups—church, Bible studies, and homeschooling—and onto our children. Homeschooling was a significant part of our family culture with our three older children, although it gave way to traditional schools when our younger two were in elementary. Phil insisted that the kids always look polished and have their hair brushed, shirts tucked in, and belts on. He would tell them to look people in the eye when talking to them, shake their hands firmly, and walk with a purpose. I had to not only set the same example for them but pretend to be a trophy wife for Phil, something I found awkward because sixth-grade me would always say, *You're nothing but a dumpster diver.*

Phil knew how much I disliked corporate events, and he'd tell me, "Go buy a new dress or whatever you need to do to feel better about going." He pressured the kids and me to conform to an image of the perfect family so he and our family would be admired by others. He would say to us, "You represent our family, and the way you look and act tells them who we are."

I felt like the real me needed to stay hidden.

The more pressure I received to perform, look good, and be somebody, the more alienated I felt from myself. The person Phil wanted me to be wasn't who I was. Depression crept in and made me push people away. I struggled to have real friendships because I felt like the real me needed to stay hidden.

Occasionally, I would let Phil know the depth of my feelings. "Phil, I think I need to see a counselor. I need to talk to somebody about why I feel so depressed, so disconnected." His response was predictable.

"Why? You have a perfect life. You have a nice house, a new car, five amazing kids—and you get to stay home. We go on great vacations and don't have to worry about money. What do you have to be depressed about? All your needs are taken care of. I wish I had your life, and so do many of your friends!"

"I guess you're right." I'd sigh, still frustrated and unsure how to fix my feelings. I was crying out for help with my isolation, loneliness, depression, and big-time anger that had taken root in my childhood. Our lifestyle of persistent stress to appear perfect fed my active anger, and after the 16,000 Movies revelation, I decided to attend an anger-management class at church.

I wore my mask well to hide my anger in public, but when I would sometimes discreetly share I was attending an anger-management class, friends would say, "What? You have anger issues? No way!" They never witnessed my volcanic eruptions and explosiveness.

The anger-management instruction was to share my feelings more, read my Bible more, and exercise more. I didn't have anyone to share my feelings with, not even in that setting, and I didn't read my Bible. I did try to exercise more, something my kids would suggest when they saw my aggression building.

The more I withdrew from honestly confronting my feelings, the stronger the bondage of anger, unforgiveness, depression, isolation, and fear grew inside me. I further isolated emotionally from Phil, my kids, and my friends. I didn't know it then, but I should have walked into that anger class and said, "No, there has to be more here. I wasn't born with this anger. It had to have started *somewhere*. There has to be a root. I think the Holy Spirit can help me find it."

Like me, no one pushed back against the prescribed "more" formula: more sharing feelings, more reading the Bible, more exercising . . . and I didn't know any better solution.

My discovery of Phil's secret shopping at 16,000 Movies had further fueled my anger, and the porn betrayal had not been resolved between us. Like my grief, the issue had been swept under the rug with all my other hurts and anger, where no one could see them. But they still reacted in me like fertilizer to weeds.

Although my anger had grown exceedingly when I'd discovered the porn videos, that wasn't when the seed had first been planted. Recently, I had asked God to show me the source of my anger, and He had brought to mind a devastating event I had blocked from my memory. At six, I had seen my older sister and brother walking one afternoon with a few of their friends down a dirt road near our home in rural Brazil. I had run as fast as my little legs could to catch up. My brother spun around and yelled, "Go home! We don't want you with us! Stop following us!" As I continued running toward them, I could see them talking in whispers.

They stopped in front of a big pile of horse manure, laughing like someone had told a joke. My brother, John, bent down and picked up a handful of manure, and the others followed suit. He took the first shot, which landed on my chest. Soon, everyone was pelting me with horse manure. It was coming from everywhere while my brother pointed his finger at me and laughed. My humiliation and rejection from them discarding me as though I was manure were a big joke to him.

I tried to dodge the dung as I screamed, "Why are you doing this?" Tears streamed down my face, and I begged them to stop. I didn't know what else to do, and no one, not even my sister, stepped forward to protect me.

Anger rose to my defense like a warrior within me. I picked up handfuls of manure from around my feet and threw the excrement back at them the best I could. It was of no use; I was one scrawny six-year-old against preteens.

That day, anger, as a larger-than-life entity, had made its home in me and thereafter remained alert, always ready to protect me. I had accepted that power subconsciously and thereby collaborated with the enemy of my soul, the devil—anger would always be my trusty defender.

After the humiliating event, John had given me a nickname, Galinha Garinze, a Portuguese term meaning "a person of small stature who is like a crazy mad chicken." As adults, my siblings would frequently recall that name, laughing as they asked me if I remembered it. I did, but not the humiliating childhood event associated with it, nor was the event ever brought up in conversation. Though their question was asked in jest, it remained a sensitive wound in me that reminded me of the anger I still carried and the lie planted in me on that degrading childhood day: *you don't matter, and no one wants you around.*

Having anger issues long after but not recalling that fateful day from childhood made me think anger was simply part of my personality and that I should learn to live with it. Like my anger about Phil's porn videos, what happened to me that day as a little girl had been left unresolved, an unseen part of what I was experiencing as a corporate wife, mom, and friend.

After God pointed me to the transformative manure incident, I discussed that childhood fight with my sister. She said that after the conflict, I had remained full of anger, but she had never known why.

As a wife and mom, my life appeared to others like a nice, beautiful, neat package with a bow on top that everyone wanted and admired. But if anyone were to open the package, they'd see impenetrable, dry, arid ground. Nothing growing, just tumbleweeds blowing across the plains of nothingness. My anger, pride, self-righteousness, and wounds were the groundskeepers, ensuring the desolation for over fifty years.

PHIL

It was Saturday afternoon, and I settled into the seat as the plane lifted off, headed to Saudi Arabia with a stop in Dubai. The rush of packing the night before and leaving for the airport had given me a momentary reprieve from the anxiety that had pushed me to take sleeping pills all week. But as the aircraft doors closed, the fear gripping me since discovering the bump began to morph into panic. With thirteen hours of solitude ahead of me, my thoughts freely swirled, convincing me I could lose everything: my marriage, my kids, my church relationships, my money, and maybe even my job.

I had for some time thought about retiring in just a few years, and the STD crisis had quickly thrown the rest of my life into a state of uncertainty. *I might not have anything left.* Despair took control of my mind. Although I wasn't considering suicide, I understood how people in my situation could. I'd heard the stories. Someone commits suicide, and no one knows why. "He was a great guy with a great family and friends. Everyone admired him." Yes, I considered that story would be mine, but I knew I couldn't leave that legacy to my children. Suicide wasn't an option.

Sobs shook my body from somewhere deep inside me I'd never known existed. I shifted to face the window so no one could see my out-pouring emotions. While others in flight enjoyed their meals and got ready for sleep, my mind enacted scene after scene telling Priscilla about the STD. I couldn't eat, sleep, or stop crying. I was in the lowest pit of my life.

After I'd cried for five hours, my almost incoherent thoughts turned to God. Could He be doing something in this carnage? Could this circumstance be part of His rescue plan?

Five months earlier, we had changed churches, and the music style reminded me of Psalm 32:7: "You surround me with songs of deliverance." Such songs had planted in me seeds of healing, deliverance, and overcoming my problems, which had taken root. I had begun to believe that maybe change was possible. Maybe there was a way out of my sex addiction. I had also reasoned that over forty years of meditating on porn had broken my mind and that God wanted to heal my thinking like He could heal any other ailment. I had even developed and taught a Bible study to my community group that I'd titled "The Healing of the Mind." The group didn't know I was actually talking about *my* mind.

Now, there I sat on a plane in panic, desperately wanting a pain-free healing. I mused I could visit a church in another city—no one there would know me—and maybe there would be an altar call. I would walk down the aisle, someone would pray for me, and I would be instantly healed. No one would know, and I could keep everything secret. My sin wouldn't have to affect anyone.

I didn't know how any of this could happen—apart from my growing belief that God could heal my mind. So I started calling out to Him for rescue. Not a timid, hopeful prayer but a bondage plea, like when Israel cried out to God for rescue from the land of Egypt:

> Now it came about in the course of those many days that the King of Egypt died. And the sons of Israel groaned because of the bondage, and they cried out; And their cry for help because of their bondage ascended to God. (Exod. 2:23)

Israel had been in bondage, slaves in the land of Egypt, and I was in bondage, a slave to sexual immorality. Could it be that God was hearing my bondage cry and putting together a rescue plan?

After five hours of emotional desperation with nowhere to turn, I decided to send a text to Jay, one of my best friends. "Jay, where are you? I need to talk to you." Within minutes he responded by text.

"I'm right here. What do you need?"

"I'm on a plane. Can you call me?"

My phone rang. "Jay?"

"Phil, what's going on?" His usually friendly voice sounded serious—he likely sensed something behind my urgency.

"Jay, I'm in deep trouble."

Jay and I had been friends since high school. He was a strong Christian and someone I could trust. I'd mentioned to him in the past that I sometimes struggled with porn, but it was the kind of vague conversation that just about all men have about sexual sin.

This time my conversation with Jay was different.

"Jay, I may have an STD. I've been hooked on porn and going to massage parlors for years, and I've been too ashamed to tell you or anyone else. I need to tell Priscilla, and this is going to destroy her—and my family and quite possibly my life." I gushed on with transparency for the first time. The ruse was up. The game was over. It all spilled out.

Jay listened intently and responded without judgment, asking short questions to better understand the whole story. Finally, with conviction, as if he was giving me words directly from God, he said, "Phil, I know someone who's had success helping men deal with this. I've mentioned him to you from time to time at our monthly breakfasts—Paul Speed. He and his wife, Jenny, are the founders of Whatever It Takes Ministries. He's the only guy I know who has helped men gain real, sustainable freedom from sexual sin. I'm going to ask him to call you right now." Jay's confident voice was the first ray of hope I'd felt since discovering the STD, and I was able to stop crying.

I recalled my breakfasts with Jay from several years past and his mentions of Paul Speed. Jay had told me back then that Paul held weekend retreats for men who struggled with sexual sin, and Jay had invited me to attend a retreat. At that time, he'd been poking at a sensitive area in me, and I had waved off the invitation. "Jay, I've been to five years of professional counseling and have heard just about everything. But I'll think about it." What I'd really meant was that I'd think about not going. During those monthly breakfasts, Jay had brought up Paul's name a couple of times, and each time, I had deflected, wanting to keep my sin hidden and feeling that I could manage it on my own. I believed I would overcome and confess my sin in my later years to Priscilla as a conquered sin.

There was also another time when my heart and thoughts had been confronted about my sin. A friend had openly confessed his sin about going to massage parlors and having sex with strangers. He had been very forthright and let me know that he had received healing and was moving forward in a healthy way, free from the bondage. In my self-righteousness, I had nodded to show my empathy and concern and thanked him for being honest, but in my hypocrisy, I had refused to come clean about my own double life.

Recalling those lifelines God had given me and my refusals to take them, I saw with clarity that He had been pursuing me all along. I had been too proud to expose who I really was. This time I'd take His lifeline and hold tightly to His promise: He "gives grace to the humble" (I Pet. 5:5 ESV).

Within minutes, Paul called me. He summarized his testimony from fourteen years earlier, which mirrored many of my issues. In my desperation, I blurted out everything I'd shared with Jay.

"Well, Phil, I've got good news for you. There's a way out."

I was ready for anything. I had no other options. "What is it?"

"The key isn't years and years of counseling, memorizing tons of Scripture, safeguards on your phone, or accountability partners."

"That's good because I've tried all those things, and they didn't work for me. What's the way out?" I was hopeful, hungry for answers, and genuinely intrigued because the list he'd rattled off included all the things men are commonly told to do but that many times result in little success in breaking free.

Paul paused; then his instructions were slow and measured. "You need to embrace humility and become completely transparent, confessing your sin to your wife and then to your children, family, and others who have been affected by your hypocrisy."

I felt like a syringe had suddenly been jabbed into my heart and was slowly drawing the blood of my secrecy out, the very thing I had labored so intensely to hide for over forty years. Paul continued, "Phil, you have a pride problem, and God wants to fix it. He resists the proud but gives grace to the humble. You need to take steps of humility through your confessions, and when you do, you'll experience God's amazing grace and healing in your life."

The truth of Paul's counsel settled in and over me as if the Holy Spirit had pulled back a veil and allowed me to see His escape plan. Yes, God's plan was scary and daunting. It would destroy my self-righteous, egotistical reputation, but that was the proud man God was resisting and had resisted for most of my life. I needed a way out— God's way.

Paul went on to explain that I needed to take full responsibility for my choices. I couldn't blame Priscilla for anything, and I could no longer minimize my sin. I also needed to share with her the details of what I'd done and answer her questions openly with transparency. Without details, Priscilla's imagination and fears could create scenarios much worse than what had occurred. I couldn't protect myself any longer.

"You're right," I affirmed and thanked Paul. "I'm going to talk with Priscilla when I get home."

Peace flooded my soul as I disconnected the call. I sensed Paul's counsel was indeed God's rescue plan, and I thought about how I had ignored many previous lifelines He had thrown my way.

I disembarked in Dubai and found a sofa to wait for my next flight. Church in the United States was beginning at that time, and I found the livestream service, opening with the popular song "Come to the Altar" by Elevation Worship:

Are you hurting and broken within
Overwhelmed by the weight of your sin
Jesus is calling
Have you come to the end of yourself
Do you thirst for a drink from the well
Jesus is calling

O come to the altar
The Father's arms are open wide
Forgiveness was bought with
The precious blood of Jesus Christ

Leave behind your regrets and mistakes
Come today there's no reason to wait
Jesus is calling
Bring your sorrows and trade them for joy
From the ashes a new life is born
Jesus is calling*

---

* "O Come to the Altar," by Pastor Steven Furtick, Chris Brown, Wade Joye, and Mack Brock, Spotify, track 4 on *Here as in Heaven*, 2016.

Although I'd heard the song many times, this time was different. The person hurting and broken within was me. I was the one overwhelmed by the weight of my sin. I sat and cried, no longer caring who saw me or what they thought.

The rest of the trip was without incident, and five days later, I boarded the flight home.

As the plane made its approach into Orlando, I thought about Jay and my experience with him and God thirty years earlier. I'd taken a job at an accounting firm in Tampa, and unbelievably, Jay, who had also majored in accounting, wound up taking a job at the same firm. We'd rented apartments in the same complex and enjoyed redeveloping our friendship. A year earlier, I had become a Christian, and in reuniting with Jay, I'd shared my newfound faith with him.

One evening, he had accepted my invitation to join me at church. During the altar call, he had turned his life over to the Lord Jesus.

Now, as I watched the online church service from the airport, I realized that God's rescue plan for my life had been put in place over thirty years ago. Jay, whom God had saved years prior, had been used by Him to set me free. I was blown away by God's love and plan for my life.

The plane landed, and anxious thoughts dominated my mind as I contemplated the mission ahead to come clean with Priscilla. Just thirteen hours earlier, halfway around the world, the ominous, forthcoming event had seemed far away, with plenty of time to work out details. However, with the plane door now opening, my chest tightened as I imagined how Priscilla would react when I suddenly exposed that I'd been harboring secrets and lies our entire marriage. I wasn't confident she would forgive me, but I was confident that my confession to her was what God wanted me to do.

God, help me. Help us.

In forty-five short minutes, Priscilla would see me for who I really was. There would be no turning back to who we were before.

| Savage Questions for Reflection |

1. Have you been in a situation like Phil's, where you felt you were in the lowest pit of your life? What was the circumstance? How did you get out? Or have you not yet gotten out?

2. What seeds of sin were planted in your life? How were they planted, and how have they grown? What effects have they had on you? What effects have they had on others?

3. How is your outward appearance different from the person you are on the inside?

Chapter 3

SECRETS SHATTER OUR MARRIAGE

Be sure that your sin will find you out.

—NUMBERS 32:23

God's voice is always calling us out of hiding—that's how you know it's God's voice.

—JEFFERSON BETHKE,
*IT'S NOT WHAT YOU THINK: WHY CHRISTIANITY IS ABOUT
SO MUCH MORE THAN GOING TO HEAVEN WHEN YOU DIE*

PRISCILLA

I eagerly awaited Phil's arrival, wearing a cute outfit and the tempting scent of Hypnose, his favorite perfume. I heard the garage open and hurried to the door. I wrapped my arms around him and gave him a tight squeeze and tender kiss on his lips.

"I missed you!" I whispered in his ear. I felt his jaw clench, and I pulled back, looking at his face. "Wow! You look tired!" His normally wide blue eyes were bloodshot and drooping. He seemed drained. "Weren't you in business class last night? Didn't you sleep?"

PHIL

Priscilla's bubbly welcome made me feel all the worse, but she was pleasing to my eyes. She wore fashionable white shorts and sandals that revealed bright-red toenails, and her soft pastel blouse and subtle makeup enhanced her natural Brazilian beauty, accentuated by her long, curly hair. Her fresh look said, "Welcome home! I missed you!" I cringed as I pushed her to the side and walked into the kitchen, keenly aware that my no-holds-barred confession would soon rip her apart.

Not wanting her to see my despair, I averted my eyes, looking around the kitchen like I was seeing it for the first time, wondering how to answer her question. I resorted to my natural inclination of giving a truthful yet lawyerly answer without being completely open or transparent. "I had a very hard week. I couldn't sleep. Too much on my mind." It was a puny start; there was considerably more that needed to come out.

PRISCILLA

Trying to be upbeat, I quickly changed the subject. "Hey! I just finished working out, and I'm starving." Phil wheeled his bags into our bedroom. "Are you hungry? Want to get some sushi?"

"Sure. Give me a minute to change."

I was anxious to catch up on a week's worth of activities. Since the kids were at school and two weeks had passed since Phil and I had been intimate, I had mentally prepared myself for arrival sex, knowing we would have more time after lunch than after the kids went to bed. I hated "quickies" and wanted to have more than just a physical encounter.

At the restaurant, I did most of the talking. I figured jet lag was making it difficult for Phil to be peppy. He asked a few questions about our kids, but his head was still in business mode. He was never fun when his mind was on work. It usually took a couple of days for him to settle into being home. It was what I called *reentry*, the process of reconnecting emotionally and sexually, part of the dance—not only for us but relationally for our whole family.

We hurriedly finished lunch and headed home. I held the door open for our dog, and strangely, Phil waited for me. When I turned to look at him, his eyes were downcast, sad, and full of dread. He gently took my hand and led me toward the kitchen table. We sat, facing each other, and something seemed off.

Phil struggled to get out the first word as his eyes dropped to the table. He stared at his folded hands and said, "I have to tell you something." His lips tightened, and his brow wrinkled, and I felt a tightening in my stomach. His chin began to quiver, and his shoulders slumped, communicating he had something big to say. Fear rose in me. His breathing became short and rapid, broken only by quiet sobs that slowly racked his body like waves washing onto shore. My pulse accelerated as my thoughts went back eighteen years to the very serious porn videos conversation at this same table. *Oh, dear Jesus! What has Phil done? Was he fired? Did he do something immoral?* He lifted his head, and tears streamed down his face. I waited, not breathing, and watched him wipe them away with his hands. I had never seen him cry like this before, and I could manage only a weak "Are you okay?"

"No, I'm not," he said, almost unintelligibly as he shifted in his chair. Phil's answer made me hesitate, realizing this must be something really big.

I finally managed to eke out the next obvious question, though slowly, emphasizing each word. "What did you do?" I wanted to know and understand what we were dealing with, but Phil continued to look down and seemed unable to reply. I eventually found enough courage to voice my greatest fear. "Have you been with someone else on this trip?"

He could barely force his reply out between sobs, which were now more frequent and intense. "No, not on this trip."

Thrown by his response, I wrestled with the sudden onslaught of questions firing in my head. *What does "not on this trip" mean? On another trip, he was unfaithful? How could this be? He always calls me when he's out of town, and when in town, he's always with me.* I gripped my chair and leaned back, bracing for what might come next. The weight stole my voice. I whispered, "Not on this trip? Then when?"

Silence.

Phil's head rested on his arms, his hands covering his face. He was breathing heavily like he was searching for the strength to answer. He uncovered his eyes, and his lips began to move; then ragged words stumbled out. "I've been living a double life."

Stunned, I instinctively recoiled from the stab to my heart, and a tidal wave of more questions pummeled me. *What's happening to us? This doesn't make sense . . . a double life? How can he have a double life? I know where he is all the time—and his calendar is always booked. He's never out at night. He spends his free time with us . . . how is this possible?* I couldn't wrap my brain around his words—*double life*. It sounded foreign, so out of left field. *What does that even mean—a double life?* I wasn't prepared for this and felt myself falling apart and needing answers. "What do you *mean* by a double life?" Although I'd asked the question calmly, inside I was preparing for a hurricane. I felt the gusts pushing my emotions to a breaking point. *There has to be a reasonable explanation. This can't mean what I think it means . . .*

PHIL

Paul Speed had told me, "You can't minimize your sin, and you need to share everything with Priscilla so she won't be left hanging to imagine details worse than what you've done." He'd said that secrets create fertile ground for seeds of immorality to grow, and anything left hidden would be like a hook, pulling me back into my past sinful thoughts, temptations, and behaviors. And he'd said, "If you want to be truly free, you have to expose all your secrets and shame."

I was ready to unload the weight of my sin, no longer wanting to protect myself. I couldn't bear the burden anymore. But where to start? I'd done so much wrong.

Priscilla searched my face as I struggled to release the truth. Her mouth had straightened, and her eyes told me she wanted to know and understand what I had done. I tried to talk, but only groans with sobs escaped my lips. *Jesus, help me.*

Utterly broken, I began my confession. "I've been going to massage parlors, but not like the ones you go to." Priscilla's patient approach to drawing me out faded as her wide eyes narrowed and her lips pursed.

"Where?" she demanded tightly.

With another step of humility, I answered with clarity, knowing I had to be HOT to become healed. "The places I've traveled, and here in town. I'm so sorry. Oh, God, help me," I cried as I uttered the first details of my sinful life, words that began to describe the longtime shame burning inside me, details I had never told anyone.

PRISCILLA

Phil's words were a gut punch, taking my breath.

A battle began to form in my head. *Is it better to know or not know what he did in those dark, degrading places?* I imagined all sorts of scenarios and wanted to run and hide. *But if I don't ask questions, how will I ever know the truth? Will knowing be any worse than the images running through my imagination? If I know the truth, at least I won't live in fear of the unknown.*

I concluded that truth had to be more powerful than the lies stoking my fears. Still, I felt desperate to flee. I stood and turned, hands on my hips, and wildly looked around, but there was nowhere to run.

I turned back to Phil, placed one hand on the table and the other on the chair next to him. I leaned over him in a fury and fired off questions like a seasoned prosecutor, giving him only seconds to answer before shooting the next volley. "How many times did you go? How much did you pay them? What did they look like? Were they pretty? What were they wearing? Was this why you carried so much cash? Where were your hands? Where were their hands? What did you say? What did they say? Did you go back to the same woman?" My questions were demands, full of anger and rudeness, short, and to the point. I needed answers to center my mind on what had actually happened rather than focusing on my fears.

Hurry up, Phil, explain! I don't know how much more I can take!

PHIL

What started with one very direct question became a torrential downpour, question after question. I'd barely answered the first before the next one hit. I talked faster and faster, although each answer just turned into another question.

As I shared the details of my secrets and shame, Priscilla's face and body contorted with an uncontrollable rhythmic bounce to my every word. She stamped her feet in disgust as each syllable of her demands for an explanation was formed by sobs, creating new bends to her lips and eyes as her tears flowed.

PRISCILLA

Phil answered all my questions in detail. His words painted an ugly picture of betrayal. I knew what the women had looked like, what they'd worn, and what they'd said and done. More importantly, I knew what Phil had done. Although I'd never seen a nervous breakdown, his behavior looked like one. He was crying nonstop, his confession broken only when he begged for forgiveness.

As the details became clear, I realized he'd participated in more than massages with something extra. He had participated in activities previously reserved exclusively for me, enjoyed in the intimate confines of our bedroom.

Phil receiving pleasure was one thing, but giving pleasure to other women was something entirely different. It was as if he'd taken a precious gift, wrapped and presented only to me, then ripped it out of my hands and given it to another woman. The reality was more than I could bear. My knees grew weak from the anguish in my soul.

Phil had always been a pillar of strength, my personal strong tower I could run to for protection, and he'd turned into my torturer. "How dare you, Phil!" I hissed, my intense pain making it hard for me to get out anything more than the agonizing statement gorged with disgust and rage. I had devoted my life to Phil, to making him look good, to creating a perfect family picture that mirrored to the world that the Fretwells were people to be admired and emulated, and Phil had shattered that mirror into a million pieces. The shards had created so many wounds in me and our marriage that no one would ever be able to heal them, let alone Phil or me.

He tried to touch my hand, as if to say, "I'm sorry," and I pulled from his reach, repulsed. I paced from the sink to the table, wanting an escape so I wouldn't have to step on the broken pieces of our life. Our marriage was crushed and irreparable. I was crushed and irreparable.

Having no place to run, the lifeblood flowing out of me, I fell into a chair and stared at him. My husband had chosen to betray me for moments of illicit pleasure rather than choosing me. The realization was unbearable. Voices chanted in my thoughts in a maniacal chorus, *Lies, lies, lies! Everything you've known were lies. All your family celebrations, the milestones in your life, the vacations together, your perfect family pictures . . . all lies!*

I tried to reject the voices, but they consumed me, each word a painful stab impossible to escape or deny. My whole being cried, *Phil, have you lied to me all this time? All these years? Did I not mean anything to you? Do you even care about our family?*

PHIL

Although the emotional pain I'd experienced on the plane had been monstrous, it was nothing like the agony of confessing to my wife and witnessing the visceral effects in her. On the plane, I could only imagine her reaction. In the reality of our kitchen, she was ablaze with anguish, anger, disgust, and despair, painting a horrendous picture of what my sin had done to her heart. Her every move, tear, and word dripped with fury from my betrayal, paralyzing me as our tears flowed uncontrollably under the tormenting weight of my sin.

The pace of her questions had slowed, and she now sat in lifeless silence. Neither of us knew what more to say. I had shared everything, which made clear to her why there had been distance between us for so many years, why I had for so long disconnected from her emotionally, and why she'd had angry dreams of betrayal. There had always been a secret life embedded in our marriage that I'd worked hard to keep hidden, desperate to protect her (and me) from pain.

Through the years, I'd never thought I would take my guilt to the grave, but I'd believed that rather, one day, maybe in my eighties, I would share my long-past secrets and shame with Priscilla. I'd imagined I would have figured out long before how to shake the temptations and be out of my dark lifestyle by that later point in life. My indiscretions would be long past, and I'd feel good about myself and be able to tell her, "Twenty years ago, I had some problems." I imagined her graciously forgiving me and saying, "Let bygones be bygones."

The problem with my logic was thinking I'd get better. I had been contemplating this plan for most of our marriage, but all I had done was get worse. And now the physical manifestation of my sin through a possible STD had obliterated any possibility of waiting until I was eighty to confess my double life. Clearly, I had a seriously destructive problem in my brain, and it was unlikely my reality would get easier with the passage of time.

I thought back to Paul Speed's words: "When you don't know what to do next, humility is always the answer." Although I had just shared my sin in true brokenness with Priscilla, I knew I needed to take another step deeper into authentic humility. I had always been self-sufficient, but I now sensed that Priscilla could be part of God's plan to help me overcome addiction and heal. I pointed to my head and, in desperation, pleaded, "Priscilla, I am *so* sick. My mind is broken! I need your help to get it fixed. Will you help me?"

PRISCILLA

Phil's words were soft, contemplative, and humble, reflecting a brokenness I'd never before seen in him. Although his request was simple, it was a profound switch in his attitude toward me. He had never asked for my help with *anything*, except chores related to the kids, our home, and making him look better. He had always been self-assured and in charge. It was unnerving to see him bent over in weakness, needing something only I could provide. But my emotions were still raging, making me want to extract vengeance rather than provide help. *Hell no! After what you've done, you're on your own!* But still, his quiet plea—"Will you help me?"—got my attention, and his typical arrogance was replaced with brokenness and contriteness I'd never witnessed in him. He looked so lost. His shoulders were slumped in defeat, his head was bowed, and his red eyes begged, *Please help me; I can't do this alone.*

As I further pondered his appeal, in sight of his radical loss of pride—a man I barely recognized—a tiny feeling of mercy, a sliver of compassion, opened my heart. *Phil is my husband. We've been married for longer than I've lived without him, and he's the father of our five children.* Still enraged and a slave to my broken heart, I guardedly agreed to at least help him find healing. I couldn't promise more than that.

"Okay, we'll get through this. I'll help you get fixed."

PHIL

Priscilla's resilience prompted a flashback to my past confession of the porn videos I'd brought into our home. She and I had trudged through that crisis by keeping a lid on everything. We'd chosen an easier path: hiding our pain by sweeping the issue and all its tentacles into our separate closets, wrestling through our feelings in the dark, independent of each other. Now, eighteen years later, we again faced the same option: simply lock it all away.

Although I was relieved to hear she would help me, I knew we couldn't take the same road this time. Perpetually hiding my sin had fostered only further decay and stench. I was searching for healing that would eradicate my sinful desires. If such radical healing was possible, I was willing to write my sins on a billboard if that was what it would take. I looked at Priscilla and shook my head. "No, I have to tell our kids."

She jerked her head toward me, her eyes searching mine, trying to process my words. "Our kids?" she stammered, as though unsure she had heard me correctly.

"Yes, our kids. I have to tell them. This secret life is killing me—it's killing us and our marriage."

> We wrongly believed our well-intentioned facades were for the benefit of our children, which encouraged us to embrace hypocrisy as a necessary way of life.

As agonizing as it was to have confessed to Priscilla, the thought of being HOT with our kids felt even worse. We prided ourselves on "raising our children right" by homeschooling and doing plenty of religious things such as going to church, praying before meals, and occasionally reading the Bible with them. We believed if our kids saw us as model Christians, they would be model Christians. If we looked successful, it would ensure their success. So I'd pursued becoming a leader in the church, teaching Bible studies, and making sure everyone, especially our children, thought we were great Christians. We believed if our children knew we had failed (in anything), we would be handing them a pass card to do the same. We thought the keys to their successes were rooted in following our example of looking good and becoming somebody. Our false beliefs had kept us from presenting our honest frailties and limitations to our children and others. We wrongly believed our well-intentioned facades were for the benefit of our children, which encouraged us to embrace hypocrisy as a necessary way of life to gain respect, acceptance, and accolades. It was the wide road of destruction, the path of pride.

"But not Anna Hope and Becca!" Priscilla gasped. "They're too young! They're only nine and eleven!" Anna Hope and Becca were the youngest of our five children. We had adopted them from China when they were under three years old, and Priscilla had been their constant protector and comforter. She reacted to every issue as if it exacerbated some unseen pain or deficit from their past.

"Yes, Anna Hope and Becca too," I whispered, hanging my head.

"No, no, no!" Priscilla pleaded as she doubled over, hands on her knees, heaving like she was going to vomit. Her mama-bear instincts had emerged in wails of anguish, and I was the cause. *Our young daughters' lives will be tinged with my vile transgressions and painful disappointment that their dad is not worthy of being their hero.*

Priscilla was visibly spiraling out of control, and instinctively I was compelled to rescue her. I couldn't lose her on this one point. "Priscilla . . . Priscilla, we don't have to decide right now. We can just take one step at a time. Just one step." She nodded, and we wept as we contemplated how my confession would shake our children's whole world.

Sharing my sin with our children was going to be daunting.

PRISCILLA

Phil's decision to share his sin with Anna Hope and Becca sickened me. *How can he even consider ruining two little lives with his wretched truths? It's not fair to them! They're innocent! How has his problem now become everyone's problem?* Nothing made sense; my world and thinking were upside down.

Seeing my shock and struggle to accept that we had to share his sexual sins with our little girls, he quickly shifted gears. As he continued talking, I was speechless.

PHIL

"Priscilla, there's an organization, Whatever It Takes Ministries, and I talked with the founder, Paul Speed. The ministry helps men and women who are experiencing trauma like we're going through. They have weekend retreats for men and women, and I've already signed up for the men's retreat. It's in two weeks. It's called 4 Days 2 Freedom. They have a women's retreat too, 4 Days 2 Hope. It's run by his wife,

Jenny, and starts this Thursday in Atlanta. I've already registered you and bought a plane ticket. I think it will answer your questions about the steps I should take to heal my mind. Can you do this for me? I need your help."

PRISCILLA

What? He's asking me to take the first step toward fixing his problems? They're not my problems to fix! They're his! He's the one who's been unfaithful, and he's the one who needs to fix this!

And how can one weekend away from this nightmare possibly fix his problems? I wasn't so sure, but the thought of an escape from facing Phil every morning was, frankly, a salvation. My soul was screaming, *Run! Get away!* Leaving for a retreat felt far better than staying home with Phil. "Okay, I'll go."

I realized it was time to pick up Anna Hope and Becca from school. I grabbed my keys while struggling to pull myself together. As I left, Phil and I exchanged a painful glance but said nothing.

PHIL

Déjà vu hit me as I recalled the previous time, eighteen years ago, I'd sat alone at our kitchen table in despair, my mind racing. I'd made the initial call that connected me to Brian for five years of counseling.

Had I really wasted eighteen years?

Although I was relieved that Priscilla now knew about my secret life, questions without answers circled my spirit like scavengers seeking roadkill. Part of me still felt dead and decaying in my sin. *How will I tell my children? How will this affect their lives? Will they still love me? Will Priscilla ever forgive me? Will we get a divorce? Can I ever control my lust? What happens if I ever fail again?* I had been unsuccessful in the past at curbing my sinful lust, even after five years of counseling. I didn't yet have any confidence this time would be different.

My dad had remarried three days after his divorce from my mom

---

was final. I was ten years old. I never learned much about their circumstances, but it was clear to me he had committed adultery. By the end of his life, my dad had been married seven times.

The first summer my sister and I had visited his new family, our new stepmother, Mamma Patty, had rushed into the family room one afternoon, quickly gathered us and her kids, and sent us to a neighbor's apartment. She had hurriedly moved us along without offering an explanation. She'd only said she and my dad had to go somewhere.

When they'd returned, several hours later, my dad had explained he had accidentally shot himself, and the bullet had entered his chest and exited his shoulder, amazingly missing his vital organs. As he had calmly shared the story, he'd removed his shirt and showed us the bandages on his chest and his back. He'd said he had been cleaning his revolver and the gun had accidentally fired.

His story hadn't made sense to me (and never would). He was former military and certainly knew how to handle guns.

At the time, I had wondered why it was so important for him to clean his gun. How, or why, had he left a bullet in it? How had he accidentally pointed it at his chest and then accidentally pulled the trigger? I didn't know much about guns, but making sure a gun was completely unloaded before cleaning it was something everyone would know to check and double-check.

Over the years, I invented my own answers. The shame and guilt of my dad's adultery had become too painful for him to bear. Seeing my sister and me struggling with his new family, he had let his regret consume him with unbearable pain. In desperation, he had turned to his gun.

It would be forty years before I broached the topic with my dad. His denial of a self-inflicted gunshot wound and absence of a truthful explanation for why he'd shot himself remained unchanged and still unbelievable.

The example of my dad's adultery—and, I believe, his attempted suicide—kept one fear ever before me: "You are going to be just like your father, destined to suffer the same fate." With every failure through the years, that was the message the enemy whispered in my ear.

Priscilla and I had made a vow at the beginning of our marriage that we would never use the D-word. Yet here we were, dealing with something that had the potential to take us there. Becoming divorced, like my father, was one thing I desperately wanted to avoid. In that moment at the kitchen table, the enemy of my soul, the devil, resurrected in me his familiar refrain. "See, you're just like your father!"

In my desperation to prove him wrong, I took a step toward truth, toward humility, toward freedom. Coming clean to Priscilla, about not only my sin but also my past wounds and what was going on inside me (something my father had never done with my mother), gave me hope.

As memories pulsated in my head, I gained new insight, the final puzzle piece that formed the complete picture of my addiction. I saw clearly the lies I had believed:

- A little porn use is acceptable.
- Every man needs to learn how to accommodate this "normal" level of lust because it's uncontrollable.
- How can we really be responsible for sin that is uncontrollable? We can't.

In truth, porn is the destroyer of spiritual, emotional, and physical intimacy—not only of a marriage but also of the whole family.

Allowing porn into my mind was not a victimless crime. Believing the lies had led me further into darkness, despair, and lustful desires than I had ever imagined I would go. Lust was the overwhelmingly powerful vehicle that had driven me toward adultery.

It was hard for me to accept the label *adulterer*. I preferred to think I just had a problem with porn. But in Matthew 5:28, Jesus said, "Everyone who looks at a woman with lust for her has already committed adultery with her in his heart."

The fact was I had been an adulterer for many years before going to a massage parlor. I had never done anything outwardly that had not first taken root inside my mind. I had thought the solution to my sin was controlling my outward actions. But I also knew Romans

12:2 and brushed it aside: "Do not be conformed to this world, but be transformed by the renewing of your mind." Yes, the truth was I was an adulterer and needed an inward transformation, a renewing of my mind, to be an authentic man of God.

> I needed an inward transformation,
> a renewing of my mind, to be
> an authentic man of God.

PRISCILLA

In the car, headed to pick up our girls from school, I breathed a sigh of relief, thankful to get away from my antagonist, if only for a few minutes. Anna Hope and Becca would soon be in the car, and I felt like a mess. In the visor mirror, I saw my bloodshot, puffy eyes and swollen nose. *Maybe they won't notice.*

I managed my brightest "Hi, girls!" as they hopped into the car. Little Becca questioned me right away. "Mommy, have you been crying? Is it a happy cry or a sad cry?"

I decided to be honest. "It's a sad cry, baby girl." Becca twisted her little body to face me. "Can you talk about it?"

"No, not right now. I will later." We rode home in silence without the usual chatter of their day's events.

In the days that followed, I cried nonstop. I couldn't accept the reality of what was happening to my marriage and the threat to my family. I was in denial, the first stage of working through my grief. I isolated myself from Phil, and we spoke only about things necessary to coexist.

While I counted down the days to my upcoming trip to the Atlanta retreat, the whole kitchen scene replayed in my head. The events of the past week had certainly pushed us over the edge and further apart. But the truth was we'd been disconnected emotionally and sexually for years. My angry dreams meant something after all. I wasn't crazy.

PHIL

The week before 4 Days 2 Hope, Priscilla and I treaded water. I didn't sleep well and rose between two and four every morning. My thoughts were dominated by memories of Priscilla stamping her feet, crying, and screaming at me—a picture of savage pain: wild, untamed, and full of force. I didn't realize it then, but that picture would become a powerful deterrent against allowing my desires to feast on lustful thoughts again.

Massage parlors had always been linked in my mind to pleasure, and now they were indelibly linked to my grievous confession of sin and the excruciating picture of Priscilla suffering unbearable pain. I never, ever wanted Priscilla or me to again experience that crippling horror.

But there was one thing I had been too afraid to tell Priscilla about: the hard white bump that had instigated my emotional crisis and sent me reeling in fear. We had already agreed that we should both get tested for STDs, so what would be served by telling her about the bump? It would create only fear and wouldn't change the outcome of the testing. So I decided not to share it.

One morning, as I got out of the shower, my finger went to the familiar hard white bump, reminding me I had reaped what I'd sown. I gave the bump a slight squeeze, and it popped! It wasn't a wart at all! It was more like a pimple but with no redness or remaining mark. As mysteriously as it had appeared a couple of weeks prior, it had gone, never to return. I was incredulous. I had gone down this painful, heartrending path based on believing I had an STD, which wasn't an STD at all!

I briefly wondered what life would have been like if I had waited to confess. Maybe I wouldn't have had to go through all this pain, but neither would I have realized the taste of true freedom I had experienced since confessing. In God's providence, He knew exactly what I needed to push me over the edge and when. He had allowed the physical bump to destroy my resolve to keep my double life secret. It was more amazing evidence of God's love for me and confirmed that He was truly moving in a supernatural way I had never experienced. He was refining me to become the man, husband, and dad He'd created me to be.

As Priscilla and I prepared for our back-to-back weekend retreats, I began to clearly see that my pain was also a vehicle, moving me to where God wanted me to be. Rather than numbing my pain, I needed to feel it. Numbing had been my way of life, beginning with my parents' divorce, when I'd discovered that the drug of porn could provide that fix anytime I needed it. I'd never imagined how far this drug would pull me into darkness, fear, and desperation. Had God not intervened, porn would have taken me even further down the wide road of destruction.

As we pulled up to the airport curb at departures, I retrieved Priscilla's luggage from the trunk and gave her the handle. She turned to walk toward the airport entrance and, with a sidewise glance, said, "I'll send you a text when I get there."

"I'll be praying for you," I responded, trying to show her newfound care and concern. She left without a hug or further words.

As I watched her walk off, I thought about the name of her retreat: 4 Days 2 Hope. The time frame didn't seem plausible. *Only four days? After what we've gone through?* Even four years seemed like a stretch, but I didn't have any other answer in my hip pocket. No clever way to get a redo. Nothing to rely on but faith and hope. The only way out was forward. The next four days had the potential to either make or break us.

I felt entirely broken.

I didn't realize God was doing more than changing me; He was planning to change *us* and the trajectory of our entire family. We would soon discover He had a radical, savage plan, too wonderful for us to even imagine.

| Savage Questions for Reflection |

1. Have you ever experienced a marital crisis? What happened, and how did it change you? What are the lingering effects?

2. Have you told your children about any of your failures? Why or why not?

3. Have you or your spouse ever revealed something that caused significant pain in your marriage? What happened, and how did truth affect your relationship? How did healing occur, or what is needed to be healed?

Chapter 4

UNLOCKING THE DOOR
TO FORGIVENESS

Be kind to one another, compassionate, forgiving each other, just as God in Christ also has forgiven you.

—Ephesians 4:32

Forgiveness is the key that unlocks the door of resentment and the handcuffs of hatred. It is a power that breaks the chains of bitterness and the shackles of selfishness.

—Corrie ten Boom

PRISCILLA

I relaxed as Phil pulled away from the airport drop-off, glad I didn't have to be around him for four days.

I made my way through airport security and later found my seat on the plane. *Thank you, Lord—nobody is beside me.* I just wanted space and to be left alone.

As I sat in complete silence, I felt almost comatose. Phil's revelations had left me numb, and I wanted to curl up, fall asleep, and not wake up again. But questions about him kept my thoughts running in circles, prickling my mind and sending sleep far away. I had never been to a women's retreat where I didn't know a single person, but I was thankful I wouldn't have to make small talk or share what had happened five days ago. I could just listen to the speaker and take notes on how to fix Phil once and for all. I decided to make a list of questions to ask Jenny Speed, hopeful her answers would be the checklist to fix my husband and free me from the mess I was in.

I boarded a van with six other women for the two-hour ride into the mountains of north Georgia. Our driver, Lisa, welcomed us to 4 Days 2 Hope. She was kind, and her smile was genuine, as if she had also experienced the heaviness we each carried. Most of us sat in silence, nursing downcast faces that showed our inner turmoil and pain.

Once inside the rustic cabins and throughout dinner, we did what most do: we made superficial chitchat and awaited the first evening session with anticipation.

Jenny Speed was a petite, slender woman with soft brown hair and eyes. She had an athletic build and was wearing jeans and a blue top emblazoned with "Whatever It Takes," the name of her ministry. Her deep southern accent was paired with a New Yorker-badass attitude, but her contagious laugh and unpretentious style made it easier to let our guards down.

After her brief welcome, the leaders each shared what had brought them to 4 Days 2 Hope many years ago. Some stories were similar to mine, and others totally different. The common cord that united us all was pain. Their sharing set a tone of transparency.

We were listening intently, seated on couches and overstuffed chairs, when Jenny suddenly directed her attention to us. "Ladies, there's a reason why you're here at Hope. Tonight, we want to hear from you. How did you hear of 4 Days 2 Hope, and what brought you here?"

Thick silence enveloped the room, as if the air had been sucked out. We all looked down and avoided eye contact. No one wanted to go first. Jenny patiently ignored the silence and simply waited. It was broken by the woman sitting next to me. All eyes in the room pulled toward us as she shared. Her story was one I'd never forget. "I was a prostitute, pimped out at the age of thirteen by my mom. I was addicted to drugs and eventually became a pusher. I was made to do things I never imagined. Then Jesus came into my life and set me free." Her soft smile pulled oxygen back into the room, and we all seemed to take in a collective breath. "Now I'm back on the streets—but I peddle Jesus instead of drugs." We smiled, and her lips tightened into a thin line as she continued. "I started a ministry for hookers, but now my husband is messing around with them."

She described the incredible pain she'd felt as her husband had pursued the very women she was ministering to. Her pain connected with mine, and I felt united with her and the other women, my sisters of sorrow.

"Thank you for sharing," Jenny said. "We're glad you are here." She looked around the room and asked, "Who's next?" My heart pounded, and my chest burned. I hadn't come to the retreat to share. I wanted to keep my pain hidden and simply learn. It quickly became apparent there was no place to hide at this retreat. It was a place for revealing, and I would have to speak. *Why not? My story is no worse than hers.* I slowly raised my hand and volunteered to share. Through my tears and sobbing, I spewed all the details of what had happened only five days prior. My anguish hemorrhaged over Phil's betrayal.

Jenny studied my face as I shared, and when it was clear that nothing was lingering inside me, she said, "I'm glad you're here. We've never had a woman come to Hope as early as five days after her husband disclosed his infidelity. You're the first. You're at the right place. This weekend is for you."

Still reeling from my boo-hooing, snot-running, Kleenex-swabbing testimony, I was comforted by her genuine words, which helped me catch my breath. I'd never cried so much in front of strangers. All the women there had gone through something similar and felt the pain of betrayal, abandonment, unforgiveness, abuse, or other deep wounds. We were sisters in crisis, and I felt compassion without judgment. I was glad I had come.

Each woman shared heart-wrenching stories of why they were there. Everyone was in a real mess, and I felt relieved that I wasn't alone in my desperate situation. After almost two hours, we took a ten-minute break, and I went to my room. I had turned off my phone, not wanting to be distracted, and decided to send Phil a text: *This is an amazing retreat, like nothing I've ever been to before. These women are real. I'm glad I'm here.*

PHIL

Priscilla's text was a fresh injection of hope, letting me know the retreat wasn't just another women's retreat of games, spa appointments, and laughter. She was a bottom-line person, and her message meant something truly out of the ordinary was happening.

For the first time since coming clean, I was alone at home. In the past, I'd looked for new massage parlors, even on the way home from the airport, so I could later research them on the internet. Then I'd quickly eat dinner with the kids and go to my office to look at porn. But this time, pain consumed my entire soul, and there was no room for lust. I had no sexual desire. All I wanted was reconciliation with Priscilla and a clear word from God about the way forward—that was it. I no longer cared about my career, reputation, or money. I wanted only healing and restoration.

PRISCILLA

The next morning, Jenny rounded us up. "Come on in, ladies. Get your coffee, water, bring your notebook, and take a seat. We've got work to do." She spoke with confidence tinged with jest. She was the main speaker for the session, and her gentle yet straightforward approach intrigued me. She was so natural and seemed to like her own skin. She was not there to put on a show—she was just real, down to earth, like she was saying, "I'm not afraid to be me." As she spoke, it was as if she could read my thoughts, and I wondered how she could know me so well.

Jenny described the five stages of trauma—denial, anger, grief, fear, and healing—providing examples of how she and Paul had worked through each stage. She paused, looking around the room. "Ladies, what stage are you in? Are you stuck in a stage? Are you in a whirlpool of all the stages?"

For the first time, I saw myself in a whirlpool of emotions, stuck since the 16,000 Movies confession eighteen years ago. I had fluctuated between anger, grief, and fear, and had shut down my emotional connection with Phil to cope with my pain. I had focused on self-protection and keeping my mask on so no one could really know me. Anger had been my life, my reality, my go-to reaction when the least little thing hadn't worked out right. Rather than addressing my anger, I had tried to hide it and pretend it wasn't there. My pain was now banging on the door of my heart, screaming for healing from my grief.

The weight of unresolved grief was dreadful, and my fear that Phil would return to porn was continually in front of me, trapping me in hopelessness and despair. But as I sat there, facing it all, the whirlpool felt even worse because the situation in our marriage was no longer just porn. It was a whole double life of immorality.

All my emotions felt constantly bundled up in the washer of life, permanently set on one never-changing cycle: perpetual agitation. As the load churned in day-to-day life, each emotion would erratically surface. I was stuck in unresolved trauma and had kept the washer lid shut tight, but Jenny had just opened the cover, and I was now seeing the full load of our swirling dirty laundry.

How could I have been so blind to this for eighteen years?

Jenny acknowledged that some of us were probably struggling to see past our current trauma, and she encouraged us to ask the Holy Spirit to reveal the wounds from deeper in our pasts. I closed the lid to my present crisis and asked the Holy Spirit to show me my past wounds and the lies I believed.

I remembered the impact of rejection from my siblings, including the manure fight. I had never felt accepted or included, and I'd believed this lie: *You don't belong in the family. No one wants you, and you're not one of them.*

I didn't understand how my parents had ignored my siblings' verbal abuse against me. They hadn't protected me, which had made me feel unworthy, unloved, of no value, with no sense of belonging.

I also remembered teachers who had made me feel stupid and

bullies who had beat me up. I had wanted *someone* to stand up for me, and not even my parents had seemed to care.

Never before had I contemplated so clearly, and directly, my past wounds. Jesus was shining His spotlight on my heart to help me see beyond all the shadows. My entire life, not just the past eighteen years, had been a whirlpool of never-ceasing emotions cycling randomly to the surface and back into the deep without ever moving into the next stage: true, healthy healing. My wounds had remained buried, never healed because I'd shut that lid and not opened it.

Jenny asked us to do a simple exercise: "Think about who you place your trust in—God or man—then personalize Jeremiah 17:5–6."

The blue ink in my workbook screamed at me: *Priscilla had trusted in Phil.*

> Cursed is <u>Priscilla</u> who trusts in <u>Phil</u> and makes <u>Phil her</u> strength, whose heart turns away from the Lord. <u>She</u> is like a shrub in the desert, and shall not see any good come. <u>She</u> shall dwell in the parched places of the wilderness, in an uninhabited salt land. (ESV; author input)

I had never before seen how much I'd made Phil my god, counselor, fixer of all things, provider, friend, and lover of my soul. *I wholly misplaced my trust such a long time ago, beginning with my earthly father.* He hadn't fully protected me as a young woman, and I had trusted in him rather than my heavenly Father. Now, after all these years of marriage, I was seeing how I had clung to Phil instead of Jesus. I had placed all my hope and trust in a man, when all my hope and trust should have been only in Jesus, the true lover of my soul, my true Friend and Father. It was no wonder I'd held on to so many disappointments in our marriage—and no wonder the chasm between Phil and me (and me and God) had continued to grow. No man could have ever lived up to my needs and expectations of him as my god.

I was also seeing my idolatry for the first time: I had erected more than one god, and none of them was my Creator, the living God.

I continued looking at Jeremiah 17:7–8.

Blessed is the man who trusts in the Lord, whose trust is the Lord. He is like a tree planted by water, that sends out its roots by the stream, and does not fear when heat comes, for its leaves remain green, and is not anxious in the year of drought, for it does not cease to bear fruit. (ESV)

God's words, written so long ago, now poked through my whirlpool of emotions, giving me spiritual clarity of each piece of laundry in the load. A true revelation. While the dirty water churned endlessly inside me, I felt parched, dwelling in a wilderness like a tumbleweed with no root, no life, no living water . . . blown at will by the scorching breath of the enemy of my soul across the vast desert of life. All because I had trusted in earthly men since birth instead of being rooted and watered by Jesus.

I longed to be the strong, flourishing tree rooted beside the beautiful stream, bearing fruit in every season, with no fear of drought or heat that life inevitably brings.

For all those years, I had misplaced my trust. I had been the one in the wrong. Jesus had not been my first and only love; I, too, had been unfaithful—to my heavenly Father. My misplaced trust was now so clear to me, even as I grappled with a shattered marriage and my lost dreams of living happily ever after and growing old with Phil. Everything was now a heap of oozing filth that produced nothingness.

Lord Jesus, what have I done? I've rejected You for so long.

With the light of truth piercing my heart, showing me the facts of my problems, my cocoon of numbness and protection began to dissolve.

In the midst of my reflection, I was jarred by a gentle voice inside me: "Priscilla, I didn't bring you here to fix Phil. I brought you here to fix you." That was the first time I'd heard God's voice so clearly. His words were clear, soft, and true. I needed Jesus. I needed to be well and to be healed by Him. His words held me so tightly I couldn't move.

In awe and brokenness, I sat there thinking, *That was God speaking to me! And He really does love me!* I was stunned for a few minutes by what I had just experienced. My entire reason for going to Hope had been to fix Phil, but God's entire reason for me being there was to fix me. He was pursuing my healing, just like He was pursuing Phil's healing. Yes, the pain of Phil's betrayal was real, but the power of God's voice—opening my eyes and heart to His love for me—was overwhelming. I had often heard people read God's Word, but hearing God's voice directly inside me from His Word and Spirit was the beginning of my healing.

The next morning, Jenny began with a session on forgiveness. I had always thought forgiveness was more like forgetting and putting the offense in the past: forgive and forget. The problem with my thinking was that all the ugly emotions and pain quickly surfaced whenever a past offense was brought up, which meant I hadn't actually forgiven. My response to forgiving had been to stuff offenses in the overfilled, broken laundry tub, and my effort to forget them had been to close the lid. I had never truly forgiven because offenses were never truly washed so they could heal.

When the 16,000 Movies incident had happened, I'd tried to forgive Phil and forget, believing the lie that time heals all wounds. Now, eighteen years later, I was awakened to realize I had not forgiven Phil nor forgotten how his betrayal made me feel. The memory of that day was still breeding anger, resentment, and bitterness. "Time heals all wounds" was another lie. The truth was closer to "Time causes wounds to fester."

My wounds had scabbed over, but underneath was a dangerous infection, continually eating at my soul, fueling my feverish anger. That day at Hope, God removed my scabs, and I could see the pus of unforgiveness had been hidden and poisoning me for so long.

During the first evening, when Jenny had asked us, "Where are you?" I'd seen myself only as a victim of Phil's betrayal, so that was where I had thought I was on the journey. Now I clearly saw I was actually in bondage to unforgiveness, and that bondage was threatening to destroy the rest of my life! Although I had thought forgiveness was primarily for Phil's benefit, I now saw the truth: forgiveness was for me too.

Intellectually, I knew I needed to forgive Phil, but I was still drowning in that whirlpool of emotions and didn't *feel* like forgiving him. The pain was powerful. In the past, my expressions of forgiveness had occurred after I no longer *felt* offended. In other words, I based forgiveness on my feelings. God showed me that true, healing forgiveness is based on *faith*—believing He provides the power to do what He commands and that my feelings of forgiveness will follow, not precede, my forgiveness of Phil.

> True, healing forgiveness is based on *faith*—believing He provides the power to do what He commands and that feelings of forgiveness will follow.

I had heard the Bible enough to know that Jesus commanded us to forgive, and now I knew that truly forgiving Phil and others was possible by *faith*, not feeling. To be freed, I needed to believe that Jesus had given me the power to forgive, even when I didn't feel like forgiving.

My next thoughts were tentative as I pushed into this new and unknown place in my thoughts and heart that Jesus was spreading out before me. He was holding out his hands to me, calling me by name. I slowly let words trickle from my mouth that I didn't *feel* in my emotions, declaring what I knew to be true rather than how I felt. "Lord Jesus, I know I can forgive Phil because You have forgiven me of so much."

With that simple prayer, I asked God to help me forgive Phil by faith, not feeling.

I was determined to figure out how to unlock God's power in me, by faith, to forgive Phil in the face of so much lingering pain. My thoughts were broken by Jenny's voice.

"Ladies, forgiveness doesn't mean forgetting. It means *you choose* to release into God's hands the one who wounded you."

It was suddenly so clear: I had never released Phil into God's hands!

I had been fighting for control. I had wanted to be his continual judge, reigning above him and exacting payment and revenge. He had hurt me, and he deserved to pay! That mindset and heart posture had pushed God aside and positioned myself in His seat; I had not trusted that He could deal with Phil without my help. I had seen Phil as my problem and myself as his judge, and I'd chosen to hold on to the offenses while simultaneously trying to hide them from my thoughts and pretend they had never occurred.

Then it happened.

Everything shifted into its rightful place when I moved from God's seat and relinquished to Him my hold on Phil, with a simple request: *God, Phil is your problem. You deal with him.*

A weight was off my shoulders, cast directly onto God's, where it should have been all along. I was no longer the judge and jury and no longer the victim. I was the victor because of Christ.

On our last night at Hope, we broke into small groups of three to four women for prayer. I was accustomed to praying at church, but this was different. Jenny said in her southern twang, "Ladies, I know some of you are Pentecostal and Charismatic, and some of you are Baptist and Presbyterian. So for you Pentecostals, we're gonna do some deliverance, and for you Baptists, we're gonna break some strongholds! Whatever you want to call it is fine; you have an opportunity to experience the power of the Holy Spirit tonight."

I had no clue what to expect. I hadn't been in this position before, and it felt strange to this former Baptist, Methodist, nondenominational girl. All I knew was that I was at the end of myself and the beginning of letting everything go by giving it all to God.

I looked at all the pages I'd written, including the inventory of all my wounds, shame, regrets, and mistakes—and there I saw it, written in blue ink: I had been the rebellious one toward God for most of my life. I had been apathetic toward His word, His direction, His voice, and even His presence. Now I was in the presence of a Holy God, seeing and feeling the weight of my own sin. For the first time, I was bowing down before Him, confessing and agreeing with Jesus that I had chosen my way in the past instead of His. I had looked out for my own best interest, tried on my own to protect myself, and consequently denied Him access to my life, my heart, and my mind. I had betrayed His love for me. I was the adulterer. The very judgment I had leveled at Phil only a few days ago was now squarely pointed at me.

After our small-group leader prayed, each of us renounced the work of the enemy in our lives and asked the Lord to take back from the enemy what he had stolen. We all prayed in agreement. In the middle of our desperate cries for help, Jesus was there with us—in unconditional love, grace, and true, healing forgiveness.

I prayed an honest, no-holding-back, gut-level prayer before my Lord. I confessed all my junk, my regrets, and the ill decisions I had made. I renounced my rebellion, apathy, critical spirit, fear, bitterness, anger, and unforgiveness. In that moment, I realized more fully how much Jesus loved me, and the full weight I had been carrying for most of my life lifted.

I felt free.

The churning had ceased, all the dirty water had drained out, and the living water of Jesus was pouring over me and filling me.

Around midnight, after about three hours of prayer, our group adjourned as new women in Christ. We walked lighter and taller; we now carried a radiance in our souls that we had not carried in.

I remembered Jenny's encouragement from earlier in the day. "Ladies, if you want reconciliation with your husband, you have to take one hundred percent responsibility for your portion of the problems in your marriage. If you think you're blameless"—she pointed upward—"you should get up on that cross with Jesus. Whether your part of the marriage problem is two percent, ten percent, or fifty percent, you have to take full personal responsibility and ask God and your husband to forgive you."

I had wondered what my percentage was, and that second evening at Hope, God made it clear to me. It wasn't only Phil who had messed up royally by living an immoral life. I had made my own choice to live in hypocrisy and idolatry, wearing a mask of the good Christian wife and mom while, under the surface, my heart was desolate, dry, hard ground with no life and no growth. Yes, Phil was an adulterer and had chosen to do immoral things, but I, too, had chosen to betray God by putting Him in the back seat instead of the driver's seat—and not even allowing Him in the front seat beside me. Until that evening, I had not relinquished the driving to Him but, in essence, had said, "I got this. I can do it. I can make my own decisions. You just sit back there and watch me drive. I'll call You when I need You." I had traded the immense and powerful love of God for the love of myself and the world. I was an adulterer, just like Phil, and my adultery had undoubtedly contributed at least 10 percent toward the distance we had begun to experience in our marriage long before Phil's confession. We had both created a massive cavern between us.

That evening, in reflection and revelation, I took 100 percent responsibility for my portion of the problems in our marriage.

Phil had always been at the top of our family pecking order, where he had placed himself since the day we'd married. I knew it, my kids knew it, everyone knew it. The moment he'd confessed, he had let go of that top rung, and in my eyes, he had dropped far below me—and I had quickly grabbed that top spot. I'd agreed with Phil that he was a wretched bum for what he had done to me, our marriage, and our family. Now, having seen my own sin through God's eyes, my own shortcomings, my own adultery, I had to be willing to loosen my grip on the top rung, let go, and trust God to be my safety net.

I slid down that ladder and found myself seated *beside* Phil, resting with him.

He and I were now equal sinners, clinging only to Jesus in likeminded faith that He was at work in our lives, our marriage, and our family. Our eyes were now fastened upward to God, seated in His rightful place in our hearts and lives: on the top rung.

Seeing my sin made it impossible for me to continue holding Phil in judgment. Yes, the awful feelings were still there, and I still felt the sting of his betrayal, but my self-righteousness was gone. I could no longer demand revenge, retribution, or penalty on Phil because my Lord Jesus was not demanding those on me. I asked Jesus to let me participate in His forgiveness of Phil. God was the author of forgiveness, and any expectation I'd had that I could ever forgive Phil without God's power had been misplaced.

That evening at Hope, I completely forgave Phil and released him to God. And I stood on God's forgiveness.

From across the country, women had come to participate, as complete strangers, in 4 Days 2 Hope. Four days later, we had walked together through trauma, betrayal, wounds, and heartaches and ended up sharing the rawest parts of who we were. We had found commonality and connection, which had created a sisterhood. And we had found true hope. Maybe such honesty, openness, transparency, humility, and unity were what Jesus wanted all along for the body of Christ. It was not likely I'd see some of the women after that weekend, but the few I would see on occasion would be real about what they had faced and what God was doing in their lives. No masks, no hiding, no pretense . . . and no shame.

On the flight home, I realized I'd been running on fumes. My exhaustion pushed me deep into my seat. I was spent. There was nothing left of my energy, but I still needed to face what awaited me at home—and that would be far from a bed of roses. A slight uncertainty entered my heart. *How do I walk this out, not just on paper but with Phil?* I didn't want to go home and just kiss and make up, forgive and forget. No! I wanted a restart, a new beginning. I couldn't go back to what we'd thought was our normal, mediocre-at-best marriage. I had to draw a line in the sand and say, "No more normal."

PHIL

I pulled into arrivals and saw Priscilla walking out of baggage claim. My heart sputtered as I wondered what type of greeting I'd receive. Maybe a hug? A small kiss? Maybe an "I forgive you for everything, Phil" and a big kiss?

I stopped at the curb and jumped out, looking for a signal from Priscilla that all was well. "Hey, Priscilla! How are you doing?"

"I'm so tired," she uttered wearily. "This was a long weekend. No sleep." She handed me her luggage and turned to get in the car. No big or small kiss—not even a warm hello. Her demeanor suggested an "all is well" moment wasn't in my immediate future.

On the way home, we shared chitchat mostly about whether the girls had been okay without her, sprinkled with a few tidbits of her weekend experience. It became clear that something amazing had happened, and while she still seemed hurt, the screaming and stomping of feet were now gone. I was thankful.

When we arrived home, Priscilla quickly wheeled her luggage into the bedroom while our girls ran in shouting, "Mommy! Mommy!" She gave them big hugs and kisses, lingering while they enthusiastically embraced her and told her how much they'd missed her. Their interactions were warm. I watched from the sideline—I obviously wasn't part of Priscilla's eagerness to connect emotionally. She walked them to their rooms to say good night and returned to our room a few minutes later.

"Phil, I want to talk about our bedroom situation." My heart sank. "You have two choices." Her tone was matter-of-fact and unemotional. "You can either sleep in the guest bedroom or pretend like we're sleeping in two twin beds," she said as she motioned toward our king-size bed. "You stay on your side, and I stay on mine. No touching." She had obviously spent time thinking about how she felt. My hope for a small hug or kiss had been unrealistic.

"I'll take the imaginary twin bed," I replied, hoping that maybe one day we would at least rub feet, even if by accident.

Priscilla nodded her acceptance, then turned and muttered, "I'm going to take a shower and go to bed." She shut the bathroom door, making clear I wasn't invited to join her. I climbed into my pretend twin bed.

Eventually Priscilla emerged and joined me but stayed far on her side. She said good night and turned off the light.

That's it? No kiss, no tenderness, no nothing? I rolled over. "Good night." At least I wasn't sleeping in the guest room.

PRISCILLA

I woke up at five o'clock Monday and saw the kitchen light under our bedroom door. *Oh man! Phil's already up!* I lay still for a few minutes, trying to figure out if I should get up and face him or stay put, hoping for more sleep. I decided to pray. *Jesus, I know You've forgiven me for so much, and You've forgiven Phil. I want my forgiveness toward him to be real. You command us to forgive, so it must be possible. Jesus, help me walk out my forgiveness toward him.*

That prayer was the first of many asking God to help me walk out my forgiveness by faith.

I got out of bed, picked up my robe, and walked to the kitchen. Phil was sitting at the kitchen table, reading his Bible and drinking a cup of coffee. His hair was spiked in all directions, and his eyes were red and sleepy like he'd had a restless night. There was no good-morning kiss or embrace, which had been our routine for many years. It was okay with me. I still wanted some physical distance.

I pulled out a chair and sat down. We looked into each other's eyes, and I dropped mine to my tightly folded hands. Phil asked, "How did you sleep?"

"Better here than in Georgia. How about you?"

He shook his head, letting out a soft grunt. "Do you want to walk this morning before the girls get up?"

"Sure," I replied. "Let me change and get my shoes."

> If our marriage was going to heal, the healing had to start within each of us as individuals, from the inside out.

Over the next several days, Phil and I woke up early every morning to walk and talk together. It was the beginning of unpacking the things God had revealed to me: my apathetic spirit, my unforgiveness, and the fear and anger I had carried for so long. I could tell my testimony was preparing Phil for his upcoming weekend at 4 Days 2 Freedom, and my fears were slowly being replaced by faith that God was going to do something special inside Phil. If our marriage was going to heal, the healing had to start within each of us as individuals, from the inside out. The next four days would be a defining moment for Phil, and I trusted God with Phil's heart. I had no idea God had more in mind than just changing Phil. He would change the trajectory of our entire family.

| Savage Questions for Reflection |

1. Have you ever considered what percentage of the problems in your marriage is your responsibility? What is the percentage, and why?

2. Are you holding on to any unforgiveness? Can you take a step of faith to ask God to help you forgive? Can you say "I forgive . . ."?

3. What is the deepest pain in your marriage? Have you ever shared that pain with anyone?

4. When was your closest encounter with God? What's standing in the way of receiving more from your relationship with Him? What can you do about the obstacle?

Chapter 5

RELEASING THE POWER
OF HUMILITY

God is opposed to the proud, but gives grace to the humble.
—JAMES 4:6

One of the greatest works of grace in the heart is to humble our pride.
—CHARLES SPURGEON

PHIL

I arrived at 4 Days 2 Freedom just in time for dinner and quickly found Paul Speed. He was tall and lanky, wearing shorts, a Whatever It Takes T-shirt, and no shoes. He showed no pretense, and I liked that. The last thing I needed to see was a bunch of business guys in ties.

"Hi, Paul. I'm Phil Fretwell. I spoke with you from the plane a couple of weeks ago."

"Hi, Phil. So glad you made it! You can put your things on one of the beds, and we're going to eat in a few minutes. Make yourself at home."

Paul seemed easygoing, affable, and used to handling a group. There were eight participants, plus Paul and a couple of guys preparing food. I realized all of us were there for a reason—probably because we'd reached the bottom of the pit, or our wives had demanded we come. However, no one wanted to admit it, and we busied ourselves with typical small talk about where we were from and what we did for work.

After dinner, Paul got down to business. He quickly summarized his personal story and then passed the conversation to us. "Guys, let's go around and each take a few minutes to share why you're here."

I had been to other men's retreats, and most of them had included some type of call to transparency. I had always hung back, waiting to hear how much other men were willing to share. I had even helped lead a men's retreat several years earlier and suggested to the pastor that participants not be put on the spot because it was uncomfortable. Of course, it was really me who hated opening the kimono. But this time I quickly raised my hand.

I usually relished all eyes on me as an opportunity to make myself look smart. But this time was different. Paul's candor with me on the plane about my pride problem was still fresh on my mind, and I knew there was no room to manage my image. I was going to be self-effacing with no expectation of admiration from anyone. I was in a pit and willing to do whatever it took to get out, so I shared transparently.

"About two weeks ago, I came clean with my wife. I told her I'd been leading a double life, hiding sexual sin from her for most of our marriage."

My summary weighed heavy on my emotions as I spilled what I had painfully told Priscilla in detail less than two weeks earlier. I choked back tears to continue. "I had been using porn since I was a kid but thought getting married would finally give me a God-ordained sex partner who would cure all my problems. Well . . . that didn't work, and my porn issue grew to include going to strip clubs and massage parlors, and I couldn't stop. All this time, I'd been active in my church, leading weekly Bible studies, and serving as an elder. All the secrecy was killing me.

"About four months ago, I cried out to God to heal my mind. I needed a rescue because I was so unhappy with my life, and all my efforts to fix my problems had failed. And about four weeks ago, I saw

72

symptoms that led me to believe I had contracted an STD, and it scared me to death. I called a good friend, and he connected me to Paul. Paul told me I needed to embrace humility by confessing what I'd done, starting with my wife. So that's what I did, and it was the most difficult conversation of my life. I'll never forget the picture of her in our kitchen—screaming, stamping her feet, and telling me how disgusted she was with me. But she said she would help me find healing. I know we have a long way to go, and that's why I'm here."

My brief testimony felt so different from all times past when I'd spoken to a group. Gone were my typical protectionism, posturing, and jockeying for position. I no longer wanted to be revered and seen as profound. I was as low as one could go, and the first step to freedom was to be authentically transparent and humble. I wasn't sure where to begin, but instinctively I knew a good start was being open about what a reprehensible person I'd become. Maybe one day I'd also be able to describe how God healed me. But that wouldn't be today. This day was to tear down any lingering pride, beginning with my desire to look good and be somebody. Even though the group of men was small, all with similar problems, it was a start and felt scary and beautiful at the same time.

As the evening continued, other men's stories included porn use from their childhoods. I had expected that but noticed something different about the way Paul talked about porn. In addition to the P-word, he also used the M-word—masturbation—and he used it frequently, to my shock. The P-word was socially acceptable, but I'd never heard anyone say the M-word at church. Occasionally, I'd heard it at a men's retreat, but it had been quickly swept aside, everyone feeling the awkwardness of shame it invoked. The more Paul said the M-word, the more I began to see that masturbation was the real crux of the problem related to porn. After all, porn without masturbation was just frustration. Masturbation allowed men to imagine themselves inside the porn scenes, intensifying the feelings of lust and shame that made men want to hide.

Priscilla and I had never talked about masturbation in our twenty-eight years of marriage. Even in my 16,000 Movies confession, I hadn't told her I'd masturbated while watching the movies. It was just too embarrassing, too shameful to say out loud. I had talked with my sons about masturbation, but only to tell them not to do it because once they started the habit, it would be hard to stop. This was the one thing I knew was true about masturbation, and I feared my sons would wind up like me.

Some men in the group tentatively tested saying *masturbation*, but I could tell it was uncomfortable for them. An older guy, a marine veteran, said he would "relieve himself." He couldn't say *masturbation* or any of its crude derivatives. Also, anytime I placed my workbook on top of my Bible, he'd reorder them, hiding the workbook beneath. He said, "Phil, my parents taught me to honor God's Word by not putting anything else on top of it. You need to always keep your Bible on top."

Are you kidding me? Here you are, separated from your wife, having sex with other women, hooked on porn and masturbation, and you're telling me the key to recovery is making sure there's nothing on top of my Bible? That's what the old me would have fired back, stating how ridiculous that virtue sounded. Instead, I absorbed his correction and suppressed my typical pride that would have forcefully argued my point of view with numerous Bible verses to support my position. Not this time. I could see my pride was at the heart of my desire to correct him. I could not let pride get a foothold at this retreat.

I now understood that the real problem with masturbation wasn't the physical act; it was the fantasies imprinted in my mind that enforced the belief that sex was all about me. Even then, I recalled my lust over the first pornographic pictures I'd seen as a child. And I recalled Matthew 5:28, in which Jesus said, "Everyone who looks at a woman with lust for her has already committed adultery with her in his heart." I was facing the truth: the sin of lust and adultery happens first based on what's happening inside my head, not outside. In theory, if I masturbated with no sexual fantasies, I could masturbate without sin. Those with children may have seen this when their toddlers discovered their genitals, even among company. While such times may have been embarrassing, their discoveries weren't sin but purely attaching their minds to the feelings of their biological structures, not to lust or sexual fantasies.

I came face to face with another truth: while it was theoretically possible for some people to masturbate without sin, it wasn't possible for me. I had indulged in sexual fantasies and lust through masturbation since I was probably eleven years old. The more I fantasized, the more such thoughts dominated my mind, even when I was making love with Priscilla. Fantasies and masturbation had stolen from my wife and me the moments of true passion we could have experienced together. Instead, I had allowed my thoughts to roam among my concocted fantasies, perpetuated by porn and massage parlors.

My lack of understanding what masturbation was doing to me made me self-centered, consumed only with fulfilling my own sexual desires. Thereby, I was a taker rather than a giver in my sexual relationship with Priscilla. I was seeing that God designed sexual desire to drive men closer to their wives and that I had allowed sexual fantasies to drive me to porn and masturbation. Rather than linger for an hour of lovemaking with Priscilla, my mind and body had pursued sexual release that took only minutes. It was no wonder she didn't seem to enjoy sex and had frequent dreams of my infidelity.

After everyone shared why they had come to the retreat, Paul asked, "Men, do you believe you have the power to say no to your lust?"

My simple off-the-cuff answer was, *No, that's why I'm here! If I could say no to porn and massage parlors, I wouldn't be in this predicament. I would have said no a long time ago!* I began to think maybe Paul hadn't thought about the complexity of what I was going through. *If after four days he's going to say the secret to success is "Just say no," maybe I should go home right now.*

Paul turned to Jason, who had just arrived, and asked him to share his story. Jason was young, energetic, and lively. He was a pastor's kid with a long history of sexual immorality, drugs, and alcohol abuse—and he used the word *masturbation* frequently. He talked openly about what had happened in his marriage and how it had wound up on the brink of crisis. Nothing he had done had worked to curb his sexual appetite.

Then he'd attended 4 Days 2 Freedom four years ago, and he'd not looked at porn or masturbated since.

What? Did I hear that right? He attended this retreat four years ago and hasn't since looked at porn or masturbated? With Jason's new understanding, God had transformed his lustful desires, which in turn had restored his life and marriage. His testimony got my attention and started changing my thinking about one pertinent part of Paul's question I'd overlooked: "Do you *believe*?"

My life had been a secret testament of failure that generated a cycle of sin, shame, and repentance followed by failure. As I would meditate on my defeats, I'd become further defeated and replace the truth of God's Word with a lie: *since I have no power to stop what I'm doing, I need to manage my sin to minimize the effect on my family and me.* My capacity to believe anything different had disintegrated.

God was now helping me replace that lie with His truths:

Do not be conformed to this world, but be transformed by the renewing of your mind, so that you may prove what the will of God is, that which is good and acceptable and perfect. (Rom. 12:2)

This is the will of God, your sanctification; that is, that you abstain from sexual immorality. (1 Thess. 4:3)

Flee immorality. Every other sin that a man commits is outside the body, but the immoral man sins against his own body. (1 Cor. 6:18)

I knew these verses but had put them in the category of things I should obey but couldn't. So these verses were aspirational, targets to shoot for, but not achievable because I had never *believed* I could change.

The apostle Thomas had the same belief problem, which earned him the name "doubting Thomas."

The other disciples . . . were saying to him [Thomas], "We have seen the Lord!" But he said to them, "Unless I shall see in his hands the imprint of the nails, and put my finger into the place of the nails, and put my hand into his side, I will not believe." . . . Jesus came . . . and stood in their midst, and said, "Peace be with you." Then he said to Thomas, "Reach here your finger, and see My hands; and reach here your hand and put it into My side; And be not unbelieving, but believing." Thomas answered and said to him, "My Lord and my God!" (John 20:25–28)

Thomas believed when Jesus showed His wounds to him. Jesus could have shown up with no wounds or scars, but He chose to let Thomas see what He had experienced. He knew that when Thomas saw His wounds and scars, he would believe.

As man after man in our group openly shared their wounds and scars, I began to believe that God was who He said He was.

The men who had come to testify of the freedom they had found were not merely talking about God's power—they were demonstrating that power by showing their wounds and scars, just like how Jesus showed His to Thomas. Seeing the transformation that had taken place in the alumni's lives propelled me toward seeing and believing that God could transform me as well. The familiar verses that had been only aspirational to me in the past were now possible. I began to *believe* that whatever command God gave, He also gave power to obey.

For all the years leading to the retreat, I'd thought I was lacking some intellectual knowledge that would change my life; but in reality, I was missing the power of God that comes through *believing*.

When I had read about doubting Thomas in the past, I had focused more on the next verse: "Because you have seen Me, have you believed? Blessed are they who did not see, and yet believed" (John 20:29). Jesus's response had seemed to me like a rebuke and pushed me toward thinking that people who had *not* seen the miraculous were *more* blessed than people who *had* seen the miraculous. However, with my new insight, I believed Jesus was showing Thomas He provides a way for *everyone* to be blessed—even me and the men around me who had proven to be slaves to sin. Some people have faith to believe without seeing, and they are blessed; others struggle with their faith, and still, God shows them His marvelous power and gives His grace to help them believe. Neither person is blessed more than the other.

> I'd thought I was lacking some intellectual knowledge that would change my life; but in reality, I was missing the power of God that comes through *believing*.

For the men at 4 Days 2 Freedom, many of us struggled to believe God had the power to change us. But by His grace and through the men's testimonies, we were now seeing God demonstrate His death-defying, life-transforming, miraculous power.

"Gentlemen," Paul continued, "you are all here because you've been unable to change behaviors that have caused you and your wives a lot of pain. You have to understand that you do what you do because you *feel* what you feel—because you *think* what you think. The problem isn't in your doing; it's in your *thinking*. You've never done anything you didn't feel like doing, and you've never had a feeling that didn't start with your thinking. The battle is in your *mind*, so your thinking is what needs to change. Renewing your mind is where the victory starts. Apps on your phone and accountability partners may help control what you do, but you will never be free until you change your thinking. Without changing the patterns of your mind, you'll always be tethered to counselors, phone apps, accountability partners, and other curbs and bumpers."

Wow! That was a big statement. It summarized what I'd acutely felt for the past eighteen years. I genuinely wanted to stop my behaviors, but I first needed transformation in my thinking. In the past, I had asked God to transform my *behaviors* rather than my *desires*, yet I had failed over and over. Thereby I believed transformation was not possible. In other words, I had tried to change from the outside by changing my behaviors instead of from the inside by asking God to change my thinking—and believing He could. It was clear that my thinking had always been the problem, and God's healing and transformation had to start with my mind.

As other 4 Days 2 Freedom alumni unpacked their rescue stories, my belief emerged that God could change me from the inside out. Since He had done it for them, He would do it for me.

Like Thomas, when I saw the power of God in the scars of the alumni's testimonies, a switch inside me flipped from unbelief to belief. Yes, my belief in God's power to heal me was just a spark, a flicker, a minute speck, but it moved my thoughts from thinking that healing was merely *possible* with God to believing it was *probable*. I could feel the truth of His healing power taking root in me—not only in my mind but in my emotions. It was what I had begged God to do in me only four months earlier. Just like Thomas, I was encountering the healing power of God that not only had raised Jesus from the dead but would raise and heal me as well.

Every man's testimony mentioned two essential words: *pride* and *humility*. I recalled Paul's words to me on the plane. "Phil, you have a pride problem, and God wants to fix it. He resists the proud but gives grace to the humble."

My pride had kept all my problems hidden, allowing my sinful behaviors to grow. My entire life to that point had focused on making myself look good—to feel that I was somebody. I had pursued my career and church positions so others would admire me. I had pulled Priscilla and my children along with me, asking them to look good because their appearance reflected on me. My whole life had been self-centered, full of pride. For the first time, I was stripping away the fig leaves I'd hidden my true self behind and allowing others to see what a proud, arrogant man I had become.

Paul had also told me, "You need to take steps of humility through your confessions. When you do, you'll position yourself to receive God's amazing grace and healing in your life."

I had always linked the word *confession* to *forgiveness*, focusing on 1 John 1:9: "If we confess our sins, He is faithful and righteous to forgive us our sins and to cleanse us from all unrighteousness." But I had ignored James 5:16: "Confess your sins to one another, and pray for one another, so that you may be healed." I desperately needed healing in my broken state, and I now saw how healing was linked to confession of sin and prayer.

Though I had cried out to God four months prior to heal my mind, I had wanted instantaneous healing without anyone knowing. Now, for the first time, I understood that God's healing would come when I positioned myself in faith to receive His amazing grace, which meant pulling everything out of darkness and laying it all out in the light of truth. I needed to allow God to work from the inside out. I had to be HOT to be healed.

> God's healing would come when I positioned myself in faith to receive His amazing grace, which meant pulling everything out of darkness and laying it all out in the light of truth.

Our group asked Paul many questions about transparently confessing our sins to our wives and how they would react. In general, there was a lot of fear among us. We had all managed our lives through secrecy, with the "pass card" that we were protecting our wives from truths that would hurt them. I'll never forget Paul's enormous encouragement: "We've not seen wives walk away from husbands who are truly broken over their sin."

Am I broken over my sin or just over the circumstances I've found myself in?

I recalled Priscilla's tears as she had confessed her apathy and rebellion toward God. Yes, she had natural brokenness over my sin—what I had done to her—but she was also spiritually broken over her own apathy and rebellion and her choice to trust men rather than God. I was clearly experiencing a lot of emotional pain over what I had done to

Priscilla, which caused only *natural* brokenness, the type of brokenness everyone experiences when something traumatic happens. But what I needed was *spiritual* brokenness.

I called out to God to show me my pride and break me spiritually so healing and rebuilding could begin from the inside. It was hard for me to fathom how much He had pursued me and my healing because He truly loved me. Even in the midst of my sin, God had been showing me much kindness while resisting my pride and arrogance. I suddenly realized what Romans 2:4 meant by "The kindness of God leads you to repentance."

I let God's love wash over me as I saw and experienced His kindness in a new way and felt His compassion pulling me into spiritual brokenness.

As the weekend progressed, Paul spoke about how fear controls people to the point of believing lies that shape their thinking. My thoughts turned to my number one fear the enemy had long whispered inside me: "You are just like your father and destined to turn out like him."

When I'd discovered my dad was also viewing porn, I had agreed with the lie that porn doesn't hurt anyone and had accepted that I would vainly battle the lure of this temptation for the rest of my life.

Out of fear that my children would become like me, I had laid down the law to them regarding sexual purity and become legalistic in controlling their phones, internet usage, and who they spent time with. My legalism had created emotional distance from my children and Priscilla as I'd prioritized correction over connection.

During the retreat, I journaled raw truth each day, asking God to give words for my emotions. As I processed what I was learning, I wrote:

Praying for Priscilla all the time. She is bearing my burden. She is amazing. I could not do this without her. Well, maybe. God is the real key, and He's using Priscilla.

I pray I will never forget how Priscilla wailed when I exposed the extent of my sin. It was so painful. I want to feel this whenever I'm tempted to sin.

I must be ready to never have sex again. I need to focus on restoring my relationship with God first. Restoring only a physical relationship with Priscilla will not be the key.

Oh God, please help me.

Journaling was a powerful tool that helped me practice hearing from God, helped me decipher my feelings, and tangibly reminded me of the way forward. I didn't know it at the time, but daily journaling would create a treasure trove of God's words, combined with my thoughts about what He was doing in my life.

PRISCILLA

I didn't expect to hear from Phil, so I was surprised when the phone rang on Friday evening.

"Hey! What's going on? I didn't think you'd call."

"Hey, I have a few minutes. How's it going with you and the girls?"

"Everything's fine. How's the retreat?" I couldn't make small talk while we were trying to climb the mountain facing us.

"It's going well. It's a small group. Several men have come and gone, sharing testimonies. One interesting thing—this retreat isn't very religious, if that makes sense. I mean, Paul doesn't open or close sessions with typical perfunctory prayer, and he doesn't force us to make a list of religious things to do, like reading our Bibles and praying more. He talks a lot about pride versus humility, what God wants to do in our lives, and living open, broken, and free."

It felt good to hear Phil focused on something besides just looking more religious. We had done enough of that for years. I didn't want to live in our hypocritical lie any longer.

"Priscilla, could I ask you to think about one thing before I get home?"

"What is it?"

"Think about what I need to do to help you feel safe. What boundaries do you want me to have so you're not worried about what I'm doing? Whatever God brings to your mind, I'm willing to do it. Anything. Okay?"

Well, this is certainly new. I'd never heard Phil offer to give up anything for me, and his question hit the core of my fears, where I was still living. His work would still necessitate his traveling and having client lunches and dinners. Until he'd confessed his secret life, I'd never worried about where he was, but now I had to think seriously about his future absences. "Okay, I'll pray about it."

"Great, thanks a lot. I'll see you Sunday afternoon. This retreat is really helping me see myself."

"Good. I've been praying for you. See you on Sunday."

I was encouraged. The old Phil would have been focused more on his agenda than on my safety. Something had to be happening inside of him.

PHIL

On Saturday, Paul asked us to write an identity statement about who we truly were in Christ. I went outside by the lake, sat cross-legged on the grass with my workbook, and wept. I was spiritually broken, humbled, and genuinely contrite, seeing for the first time where my sin had come from, where sin had taken me, and what God now wanted to do inside me. I begged Him for words that would adequately sum up my feelings about who I really was.

That's when I heard God's voice inside me, responding to my cry. "You have a father."

I buckled. A word from God about my dad! My fears and insecurities had told me that I would become like him—and I had come too close.

God continued speaking with an almost audible pause between each word. "You have a *Father* . . . whose name is . . . *Faithful* . . . and *True.*" I gasped, seeing His truth for the first time. My fear had come as I'd focused on my natural father. But God wanted me to focus on my heavenly Father, the only Father whose name could be consistently Faithful and True. He was the only One who could set the godly example I needed to follow. I began to write, and the words came quickly:

> *I am Phil, the son of my Father whose name is Faithful and True. I bear the imprint of His character in my body, soul, and spirit, and I seek to experience His truth in my innermost being. I celebrate His faithfulness in my relationships with my wife and family, and I embrace humility to break the chains of sin and set the captives free. I know God, I hear His voice in me, and I will follow and obey Him even when the cost is great. I trust God for His victory in my life and proclaim the favorable year of the Lord for my children, their children, and all the generations to come.*

As I later read this statement in front of our group, I was declaring for the first time who God said I really was—the truth based on hearing His voice.

I no longer had a hard heart. Softening to His molding began to change everything.

PRISCILLA

After Phil's call, I found my 4 Days 2 Hope workbook and flipped through the pages, remembering what God had done in me only a week ago. There was one final assignment I hadn't been able to complete because I had been emotionally drained and exhausted.

At the retreat on Sunday morning, we had gathered as usual for breakfast. But the atmosphere had changed. Yes, we were tired from the previous night's prayer time, but there was a new spiritual energy and openness that had not been there before.

After breakfast, Jenny had asked us to write an identity statement, which was new for me. I had never taken time to consider who I was from God's perspective.

I had opened my workbook, picked up my pen, and tried to start writing but couldn't form the sentences or even find the words. Writing and grammar had never been easy for me and had created many inse-curities. Portuguese was my first language, and when I'd come to the United States in third grade, unable to speak English fluently, teach-ers had written me off. As a result, I'd run from anything that required writing or speaking. So when Jenny asked us to write our identity statements, I froze and waited to hear from God. When she had later asked us to share our statements, my paper had been blank, and I had remained quiet. But it was okay; even though I couldn't write God's thoughts of me, I knew He had done undeniable work in my life.

Now, almost a week later, I stared at the same blank sheet. I asked God for His words to write. After many minutes, I wrote the first sen-tence, calling myself what I heard God calling me. The rest followed as I heard more from Him.

I am Priscilla, the daughter of the Eternal One. He has given me the power and authority to overcome the evil one in my life, proclaim God's goodness to those around me, heal the brokenhearted, and restore families with His truth. I will fight valiantly like Deborah to see the goodness of God restored in my family's lives.

The beautiful, God-given words provided oil to my wounds, and I sat at the kitchen table sobbing. I knew the story of Deborah in the Bible—a judge of Israel and a strong and mighty warrior. That's how God wanted me to see myself: strong and brave in the face of battle. A warrior. I would fight for victory and trust God to help me overcome this mountain of hurt and disappointment. Seeing myself as God saw me gave me hope—just as my 4 Days 2 Hope weekend had proclaimed.

PHIL

As I pulled into the garage, I remembered how I'd felt a week ago when Priscilla had returned from 4 Days 2 Hope, wondering whether I would get a hug or small kiss but receiving neither. This time I was seeing life through a different lens.

In the past, I had evaluated my relationship with Priscilla based on how sex was going—how well she was meeting my needs physically. I now knew my whole construct had been wrong. God wanted me to evaluate my relationship with Priscilla *spiritually*, not physically. I had to let go of any expectation of a physical relationship and wait for God to first heal our relationship spiritually and emotionally.

PRISCILLA

I heard the kitchen door open, and in walked Phil. He looked different. His eyes were brighter, and he greeted me with more energy than I'd seen in him the past two weeks. "Hi!" he opened. "How's it going?"

"Pretty good," I replied. My thoughts immediately went to all the times past when Phil had returned from trips. It had always taken a few days for us to reconnect. I was unsure what would happen now as we tested constructing a new relationship. I just knew there wouldn't be any arrival sex, kisses, or hugs. I still wanted physical distance and a restart in that part of our relationship.

After a few pleasantries and his hellos to the girls, Phil and I sat on the porch, seeking some private time to talk about his weekend. He opened his 4 Days 2 Freedom workbook and walked me through every page, including thirteen action steps he'd written. Many of the steps centered on confessing his hypocrisy and sin to our children, extended family, and friends, as he'd talked about before leaving for the retreat. He appeared serious, and I knew that his confessing to family members would be an arduously tremendous step for him because he had always been so focused on what others thought about him. *If he's willing to expose his sin to other people, God must be doing something incredible inside him.*

"Priscilla, I have so much more to share with you, but first, I need to apologize to you for something else and ask you to forgive me. When we got married, I should have told you about my porn problem so you would've had a choice whether to marry me. Without knowing what you were getting yourself into, you made vows to God and me. I was too proud to admit my problems and fearful you would dump me if you knew the truth. Keeping the truth hidden from you wasn't right, and I'm so sorry. I was completely in the wrong, and you probably feel you've been duped into marrying a guy like me. I should have told you before I asked you to marry me. Will you forgive me?"

I was stunned and surprised at Phil's genuine humility and plea for forgiveness for something that had happened so many years ago. If I had known about his porn problem when we were dating, I would've thought twice about marrying him. However, a confession from him back then may have pushed me to come clean with him about my past and encouraged us to be HOT with each other from the very beginning rather than twenty-eight years later.

With Jenny's words about forgiveness still ringing in my ears, I said, "I forgive you." I had to let go of Phil and his sins and put him in God's hands. I wasn't perfect, and it was impossible to change the past. God had forgiven me, so there was no way I couldn't forgive Phil.

"Thank you," he said, tears welling in his eyes. I could tell his heart was soft, and we'd had a brief moment of emotional connection. "One other thing," he prompted, pressing in once again. "Did you think about my question on boundaries?"

"Yes." His previous business trips and other connections with the world returned to my thoughts. "All your travel worries me. I know it's your job, but I don't like the idea of you traveling all over the world by yourself. And I don't want you to have any lunches alone with women. Will you do that?"

Phil paused, his eyes searching as he leaned back into the chair. "Yes, when I need to have lunches with women, I'll bring someone else with me—no problem. But my business travel is a challenge—though I've already done a lot of my travel for this year, and I don't have anything else scheduled for a few months. Can you give me a little time to work this out? What if I added someone to my team, a male who could travel with me? That way, I wouldn't be traveling alone."

"Okay, I think that will help." I didn't know what else to say. At least we would have a few months before we needed to address his travel. He reiterated his commitment to do whatever it took to help me feel safe, and we agreed to keep boundaries at the forefront.

After some time of reconnecting with the kids and eating dinner, we climbed into our imaginary twin beds.

"Priscilla?"

"Yes?"

"Paul told me that to be free, I can't bury anything in secrecy; I need to share with you the details as they come to my mind. I've started to remember some things I've done and some things that happened to me."

I didn't really know what Phil was talking about, which created fear. "What types of things?" Even though it was getting late, he seemed eager to share his thoughts, something he had rarely done.

"Well, I want to disclose everything the Holy Spirit brings to my mind about what I've done to offend you and also things I've done that created shame in me. But I'm really afraid about the memories that will come because I know those will be hard to talk about."

I was somewhat prepared because the leaders at 4 Days 2 Hope had told us that most men would have more to share after 4 Days 2 Freedom. I didn't relish hearing the details of Phil's double life, but I knew that confession was essential for healing, a way out of his secret life. I needed to ask God for the grace to hear his confessions, since my rage and anger could shut him down. My reactions would set the boundaries for what he'd be willing to confess with each new recollection. *God, give me the grace to hear and respond the way You respond to our sin—with sadness, not wrath.*

"Well," I replied, "it's also hard for me to hear, but I'm willing to do whatever it takes to get through this."

"Okay, thanks. I appreciate that. I'm trying to walk out the healing God's done inside of me. Good night," he said softly and turned off the light and rolled over—no kiss or hug. No touching was part of our restart.

PHIL

I woke up at 2:15 a.m. in the middle of a dream. I had gone to sleep fearful of remembering more details of my sin and shame. In my dream, some type of nonhuman being was responsible. He was small, blue, and muscular, with no hair or clothes, squatting down behind our bathroom door, trembling and saying, "I'm so scared! I can't remember! I can't remember anything else!" He was so real, so vivid in my dream, that when it woke me, I got out of bed, went to the bathroom door, and jerked it back to see what was behind it. Nothing. Then Ephesians 6:12 came to mind. "Our struggle is not against flesh and blood, but against the rulers, against the powers, against the world forces of this darkness, against the spiritual forces of wickedness in the heavenly places."

I spoke out loud in a declaration, as if unseen forces were listening. "I command any spiritual beings who are tormenting me to leave in the name of Jesus and by His authority!"

That felt really weird, but I remembered Isaiah 41:10. "Do not fear, for I am with you." I immediately felt God's presence, and I returned to bed and went back to sleep. The antidote to fear was remembering that my heavenly Father was with me. My fear of remembering more details of my sin and shame left me.

An hour or so later, I woke up, went to the kitchen, and sat at our table. Only seventeen days prior, our table had been the place of my confession and despair. Now it was becoming a place of spiritual insight and healing.

I opened my journal and wrote about my dream. Fully awake, I realized the dream read a bit crazy. I had always thought people who talked about demons were off their rockers. But I had seemingly experienced what they had—the work of spiritual forces the apostle Paul described in Ephesians 6:12. I wondered whether the dream had merely been the result of my subconscious preoccupation with my fears—or perhaps I was gaining an increasing sensitivity to spiritual forces I believed were at work around me.

I didn't want to settle for only an intellectual and natural under-standing of events and circumstances. I wanted to see situations the way God saw them: spiritually. So I prayed. *Father, please make me aware of things going on in the spiritual realm.*

PRISCILLA

I rolled over and glanced at the clock. It was about four o'clock, and I could see the light from the kitchen peeking under the bedroom door. Phil was already up.

I got up, put on my robe, walked into the kitchen, and sat at the table with him. We exchanged good mornings, and he told me about his dream. Having grown up in Brazil as a missionary's kid, I had seen and heard about such dreams and spiritual links, so his nightmare didn't faze me; it made sense. We were fighting a spiritual battle and should expect some dark spiritual experiences like his dream.

Moving on, Phil returned to a topic most tender to my heart. "Priscilla, I need to confess to our children. I've been such a hypocrite, and I know it's affected my relationships with them. I want to do what I can to straighten it out." He had made it clear that confessing to our children was on his action list, but frankly, I hadn't expected he would jump into it so fast. My heart sped up as I considered such a blow to our children.

"I think you should confess to Michael first because he's getting married in a month. We need to give him and Chelsea some time to absorb this and not put it right up against their wedding." Michael was our third child, now twenty-four years old, going to school full time, holding down a job, and engaged to Chelsea. Although he still lived with us, we hardly saw him.

"Okay, that sounds like a good idea. Also, I think you should be with me at all the confessions so our kids can see your face and not wonder what's happening on your side. I also want to make sure I don't leave something out that you believe is important." Then he asked, "What do you think about Chelsea being there when I confess?"

I didn't hesitate. "I think she should be there. She's going to be part of the family, and she can see how messed up we really are. It's not fair for her to learn about this later."

Phil nodded, and we both stared down, letting the magnitude of what we had just agreed to sink in.

"I'll ask Chelsea to come over for dinner on Wednesday night." I realized the invitation would put things into motion that would change our family dynamics forever. Being HOT with our kids, not just each other, was an unpredictable place to go. But it was the start of God igniting change in our entire family.

| Savage Questions for Reflection |

1. How would your spouse say your pride has affected your marriage?

2. What's the biggest step of humility you've ever taken? What additional steps of humility do you need to take?

3. Have you ever had to have a "restart" in your marriage? What happened, and do you feel like it was successful? Why or why not?

Chapter 6

CONFESSING SECRET SINS

One who conceals his wrongdoings will not prosper, but one who confesses and abandons them will find compassion.

—PROVERBS 28:13

No Christian, if he is right with God, should ever need to hide anything in his life.

—A. W. TOZER

PHIL

I got up early on Wednesday, and almost immediately, my mind went from slumber to high alert as my impending confession took front stage.

I shuffled into the kitchen, sat down at the table, and opened my Bible and journal. Michael and Chelsea would be joining us for dinner, and I planned to open my heart to them. *God, help me know what to say and how to say it. I need transparent words that will rip off the mask I've been wearing and expose my genuine spiritual brokenness. Please give me the humility I need.*

Michael was our third born and had occupied the position as our youngest child for most of his life. A thirteen-year gap stood between him and Anna Hope, our fourth child.

Michael was unpretentious and unworried about what people thought of him, qualities I should have embraced in myself but hadn't. He was quick to include the down-and-outers in his circle of influence and had no problem letting people see his weaknesses. Michael had been open with me about his porn struggles, but I had not been open with him. When the topic of his struggles had occasionally come up, I had encouraged him to stay pure and trust God to always provide a way for him to escape sexual temptations. My pride and shame, hiding my porn problem, had stood in the way of Michael seeing the real me. In my teen years, struggling with porn, I had been him; but as his dad, I'd led him to believe I was a true overcomer and that my problems were many years in the past. I had thought if Michael saw me as almost perfect, that image would encourage him not to give in to the temptations of sexual immorality as I had.

Having Chelsea with us for my confession was a bit of a wild card, but Priscilla and I thought she'd want to be invited into this moment of truth as Michael's fiancée. She was a strong woman, and I knew she'd help Michael process his emotions. They would be married in about thirty days, so the timing wasn't ideal, but it was the best I could do. It was past time to be honest, and there would never be a good time to shatter my children's image of me. I couldn't put off this confession until after their wedding.

Rather than wing it and inadvertently overlook something, I decided it was best to write out my confession, and I wanted Priscilla to vet what I was planning to say. I scripted ten points, followed by a request for forgiveness.

I heard footsteps and a short "Good morning" as Priscilla sat down at the table. Seeing how much I'd written in my journal, she asked, "What are you doing?"

"I decided to write out my confession to Michael and Chelsea. Would you like to read it? I want to make sure you believe I've covered everything."

PRISCILLA

"Sure, I'll read it. Let me grab my coffee." I hadn't slept well and needed a jolt of caffeine to clear my foggy mind.

I was intrigued with Phil's mission to confess to our children. He had always projected himself with strength, confidence, and arrogance, never disclosing weaknesses or failures. Now, our kids would finally see their real dad, so I expected he would take his time lining up his confessions.

When I'd settled into the chair and sipped my coffee, Phil handed me his journal. I read his ten points, expecting his confession would be honest but somehow result in him saving face. Instead, the confession was raw and authentic—honest, open, and transparent.

As I read each point, my coffee forgotten, I realized how much God had done in his life in a matter of days. Phil was genuinely off his high horse and walking in humility, preparing himself to take a huge, difficult, and very important step: to walk humbly before his kids. Laid out in black and white was the truth of who he was and how he'd fallen short as a husband and father.

My heart ached for Michael and Chelsea in what was to come that evening. They were living a starry-eyed dream, their wedding only weeks away, and Phil's words were going to wake them up with a jolt. But it had to be done. There was no other way.

Looking up from the journal, I said, "You covered everything. It's really good."

"Thanks," Phil said meekly, taking the journal. "How do you think they'll react?"

"I think they'll be shocked, and Michael will be really hurt."

Phil glanced down, nodding, his face contorting with raw emotions.

Boy, this is truly a different Phil. He's never let something affect him this deeply.

As the day passed, my mind kept going back to the journal and what I'd read. Even if Phil wanted to somehow contain this story after his forthcoming confession, there would be no way. After confessing to Michael and Chelsea, he would confess to our other kids, which created a tug-of-war inside me. Part of me wanted Phil to walk out the confession, take the first step in telling someone close to his heart other than me. The other part of me felt apprehensive as I wondered how each of our children would react. What would they say? Would they reject Phil? Would they reject me? We had both been such hypocrites.

Evening came, and I heard Chelsea walk in with a bubbly "Hi! I'm here, and I'm hungry!" Phil, Michael, and I were in the kitchen, busying ourselves with last-minute dinner preparations.

As we gathered around the table, I thought, *Chelsea and Michael are so happy together and in love. Thirty days before their big day, and here we are, about to pour cold water on their parade. Dear Jesus, give us the right words to say. You are here, Lord.*

After finishing the family dinner and conversations, we asked Anna Hope and Becca to go upstairs and give us some time alone with Chelsea and Michael. The girls scooted out, and the lively chitchat about the day ended. As I looked at our two young adults with their whole lives ahead of them, a somber look settled on their faces, as if they already had an idea of what we wanted to talk about.

Phil opened his journal to the marked page and took a deep breath. His face was drawn with tension, knowing that his confession was about to forever change his children's lives and ours. His breathing became rapid, and he bit his lip, signs he was going to say something he didn't want to say. He finally got out his first words.

PHIL

"Mom and I asked both of you to be here because I need to share something with you. I know you're getting married next month, but this isn't something I can put off." Michael and Chelsea shifted uncomfortably.

"Sure. What is it?" Michael said, leaning forward in his chair. Chelsea remained still, looking pensively toward me but saying nothing.

"I've written out what I want to say—not to be formal but to be complete." With that short introduction, I began to read.

I defrauded and betrayed your mother by committing adultery with prostitutes and entertaining sexual fantasies about other women while I viewed and masturbated to pornography.

I have not led our family in truth. I lied and deceived you all to make myself look better than I was. I refused to be humble but instead chose to walk in pride and hypocrisy.

I pushed you to remain pure and control your sexual urges while I was not controlling mine. I felt unable to be transparent to confess my sins to you, even when you were transparent with me in disclosing your struggles. I appeared stronger and more righteous than you, and it's all been a lie.

My sin allowed a stronghold into our family and your life that created distance between you and me. I did not model the transparency God wants for us. My lack of transparency is what led me to live a secret life. My actions may have also planted a seed of secrecy in your life because I failed in this aspect of being the spiritual leader God wanted me to be.

I pushed you to achieve and always look good because those made me look good. I pushed you so I could continue to cover the shame of my sin. Consequently, I led a life full of hypocrisy—desiring the admiration of others and using you to get there, without your knowledge and without regard for how my sin and secrecy was affecting you or making you feel.

I pursued an outwardly religious life to make me look good and encouraged you to do the same. I refused to be transparent about my life, while transparency could have helped you. I was too proud to admit my failures.

I didn't push myself to engage with you, even when I thought you may be struggling. I was more focused on protecting and hiding my secret thoughts and actions than pursuing transparency that could have resulted in your deliverance and freedom from sin.

My pride led me to elevate myself by showing a command of biblical knowledge and doctrine. I created a false impression of myself and reduced my true effectiveness as a husband, father, and spiritual leader.

I coveted a material lifestyle and placed importance on how much money I could accumulate rather than demonstrating a

*humble life and being content with what I had. I repeatedly chose
actions and paths resulting from pride rather than following a path
of dying to self.*

*I reinforced setting up barriers and fences to manage my sin
rather than being humble, transparent, and willing to die to self.*

*Overall, I have not been the father I should have been to you. I
was more focused on my lust than on you, and I was wrong. I failed
to protect and lead you, a son God gave me, and I humbly ask your
forgiveness and your permission to reengage with you as the father
God desires you to have.*

I closed my journal and waited for Michael's response.

MICHAEL

For the past year, I'd been going to a sexual-addiction recovery group at
our church. While Dad was reading his confession, I felt as though I was
back in my addiction group, simply listening to another broken man's
story. Because of my own addiction, I was very stoic as he read, and I
simply absorbed everything I could. When he finished his confession,
he looked across the table at me and Chelsea, and then he asked me how
I was feeling. I was honest as my emotions began to surface. *This isn't
group; this is real life, and it's happening to me!*

My voice rose as I tried to coherently explain to my dad how his
confession was affecting me. "About sixty-five percent of me is *so* proud
of you for sharing this with us," I said while emphatically hitting the
table. "But the other thirty-five percent is angry because you didn't share
this with me earlier. Where was this confession twelve to fifteen years
ago? My whole life, I believed you were Superman. Logically, I knew you
weren't, but I wanted you to take off your suit and show me who you
really were on the inside."

I'd always felt like my dad presented himself as someone who had
struggled with porn earlier in life but had beaten it. Like an experienced
general, he had stood behind the front lines and directed young soldiers

like me around the enemy. I thought if he had fought and beaten his porn addiction, I should have too. I thought if I fought hard enough, I could eventually be behind the front lines and have no more worry about my struggles, like him. However, what I had needed for the past twelve years was someone to be in the trenches with me, someone to say I wasn't alone in the fight and that they would fight with me.

A quote popped into my head from *Lord of the Rings: The Two Towers*.

It's like in the great stories, Mr. Frodo. The ones that really mattered. Full of darkness and danger, they were. And sometimes you didn't want to know the end. Because how could the end be happy? How could the world go back to the way it was when so much bad had happened?

—SAMWISE GAMGEE

How could my world return to the way it was? It couldn't. I was finally seeing my dad for who he truly was. There was no turning back; everything seemed to have shifted, and it felt scary. What would come tomorrow and the day after? I didn't know. What I knew was that God had written the story, and I could trust Him with how it would play out.

> God had written the story,
> and I could trust Him with how it would play out.

PHIL

Michael's words stung, but I couldn't argue with anything he'd said as his anger and disappointment had boiled to the top and overflowed into grace and forgiveness. Somehow, our honesty changed our relationship. Yes, we were still father and son, but we were also brothers who had ripped off our masks and become HOT, letting each other see the truth.

Chelsea had watched our discussion without comment, absorbing the emotions and realizing she would be marrying into a family that was undergoing significant turmoil. But I could tell by her expression that she was fully engaged. "Chelsea, how are you feeling?"

"I'm sad for Michael, and I feel that if you had been honest earlier, maybe you could have helped him. He's struggled so much. But I do forgive you." Her comments were spot on, and I could see she was already occupying the emotional position as Michael's wife, wanting to support him and do anything she could to assuage his pain. I nodded, realizing what she'd said was true.

As our time came to a close, Michael and I embraced, lingering in our emotions, our bodies shaking with recognition of what God had done in the cleansing and bonding. I was thankful that Michael and Chelsea had received my words with mercy and compassion, not just with sadness.

PRISCILLA

Being real and honest and taking off our masks was the hardest thing we'd ever done with our kids. But it was Michael—standing up, slamming his hands on the table, almost in protest—who let us know how damaging our hidden life had been. Yes, he'd also made wrong choices, but had we come to him earlier, maybe our transparency and humility would've lessened his struggles.

After Michael and Chelsea left, Phil and I hugged and cried. We'd done the right thing, but that knowledge didn't make the process any less painful.

PHIL

I was planning to meet with Tim, our oldest, at his apartment on Friday afternoon.

I had thoroughly enjoyed Tim's growing-up years. We liked adventure, travel, and debating intellectual topics. When he was fifteen, I'd taken him on a weekend retreat in the Grand Tetons. There I had told him about my porn usage as a teenager. I desperately wanted him to be free from the shackles of this sin, but I hadn't felt I could tell him I still struggled with porn. He'd listened, understood, and expressed appreciation for my disclosure.

Over the years that followed, Tim had occasionally confided in me about sexual temptations, and I had simply encouraged him that God would always "provide a way of escape" (1 Cor. 10:13). Yet I had been failing to take His way of escape from my struggles.

In the days before my confession to Tim, those memories flooded back. There was no way to recover the past. I was where I was, and the only truthful way forward was through confession.

Tim was in medical school and aggressively pursuing his education and striving for excellence. He had readily absorbed a lot of my constant instruction that always pushed him to excel. I had frequently told my children, "I abhor mediocrity," a mantra they would sometimes repeat while the rest of the family rolled their eyes. Tim had firmly taken the mantra to heart. He was sound and thorough in his thinking, always looking for reason and logic while also knowing that God's plan for his life would be the only plan that could ever provide lasting satisfaction. I had very much wanted him to be "sold out" to God and, at the same time, become a successful doctor. But in honesty, part of my hope for Tim's future had been that his success as a believer and a physician would be a testament to how great a father I'd been. What a bunch of crap. I had been so lost in my pride that I couldn't even see how out of balance I was in my hunger for admiration from others.

Friday afternoon quickly arrived, and Priscilla and I went to Tim's apartment. He met us on the driveway, and moments later, we were all sitting together—Priscilla beside me, and Tim to my right, facing me. I opened my journal, and the words communicated my emotion, my pain, and the brokenness my sin had brought into our lives.

TIM

In the days after Dad said he and Mom wanted to speak with me at my apartment, a funny feeling crept over me. I knew they had attended some conferences in the preceding weeks, but they hadn't told me the topic or purpose or what material was covered. They had only told me the topic covered "bringing darkness to the light," which hadn't helped narrow my frantic Google searches in the days leading to our sit-down. A different part of me was scared that the conversation would be an intervention rooted in their reservations about my girlfriend.

We made brief, awkward small talk on the driveway when they arrived, and I noticed my dad held a notebook and other materials. Once we were seated in my living room, Dad began in his familiar business voice, the voice I'd heard him adopt on multiple occasions—his business meetings, teaching at church, and with car dealers, etc. His voice would take a commanding posture with matter-of-fact inflections and emotional distance. However, this time, his facade quickly crumbled when he glanced to the floor, and his bottom lip began to quiver. Confusion washed over me as he fumbled with his notebook to find a specific page. *What's going on?*

"I've been unfaithful to your mom and our marriage vows."

An emotional fog descended around me as I wrestled with confusion, sadness, shock, and fear. Minutes rolled by as my dad attempted to collect his emotions while reading his prepared confession. A tumultuous storm of emotions ensued.

When I reflected on that afternoon, one other specific detail stood out in my mind. Dad looked up from the confession—emotionally spent and depleted of tears—and with a trembling voice, fighting through feelings of failure and defeat, he asked for my forgiveness. He said he was sorry and had wanted to be a dad I would look up to and want to be like.

A thought raced through my heart and out of my mouth: "I *do* want to be like you." That stopped him in his tracks, and he began to cry again. I joined him, crying with my dad for the first time. This was not the same dad I'd known since childhood; this was a different man.

Hours passed as the three of us talked about his sin, 4 Days 2 Freedom, and what God had been showing him. After they left, I felt a sense of sadness, pride, and fear. I was sad, having lost the "ideal family" I'd grown up in, and proud that my dad was experiencing radical transformation that displayed God's power in his life—which was what I wanted and expected to experience as well. I also felt fear that his openness would eventually require me to disclose the sexual sin I'd also been hiding for so long.

PHIL

As Tim and I talked in the months after my confession, our conversations became more open and honest as we confessed to each other our shortcomings and struggles.

Several months later, Tim attended 4 Days 2 Freedom, which further created a beautiful commonality in our relationship as adult men pursuing God's best for our lives.

Tim's relationship with his girlfriend ended and he eventually met Johanna, a wonderful woman who became not only his wife but a battle partner and confidant, much like Priscilla had become for me. I was so thankful for what God had done in Tim's life.

Multiple blessings were sprouting from one act of obedience—confessing my sin—and I thought of the apostle Paul's expression of praise to God from Ephesians 3:20. "To him who is able to do far more abundantly beyond all that we ask or think, according to the power that works within us."

PRISCILLA

Finding a time for Phil and me to talk with Sarah, our second born, and her husband, Shawn, would be challenging. They lived in Atlanta, a seven-hour drive from Orlando. Phil suggested we fly there and back the next Saturday, but I thought that would create anxiety and stress for Sarah and Shawn as they tried to figure out why we were coming for only a day. We decided to wait for three weeks, when they planned to be in Orlando for a special event with Shawn's family.

Knowing they had extensive plans with Shawn's family for just about the whole time, I felt awkward asking Sarah for two hours of their time.

Sarah was naturally inquisitive and would want explanations about what we wanted to discuss. Nevertheless, I punched in her number and nervously waited for her to answer.

"Hey, Mama!"

"Oi, tudo bem?" I rattled off our traditional Portuguese greeting meaning "Hi, is all well?" Talking to Sarah was a delight, and we easily picked up conversations wherever we'd left off from a previous call.

She responded with her typical "Tudo bem!" Although she didn't speak much Portuguese, it was nice that she had picked up words and phrases here and there, which always created a closeness I loved.

"Hey, I know you and Shawn will be with his parents in a few weeks. Do you think you and Shawn can give us two hours to talk?"

Sarah paused. "Well, sure we can. What's going on?"

"Just some things we really need to talk about." I was trying to be vague, but Sarah was a bottom-line person like me, and her tone became persistent.

"Mom, what's going on?"

"It would be better to talk face to face," I said.

"Okay, let me ask you something, Mom. Is someone dying? Are you getting a divorce?"

"No to both of those questions," I assured her.

"Okay, I can live with that. No problem. We'll see you soon and talk."

I let out a sigh of relief as I disconnected the call. Funny how death and divorce are what weigh on people's minds no matter their age.

PHIL

Sarah was our first daughter and only eighteen months younger than Tim. While Tim was most like me in terms of debating and delighting in having an answer to every question, Sarah was most like me in terms of presence and persuasion. In demanding settings, she showed poise and confidence while also expressing spiritual insight and tenderness. Sarah could sell anything, quickly persuading girls in high school to join the track and cross-country teams when no such teams had existed. She was beautiful like her mother and didn't mind being different from the crowd. Sarah viewed herself as the trendsetter, such as the time she had started wearing two different-colored socks in elementary school. She was also eloquent and expressive—she could articulate her thoughts well without appearing stuck up or condescending. I admired her a great deal.

I had never talked with Sarah about my porn addiction—not even what had happened when I was a teenager. I had felt I needed to protect her from everything, including boyfriends, and had seen myself as the shotgun-toting dad. I knew my discussion with her and Shawn was going to be hard.

PRISCILLA

The weeks passed quickly, and soon, Sarah and Shawn arrived. We exchanged hellos and pleasantries with the awkwardness of the elephant in the room. We all sat down, and Phil opened his journal and transparently shared his confession. For the first time, he was revealing his heart to Sarah and Shawn.

SARAH

My father's face crumpled, and tears began to well up in his eyes when he started reading. "I have not been faithful to your mother. I have broken my marriage vows to her." He hung his head, looking at his journal in his lap, and continued sharing, giving examples of exactly how he had broken his vows to Mom.

My mind reeled from the details, and my thoughts were a bombardment of questions and cries of disbelief. *How is this possible? My dad's an elder in the church! He leads Bible studies! He was leading a double life all along?*

I tuned back in to listen more closely to the details. He shared about his first exposure to porn, and the details grieved me. I felt so sorry for him. He seemed almost like a sorrowful child. His confession was so genuine and sincere, with true brokenness and vulnerability I had never witnessed in him before.

As his admission ended, my mind jumped to a confession I'd heard earlier that week, echoing a similar theme. My husband, Shawn, had confessed to using porn and had shared his desire to go to counseling for the issue. We had discussed porn before, so his disclosure hadn't completely shocked me, though the details had been vague. I hadn't been overly concerned but had been mostly pleased that he desired to put effort into fixing the problem.

My reaction to Shawn's recent confession had aligned with my religious spirit I hadn't been aware of until that week. In conversation with a friend, God had revealed to me that my relationship with Him was built on my self-righteousness from pride. I had been in a kind of crisis of faith when I'd realized all my religious acts had been from an effort to earn the Lord's favor. I'd had no idea how to interact with Him without trying to earn His love, so I had apathetically stopped trying.

When my dad finished his confession, a few thoughts were highlighted in my mind. First was the divine timing of three revelations—Shawn's confession, my realization of pride, and my dad's confession. Second, I realized what Shawn and I needed in our marriage: openness, transparency, humility, and the realness of the Lord. Third, I still loved my dad, and I forgave him.

I knew there would not be time for me and Shawn to process all of this for another two days, though I desperately wanted to.

Right after Dad's confession, Mom and I had to get on the road to travel an hour to a bridal shower with two male college-aged Japanese students traveling with us. Yes, my tears flowed, and Mom allowed me space to process Dad's confession.

Our concern regarding the two young men in the back seat fell aside as I told Mom how I was feeling. "My whole life feels fake." All those picture-perfect family moments and experiences no longer felt so golden and shiny. I knew now what was really going on with the man behind the curtain, and I was crushed.

As we arrived at the bridal shower, I dried my face and slapped on a Band-Aid smile to try to stop the hemorrhaging of emotions bursting from my soul. For the next few hours, I needed to pretend that my life was still golden and shiny.

At the shower were some familiar faces among the many strangers who attended the bride and groom's church. *How many of them are unfaithful to their wives? How many of them live a double life? How many are paying for sexual experiences?* I assumed all of them. It was hard to be present, smiling and chitchatting, while sharp accusations pierced my thoughts.

I desperately wanted to process my dad's confession with Shawn, but the weekend was packed with wedding events and sharing time between two families. So we'd agreed to put that conversation on hold until we had enough quality time to talk about it. We would have six and a half hours on our drive home to Atlanta.

As we left Orlando, Shawn and I finally had a chance to debrief together and process all that had happened over the weekend. We prayed and felt that we needed to confess to each other anything the Holy Spirit brought to our minds. They weren't all sin, but some were things we'd never mentioned to each other that had shame or guilt attached. Our new transparency shifted our interactions with the Lord and each other. The Lord became so real to us, His presence with us, in a way we had never before experienced. Finally authentic with each other, we were fully known in a beautifully broken way. My dad's confession in true brokenness had changed the trajectory of our spiritual walk and our marriage.

PHIL

I had longed for a daddy-daughter relationship with Sarah like the ones portrayed in movies. The dad sacrifices all for his daughter, who lovingly rests her head on his shoulder. While Sarah and I had a good relationship, it operated more in a business fashion—me making sure she had everything she needed to be successful in life and her reaching out to me when she had problems. I knew we loved each other, but

I wanted an emotional intimacy that would allow us to feel that daddy-daughter love rather than just acknowledge it. I had never suspected that my secret life was the barrier to obtaining the kind of relationship with my daughter that I longed for.

In my desperation to hide my true self, I hadn't let anyone too close for fear they would figure out who I was. That wouldn't be pretty. So I'd kept my children at arm's length, pulling them in with one hand while holding up the other to protect them from my secrets.

After my confession, everything changed in my relationship with Sarah. She leaned into me, and I into her, and I saw in her the beautiful, courageous, and wise woman God had blessed me with in a daughter—and now a beloved, intimate sister in Christ. Over time, our goodbye hugs were no longer perfunctory. We lingered in the arms of love without barriers, not hiding our emotions (including our tears) but instead reflecting the beautiful new way we now knew each other.

My relationship with Shawn also changed. For almost two years before Shawn had married Sarah, I'd met with him for breakfast several times a month to get to know him and monitor how he and Sarah were doing. Even in our first meetings, I'd asked Shawn whether he and Sarah were maintaining physical boundaries. I had also asked about his history of using porn. I had been such a hypocrite. I had put him on the spot with tough questions while never owning up to how much sin I was hiding.

I had feared Sarah would marry someone like me, so I had done what I could to reduce the risk. However, my posture had put Shawn and me on two different levels. I had acted like a general and treated him as my subordinate infantryman in the trenches, just like I had treated Michael. After my confession, I apologized to Shawn for how I had presented myself to him and the pressure I had put him under. He was gracious to forgive me, reflecting what God was doing in both of our lives.

Several months later, Shawn attended 4 Days 2 Freedom, and we developed a closeness that encouraged us to be honest, open, and transparent with each other. A few weeks after Shawn attended Freedom, he and Sarah called us about a confession he'd made. Shawn shared with us, "When I was at 4 Days 2 Freedom, I asked the men in the group for their advice about something that had happened earlier in the year. Sarah and I were at a get-together, and a woman bent over the table in front of me, and I saw down her blouse. I wanted to see more and took another look, and then a third. I asked the men at 4 Days 2 Freedom if I needed to confess to the woman and her husband. The group kicked it around and concluded I didn't need to confess. They said she and her husband didn't know what I had done, and as long as I had confessed to Sarah, that was enough."

"That makes sense to me," I said. "You can't confess to every woman you see walking down the street."

Shawn continued, his voice wavering with emotion. "Well, when I got home, I prayed about it and felt like the Lord wanted me to confess to the woman and her husband. So Sarah and I called them, and they joined us by speakerphone. I told them exactly what I had done and explained that God was doing something new inside me, and I asked for their forgiveness. They were astounded, surprised that I would call to confess my lustful thoughts. They were also very gracious and forgave me."

Wow. Hearing Shawn's experience, I was shocked. Even in my boldness to confess, I wasn't sure I could have done this.

Shawn continued. "But, you know, that confession created a special brokenness inside me. As I confessed, I began sobbing and continued to cry after we'd hung up."

"Shawn, I'm amazed at your courage. Your brokenness is evidence that you heard from God, even when the counsel of all the men said otherwise. That's really amazing! I'm proud of you!"

Sarah voiced her affirmation of Shawn as well. It was clear that God had enabled her to be in a position of compassion and support for Shawn.

PRISCILLA

God's orchestration of events was amazing—Shawn sharing his porn problem with Sarah and then Phil confessing his sin three days later.

Although I had feared that exposing who we really were to Sarah and Shawn would create distance, our transparency actually brought us closer together.

Several months later, we asked Sarah and Shawn to forgive us for being so judgmental and self-righteous during their dating relationship. Our sharing was an intimate time of transparency and healing.

PHIL

As for Anna Hope and Becca, we decided to meet with each of them separately. They were eleven and nine years old, and I knew my confessions would need to be age appropriate. We didn't want to exclude them only for them to later learn our "family secret" and wonder why we had not told them earlier what had happened in our family. Secrecy had been my Achilles' heel all along. We didn't want further secrecy in their lives.

Although Anna Hope and Becca had similar beginnings in Chinese orphanages, they had very different personalities. Anna Hope was a year and nine months old when we received her in Changsha, China. She'd had a long journey on a train and bus to the adoption center. When the bus had arrived, the children had been quickly carried by their nannies across the lobby and into a room as we and other hopeful parents had watched.

"Priscilla, I think I saw her!" We'd received a few pictures of Anna Hope while we were still in the United States and strained to pick her out among twelve children being carried past us.

One by one, a nanny called out family names. When we heard "Phillip and Priscilla Fretwell?" we jumped up, eager to hold our daughter for the first time. The nanny walked in with Anna Hope holding tightly to her. Priscilla instinctively reached out, but Anna Hope clung to the nanny, who had to pry her off to put her into Priscilla's open arms. Anna Hope was crying, scared, and unsure of what was going on.

When I stepped up, Anna Hope reached out to me, and Priscilla let go. Anna Hope became like a little tree frog hanging on to me with all her might. She slowly stopped crying but didn't let go of me—and I couldn't put her down or give her to Priscilla for even a second.

Somehow, Anna Hope had found in me the security she'd felt with the nanny. Instantaneously, I became her protector and provider. Her clinging to me continued for the next ten days as we processed paperwork in China and got ready to return to the United States. Even on the plane, I held her the entire thirty-hour trip. When I'd have to hand her to Priscilla to go to the bathroom, Anna Hope would cry until I returned.

This newfound affection was foreign to me because our kids had always preferred Priscilla's embrace, but here was this small, scared, shy little girl relying on me, preferring me, and trusting me. I had loved it, and my soul had risen to the occasion. I had silently committed to defending and protecting her and never doing anything that would hurt her or destroy our relationship. Yet nine years later, looking into her soft brown eyes, I had to tell her I had not kept my promise.

Three years after welcoming Anna Hope into our family, we had adopted Becca from an orphanage in Shenzhen, China. She was two years and nine months old, about two years younger than Anna Hope and small for her age. While Anna Hope was calm and quiet, Becca was a fireball, fighting for her rights and survival while demonstrating an emotional joy for life that few could match. She hadn't cried when she had left her nanny.

Over the years ahead, we had learned Becca was extroverted, emotional, and loving but also demanding and insistent on justice, fairness, and connection. She reacted quickly and emotionally to any sense of rejection, frequently saying, "You just don't care!" Somehow, God would have to show me how to expose my weaknesses to my little girl without making her feel like I just didn't care about her or her mommy.

It was with these different personalities that my conversations began. It was important to me to be at eye level with the girls as they took their turns sitting on my big stuffed office chair—me on my knees and Priscilla by my side.

I attempted to explain adult topics in a way I hoped could be understood by their child minds, and their reactions were similar. Their little eyes searched mine, trying to figure out what my explanations meant. They had come from a world of insecurity in China to a home of love and care. At least that was what they had thought. I could see in their faces a struggle to understand what my words meant to their security.

The conversations went pretty much the same with each. "I need to ask you for forgiveness for something I've done," I began. "God created a special relationship between Mommy and Daddy when we got married, and we made special promises to always love each other. God allows mommies and daddies to have a special love for each other, and we promised not to love anyone else in the same way we love each other. Part of our love is that we feel good when we're hugging and kissing each other and sleeping together in the same bed, sometimes without our clothes. But this special relationship is only for Mommy and me to share as husband and wife, and we promised each other we wouldn't be with anyone else in this way."

The girls each nodded as though they understood, but I was unsure how much they were truly comprehending. I continued with prayer in my heart.

"Over the past several years, I didn't keep my promises to Mommy. I broke my promises by being alone with other women, sometimes without my clothes on, and it hurt Mommy a lot. I love Mommy, and I don't love those other women. I apologized to Mommy for breaking my promises to her and hurting her, and Mommy has forgiven me. But I also know it hurts you to know I haven't loved Mommy the way I should. When a husband breaks his promises to his wife and brings other women into his life, the Bible calls this *adultery*."

I knew my adultery confession would hit Anna Hope and Becca the hardest, but I needed to share more to create a base from which we could revisit this situation as they grew older, into their teen years, dating relationships, and pre-marriage stages. "Part of my problem was that I had been looking at pictures of naked women, called pornography. Thinking about the pictures and sometimes touching my private parts made me feel good, but it made me not think about Mommy. It was wrong of me to think about other women while touching my private area. That's called masturbation."

Ugh! I couldn't believe I was explaining pornography and masturbation to my eleven- and nine-year-old daughters!

They each received my confession as simply information because their young minds could not yet attach the terms to shame and sin. Even though the confessions were shared with each daughter separately, both girls reacted about the same way—wide eyes brimming with tears. They understood enough to recognize that I had shared a serious situation in which I had made wrong choices that jeopardized their security.

Even at their young ages, they knew about divorce because they had seen how divorce had affected friends at school. Priscilla jumped in. "But we want you to know that I have forgiven Daddy, and we aren't getting a divorce." They nodded, and we could see the relief in their eyes. They each reached up to hug me, quickly saying they forgave me too. I felt a sense of relief and was glad I had established the base so our future conversations wouldn't contain new and shocking information.

PRISCILLA

Seeing Phil confess to each of our children created mixed feelings in me. One minute I'd want him to carry through with the confessions, but in the next minute, I'd question whether we were doing the right thing.

As we proceeded, we found that the confessions changed everything to better our family relationships; our family image, now freely authentic; and how our children thought about their parents.

Seeing Phil experience with our children some of the same rawness I felt was therapeutic for both of us. With each confession to our children, I saw Phil's heart ripped out, shredded, and put back together again. He felt the tearing and anguish as I did each time he delivered a confession. In that strange sort of way, Phil had decided to join me in my soul's pain, bringing us closer together.

We couldn't have known how our children would react. They each asked different questions, processing in their own way the wound to their familial security. They each forgave their father and embraced the relationship that remained, though newly tattered and frayed.

In the months that followed, Anna Hope and Becca each showed an interest in not only rebuilding their relationship with their dad but making it truly honest, open, and transparent. It was a true picture of grace.

PHIL

Over the next several years, Anna Hope and Becca were always included in our HOT family discussions about our story and how God was using our transformation to positively impact the lives of other couples, their marriages, and their families.

Four years later, when Anna Hope and Becca were fifteen and thirteen, we revisited the specifics with them, making sure we had answered all their questions and that they understood God's plan for honest, open, and transparent communication; personal sexuality; purity; and covenant marriage relationships of purity. We were glad we had openly included them in our prior family discussions over the past four years. They had seen all the couples, in and out of our home, who had asked us to meet with them about their marriages. So when we broached the subject in their teens, it wasn't a surprise to them. They listened attentively, showing curiosity and asking questions to understand better what had happened in our marriage and how to process the truth.

> God's plan is a covenant marriage relationship
> of purity with honest, open,
> and transparent communication.

The HOT environment Anna Hope and Becca had grown up in encouraged them to openly ask questions regarding their own sexuality. Being honest, open, and transparent with our children created communication that's rare between parents and their children. Our openness fostered a culture of safety and vulnerability for Anna Hope and Becca to discuss topics frequently hidden from parents. Priscilla and I often reflected on how unusual this environment was and how our confessions to our two young daughters years prior had created a comfortable foundation for communication. The girls could share their most intimate thoughts and questions without hesitation or embarrassment.

The freedom God had shown me and Priscilla reflected in our children's lives, giving us hope they would be protected from the potential shame that affects so many teens about sexuality and from secrets that lead to destruction.

PRISCILLA

As this part of our story came to a close, I took a deep breath. We had made it through the most intimidating part of Phil's action plan. I didn't know the confessions would serve merely as a primer for what was to come. God had much more He wanted to do in Phil's heart and life and mine. Although we had dealt with the current sin, other wounds and shame from our pasts were yet to be revealed.

| Savage Questions for Reflection |

1. How did your family of origin treat secret sins? How has it affected you?

2. Have you ever been hurt because of someone else's secrets? What happened, and how did it make you feel? How did the aftermath affect you?

3. What secret areas of your life have you not shared with your spouse? Why haven't you shared them? Are you willing to take a step toward becoming HOT with your spouse about these secrets?

4. What messages do you want to send to your children about the effects of secrecy? How can you share these with your children?

Chapter 7

FREEDOM FROM SHAME

Let's run with the endurance the race that is set before us, looking only at Jesus, the originator and perfecter of the faith, who for the joy set before Him endured the cross, despising the shame, and has sat down at the right hand of the throne of God.

—Hebrews 12:1–2

If we can share our story with someone who responds with empathy and understanding, shame can't survive.

—Brené Brown, *Daring Greatly*

PRISCILLA

Sitting on the stairs, lacing my shoes, I could see Phil was already dressed and waiting at the kitchen table for our five-thirty walk. He shifted toward me and offered a short "You ready to go?"

"Almost," I said. "Just a few more minutes to wake up and drink my coffee."

Our morning routine of walking around our neighborhood had become a therapy session for us as we shared thoughts, talked about events from our past, and created a safe place to dissect our feelings. Each day as we walked through our pain together, we realized that the more open we were in conversation, the more healing we felt taking place.

Early on in these walks, my first instinct had been to let Phil talk. He would go on and on like a babbling brook—the most I'd ever heard him share—putting his feelings and thoughts out there where I could see them and relate.

The newness of being open with our feelings brought to mind my recent doctor visit and my first-ever STD test. I'd felt shame and awkwardness as I had chitchatted with my doctor, though I'd been seeing her for over twenty years. I hadn't wanted to be there. *But what if I have an STD and I'm not even aware of it? Oh, God, is this the way I'm going out of this world?*

Years earlier, my doctor had asked whether Phil or I had any other sexual partners. I had adamantly told her, "No way!" I was faithful to Phil and certain he was faithful to me. In my mind, there wasn't a possibility that Phil had been unfaithful. But two days ago, there I'd been, lying on the exam table, my feet in stirrups, waiting for the exam to be over. I had closed my eyes and thought, *Phil should be here with me, telling her what he's been doing. This is his fault, not mine!* Shame had grabbed my heart and thrust me into a place of isolation, hiding, and embarrassment. I wondered if my doctor was also remembering her question to me from years ago and my emphatic claim that Phil and I were faithful to each other. I had been so concerned about my reputation that I had wanted to hide in my self-righteousness.

I hadn't explained why I'd wanted an STD test or how I had come to this place in my life, and I hadn't mentioned Phil. I had just endured the exam in silence, my shame stifling my voice. Shame had told me I couldn't use my voice to speak the truth and told me it was my fault that Phil had been unfaithful. Lying there physically exposed, I had needed to bury my feelings.

As Phil and I walked in the coolness of the Florida morning, I decided to speak about the shame and my feeling of not being protected and defended by him. I felt the tentacles of my bitterness toward him encircling my heart, and I knew I had to be honest and open with my feelings.

The sun wasn't up yet, and the darkness felt like a cloak of protection, neither of us able to clearly see the other's face. "Phil, I need to be honest with you. The other day at the GYN, I felt so vulnerable lying there, like I was taking on all the blame and had gotten myself into this mess and the need to be tested. I felt so much shame and embarrassment, like it was my fault you went out on me. Phil, you should have been there with me, protecting me by taking the blame for what you did."

PHIL

Priscilla's voice was sober and straightforward, but her slow, emphatic tone clearly showed her painful ache of shame. She was on the verge of crying.

My annual physical was in a few days, and I had sheepishly called the doctor's office to have my blood tests expanded to include STDs. I remembered how I'd felt on the phone, imagining what the nurse was thinking, even though she couldn't see me.

Priscilla's HOT description of her shame was disconcerting as I realized my situation was so minor, insignificant, and momentary by comparison. I wished again I could have a do-over and reclaim my right to be Priscilla's protector. But for the time being, all I could do was express my regret. "Priscilla, I'm so sorry. You're right. I should've been there to tell the doctor I was unfaithful to you and that's the reason you were there to be tested. It wasn't fair for you to bear the weight of that shame. You didn't do anything wrong. It was totally me. I'll never put you in that position again, and if you have to return to the doctor for another test, I'll be there and take responsibility for what I did."

Priscilla offered a quiet thank-you, wiping the edges of her eyes and nodding in agreement.

In the days that followed, I reflected on our conversation about shame and how it made her feel. I was certainly ashamed of my sin against Priscilla and how I'd disregarded our marriage vows and my place as her protector. My longtime and constant companion had been shame.

The first time I'd felt shame was in fifth grade at Middle School East in Leesburg, Florida, a small city of about fifteen thousand people where kids in first grade would eventually graduate high school with the same classmates. I had been selected to join a higher-level reading class of about eight students, including kids I'd known for what seemed like my whole life.

The class was taught by Dr. Burnham, the principal, and on the first day, he asked us to introduce ourselves and share whether our parents were married, separated, or divorced.

I froze.

My parents had divorced less than a year earlier, and I was ashamed that my mom was now a single mother. In that small town, I didn't have any friends whose parents were divorced. My mom had told me how ashamed she felt to be the only divorced person from the small South Carolina community where she'd grown up. Her tone when talking about her divorce told me I should be ashamed as well. So when Dr. Burnham asked us to share our home circumstances, my shame rose and took center stage. I didn't know what to say because I didn't want to say *divorced*, and I wasn't sure what *separated* meant. But the latter sounded better. I shared that my parents were separated.

As the other kids introduced themselves, no one else said their parents were separated or divorced, which made me feel all the more embarrassed, ashamed, and set apart. The seed of shame had been planted in my heart early and branched into a pattern of lying anytime I felt pressed to expose my shame.

I reflected on Priscilla's shame and mine regarding our STD tests and about everything I'd vowed to take to my grave. I considered that everybody has something they're hiding in shame, but few people decide to deal with it. They bury the incident and live resigned to the consequences—"I made my bed, so now I have to lie in it."

The things I'd vowed to take to my grave had happened in my adolescence, long before Priscilla knew me. Yet strangely, the shame still had power over me. I felt that if Priscilla knew my childhood secrets, she wouldn't love me anymore. She'd think I was a pervert, be disgusted with me, and want me to sleep in the guest room.

Yes, my shame was attached to things that had happened over forty-five years prior, but the power of shame still dominated my thoughts and feelings. It was hard to believe that fact because it made no logical sense. But shame doesn't reside in logic; it lives in our fear that we won't be loved or accepted if people know who we truly are, what we've done, or what's been done to us.

> Shame doesn't reside in logic;
> it lives in our fear that we won't be loved
> or accepted if people know who we truly are,
> what we've done, or what's been done to us.

At the root of shame is the fear of being rejected by people we love and want to remain attached with. More than anything else, I wanted love and acceptance from Priscilla and to remain attached with her. As a result, I had not shared with her the shameful things on my take-it-to-the-grave list.

Over the next several days, I pondered my childhood shame and asked God to help me be free. As I searched the Bible for an answer, I saw that Jesus had felt shame and humiliation on the cross. Most paintings depict Him covered with a loincloth, but many scholars say He was completely naked on the cross in view of His mother, family, friends, and foes. How humiliating and shameful it must have been to not only hang there naked but to have been beaten to a bloody pulp before even picking up the cross to carry to His destination of death.

Pulling from various translations of Hebrews 12:2, I found that the Bible says Jesus despised the shame of the cross, scorned the shame, looked down on the shame, conquered the shame, and even disregarded the shame. In other words, He didn't allow shame to have power over Him to any degree. Jesus experienced shame as people do, and yet He chose to view shame as unimportant because He knew the power shame can have over us and how that power can debilitate or even destroy

God's purposes for our lives. I realized Christ did not allow shame to take hold of Him because He knew the purpose for His earthly life.

In the same Hebrews passage, I read how Jesus conquered shame. He was able to endure the cross and despise the shame because of the "joy set before him." He saw the big picture for His earthly life—what God wanted to do through His death and resurrection—and He rejoiced. Anything other than that purpose, Jesus despised, put off, threw down, disregarded, and made small so it would not overshadow or overtake His purpose.

Shame had dwelled in a secret place in my soul for a long time, demanding that I hide for fear of anyone knowing the truth and no longer respecting, admiring, or loving me. The same feeling of shame had kept Priscilla's mouth shut at the GYN's office. But when she had decided to talk about what she'd felt, she had taken power over her shame.

As I listened to her feelings and showed her empathy and compassion, she wiped her eyes, and I could see the shame visibly leave her. Somehow, her pulling the shame out of darkness had weakened its grip on her and made it seem smaller.

I recognized I had allowed my shame to seem bigger than God's purpose for me and bigger than my ability to see that purpose, consequently giving shame even more power over my thoughts and feelings. I needed to see my life as God saw it. Everything else by comparison, including my shame, needed to be small. I needed to pull my shame and my take-it-to-the-grave list out of darkness by sharing them with Priscilla.

The next morning, I rose early, anxious about pushing into wounds I had kept hidden for so many years.

Priscilla joined me shortly, sitting down at the kitchen table and gesturing toward my open journal. "Looks like you've been writing a lot this morning. What's going on?"

I glanced up briefly, putting my pen to the side. "I've been thinking about our conversation about how you felt in the doctor's office—you know, the part about the shame."

She nodded. "Tell me about it."

"I've had the same feelings of shame about things that go back many years, to when I was a kid growing up with just my mom and sister. There are some things in my life I'm really ashamed of. Things I've always said I would take to my grave. Out of fear, I've never shared them with anyone, and I've been afraid to share them with you, afraid you wouldn't love or respect me.

"I know I was just a kid when the stuff happened, and I didn't even know you then, but they've demanded secrecy in my life. I shook hands with them, agreeing I'd keep them buried. But every time someone gets close to these areas, like in discussion or something I see in a movie, I shudder and want to run and hide. I don't want to fear shame anymore, but I feel like the devil has told me that what I've done is uncommon, weird, perverted, and very sinful. So I've kept them hidden from everyone, including you. Now, I want to be free from the past and the power of shame more than I want to hide. I feel that God wants me to start by sharing my list with you."

PRISCILLA

Hearing Phil say he needed to share something usually brought tension in me as I wondered whether he was planning to drop another bomb. But knowing he wanted to share things he'd held on to since childhood brought a totally different feeling and dimension to our morning conversation. Although I'd had no idea he needed to have this conversation, God sure knew. I became increasingly aware that God was moving our discussions from what had happened recently to what had happened early on. The childhood soil we'd been planted in had affected more of our lives than we'd realized, and God was helping us see the weeds and overgrowth. He wanted us to stop seeing our present situations through the lens of our pasts.

Unpacking old wounds and shame would require us to be continually transparent with each other.

Phil slowly flipped through his journal pages. "I don't know if I can do this," he said reticently.

"You can do it." I knew full well shame's power that always demanded secrecy.

"It's so hard for me. There are things I've told myself I'll take to my grave. I've never shared them with anybody." He clasped both hands over his brow, shaking his head in reluctance. "I want to share with you, but I'm afraid of what you'll think about me."

"Phil, it's okay," I encouraged. "Just say it." I gently touched his forearm. "I'm here. I'm not going anywhere. Nothing you say is going to make me reject you. Nothing. Besides, they happened in your childhood. We've all done shameful stuff when we were kids." He took a deep breath and slowly released it, his lips tightly pressed. His eyes were hesitant when they met mine. "It'll be okay," I assured him. "Go ahead; you can do it."

Phil began telling me his childhood stories, slowly at first, calculating and precise as he remembered the details of things he'd been involved in and done and what had been done to him. While the stories were short, he frequently paused, wrestling with each detail but pushing past his shame and fear. He allowed me to see the visual representation of his struggle between shame and freedom. Still hesitant, he ended, "That's all of it. You must think I'm a pervert."

"No!" I said truthfully. "Not at all. That's not what I'm thinking, Phil! These things happen to lots of people. I know this for a fact because all three things you mentioned happened to me too. We're not that different from each other. We've just never before been HOT about our childhoods."

The tension on Phil's face turned to surprise, then relief. "Wow! Really? So what happened to you?"

As soon as Phil had started sharing his childhood experiences, I'd known God was creating an opportunity for me to become free from my past as well.

As I told Phil my stories, a burden lifted from my soul. It had been there for so long, and I had learned to live with it. Now it was gone—like tackling an overstuffed closetful of junk hidden away for years. I would open the closet door, see the mess I'd accumulated year after year, and ask myself, "Why have I held on to this? What's this stuff doing in here?" I knew the junk no longer had value, but I didn't want to let go. This was now my opportunity to be freed from shame.

As I shared my shame, scars, and wounds with Phil, I felt immense healing from past wounds. My thoughts cleared as I cleaned out the closet of my mind and threw the junk out to the curb. "Phil, I'm so glad we talked about this." I felt free. "If we can share our take-it-to-the-grave lists, I think we can share anything. I just wish we had done this earlier. Think how different our marriage would have been if we'd been this HOT from the very beginning!"

PHIL

It's hard to describe, but somehow, in just a few minutes, my shame shrank and then evaporated into nothing. It was gone.

Priscilla's admission of shame over the same three things I'd experienced created empathy and compassion in me. Our shame could simply no longer exist. What had held power over us, over me for forty-five years, just vanished as we brought to light the things so long hidden in darkness. I recalled the prophecy in Isaiah 49:9–10 and felt like the verse was for me:

> Saying to those who are bound, "Go free," to those who are in darkness, "Show yourselves." They will feed along the roads, and their pasture will be on all bare heights. They will not hunger or thirst, nor will the scorching heat or sun strike them down; For He who has compassion on them will lead them, and He will guide them to springs of water.

You may be wondering what our three areas of shame were, perhaps wanting to compare them to the things you're planning to take to your grave. We're forgoing that sharing because comparing baggage—perhaps deciding yours isn't as bad as ours or you weren't affected by the same things—is not beneficial to your confession, freedom, and forward movement. The important point is that you carefully consider what's in *your* closet of shame and what God wants to do with *your* junk. As Priscilla says, "Everybody's got some junk in their trunk."

If you want freedom from your childhood shames, bring your junk into the light by sharing it with your spouse.

After I shared with Priscilla, I felt new power to be open with others about my marital sins, as I had with our children. I returned to my action plan created at 4 Days 2 Freedom: confessing to my extended family, who had also been affected by my sin. I reached out to each and arranged times for Priscilla and me to share our story.

Each family member had been impacted in different ways by my sin, so to address each unique offense and ask for forgiveness, I wrote the confessions in advance.

Coming clean to nineteen family members took sixty-five days. The listeners' empathy, compassion, and affirmations confirmed that God had brought me to that point of release. Admitting my sin decreased my shame, and the responsive support from my family increased my courage and confidence to continue in boldness.

Priscilla was with me at the confessions, with the exception of my meetings with my two nephews, ages twenty-four and seventeen at the time. We didn't want Priscilla's presence to inhibit them from asking questions and sharing honestly about anything they may be holding on to or facing.

After each confession, most people asked Priscilla how she was doing and whether she had forgiven me. She was always transparent with her feelings, showing her grief and tears but affirming she had forgiven me and that we were not getting a divorce.

Each confession was important, but the most poignant was my confession to my mom. She and my dad had divorced when I was ten. After being single for twelve years, Mom had remarried two other times—her second husband had been an abusive alcoholic, and her third husband had passed away. She was now eighty-four.

On a Sunday afternoon, Priscilla and I arrived at her home in Leesburg, about an hour from our house. It was the town where I'd grown up, and every time I drove along the familiar roads, memories of high school parties and marching band flooded back. But this trip wasn't going to be a party. I was dreading this confession in a different way from the others. My mom frequently boasted about my sister and me, to the point of our embarrassment, and thought I'd hung the moon. I knew my betrayals would be hard for her to face.

She answered the door with her typical energetic greeting and big hug. She'd always been bubbly and outgoing, loving to be the center of attention, much like me. She frequently talked about her exploits as a standout high school basketball player (even though she was not quite five feet tall) and that she had been valedictorian of her high school graduating class of five. Her father had died when she was nine, and she had endured a difficult childhood as her mother had struggled to manage a farm, run a general store, and care for her three fatherless children.

My mother's marriage to my father had lasted only fifteen years but had produced, in her words, "two wonderful children." I'm not sure she ever completely got over the hurt my father had caused. Even after almost fifty years and two more marriages, she'd sometimes cry when reflecting on how much he'd hurt her—all the more so when he'd remarried only a few days after their divorce was final.

It was just recently that Mom's third husband had passed away, so I'd waited for this confession to give her time for her emotions to settle.

We sat down at her kitchen table, and I said, "Mom, I need to share some things with you that I've done—things that have affected Priscilla and our family. This is really hard, but I need to be open with you."

Initially, Mom just stared at me, then slowly looked back and forth from Priscilla to me, like she was searching our faces for a clue of what was ahead. "Okay," she said hesitantly, shifting in her chair and recentering her gaze on me.

I had decided not to beat around the bush. "Mom, I've committed adultery against Priscilla, and for most of our marriage, I've lived a sexually immoral life."

Mom's jaw dropped, and she quickly looked at Priscilla, then back at me. She looked astonished as her hands folded in front of her. Her brief silence conveyed that she wasn't quite sure what she'd heard and was trying to grasp hold of the reality. "Phillip, what do you mean?"

I explained in detail, similar to how I'd confessed to our children but keenly aware that my confession would conjure up her memories of experiences with my father decades ago.

With each disclosure, she looked up, down, and around, shaking her head as she tried to process what she was hearing. Eventually, she summarized her thoughts. "Sex just makes people crazy. You can't even think straight."

We sat in silence as she tapped a pencil to her lips, alternately pursing and relaxing them. Eventually her mouth set in a tight, straight line, and she asked about our children. We shared how they had taken the news.

After a time, she paused and said slowly, "Well, we all have secrets."

Silence.

What does she mean? Is there something she needs to share? "Mom, do you have any secrets?"

She paused, her face turning pensive, as though debating how much to share. Then she looked up and formed words that sounded like they were coming from somewhere deep inside her, straight from her gut.

"Forty-six years ago, I had an illegal abortion, and I've never told anyone. Only the doctor and my mother knew. It was right after your dad left us."

I was stunned.

"I went to a bar one evening, met a guy, and had sex with him. I thought that somehow this would be revenge on your dad. I wanted to hurt him so badly for what he'd done to us." She took a deep breath and sighed. "Well, I became pregnant and told my doctor I just couldn't have this baby. I had two young children, was recently divorced, and I wasn't making a lot of money. I begged him to help me, and he gave me a phone number for a place in New York. I called, made an appointment, and flew up there. I got the abortion and returned the next day."

I vaguely remembered the situation because my grandmother (her mom) had come down to Florida from South Carolina to watch my sister and me for a couple of days. Prior to Mom leaving, she had been very secretive about where she was going. After she had returned, somehow the topic of abortion had come up, and she'd remarked, "People commonly have a D&C to remove a mass of cells the size of a pin."

It had been a strange conversation, and when she'd offered that explanation, I'd wondered if a D&C was somehow connected to her recent trip. But I had never asked her. Now I understood the explanation must have come from the clinic doctor or nurse to help Mom cope with the guilt that typically accompanies such a decision.

"Mom, I'm so glad you shared this with us. Unwanted pregnancies and abortions happen to a lot of people, unfortunately. I'm so sorry you felt that abortion was your only option. Why didn't you share it with us earlier?"

"I guess I was ashamed of what I did and what I'd gotten myself into. I was a schoolteacher and thought maybe I would lose my job if I showed up unwed and pregnant. That's the very thing so many young girls dealt with in high school, and there I was, a teacher in the same predicament." She looked down, her face scrunched with the emotion of her experience and unloading a burden she'd carried so long.

"Mom, do you believe you've been forgiven?"

Her gaze shot up. "Yes, I asked the good Lord to forgive me." She stared down again, seemingly deep in thought about having disclosed something she'd planned to take to her grave.

"Well, I'm confident God has forgiven you, Mom. You know, I think you should share this with Cindy and Bob. They really need to know, and it will be good for you to share what happened." I knew my sister, Cindy, and her husband, Bob, would encourage Mom. I was very happy she had unloaded her shame, and I wanted her to feel empathy and compassion from other people who loved her.

"Okay, I'll email them and see when they can come by. Thank you, Phillip. I love and forgive you."

"I love and forgive you too, Mom. We all have secrets, and God wants us to bring them into the light so we can be free."

A few days later, I received an email from Mom sharing that Cindy and Bob would be coming to see her the following weekend.

Cindy is four and a half years younger than me and married Bob the same year I married Priscilla. Our families spent quite a lot of time together. Our kids had all run track and cross country together, and we'd gone camping with them in North Carolina almost every summer. Cindy's smart and funny and has bright eyes, a quick smile, and an eagerness to know and share whatever God is doing in her life. She had worked as a CPA, like me, but had decided to stay home with her three kids and homeschool them through twelfth grade. She had only recently returned to the workforce, refreshing her accounting skills while staying involved with her kids.

Bob was analytical and an engineer by training, and he provided a good balance to Cindy. He thought about the details of every problem and frequently poked fun at himself and Cindy. I knew they'd provide empathy and compassion to Mom. I was excited to see what God was doing in her life and eagerly anticipated hearing from Cindy about their meeting.

CINDY

I knew Phil and Priscilla had visited Mama to share their story, so I wasn't surprised she wanted Bob and me to come by so she could talk with us "about something important." A couple of months had passed since Phil's confession to us, and I imagined the news had shaken Mama's world.

On the drive over, Bob and I wondered how she'd received what they had shared. We prepared to help her think through their confession, realizing it probably had brought back emotions from all that had happened between her and Dad. We resolved to create a safe place for her to express her feelings and hoped she was excited about what God was doing in Phil and Priscilla's marriage.

As we pulled into the driveway, Mama opened the door, anticipating our arrival. Her typical happy and bubbly greeting was subdued, and her smile was only slight as she opened the door. She quickly moved us into the family room and said, "I'm sure you know that Phil and Priscilla were here last weekend, and they shared with me about Phil's adultery." She paused as if caught in thought, and her hand went to her lips. "I just couldn't believe it." She shook her head. "They told me they'd already shared with the rest of our family. It was hard for me to believe he did all that. He's always been a wonderful son, but I know sex makes people crazy. They can't think straight." She paused, collecting her thoughts. "I felt so bad for him and wanted him to know that other people have secrets too, so I shared with him something I'd never told anyone." Bob and I nodded and gave her the time she needed to continue. "Phillip thought I should share it with you also, and that's the reason I invited you to come over today."

With that short introduction, Mama then shared her painful story and spared no details. She described how she had thought her only option was an illegal abortion.

As Mama shared, Bob and I exchanged glances, and thoughts danced in our heads about Phil and Priscilla's meeting with us only two months earlier. As they had shared their story, Bob and I had reflected on our dating story. I was nineteen when I had first become pregnant. Believing we had no other option, Bob and I had decided I should have an abortion. After becoming Christians, we had openly shared our story with Phil and Priscilla and at churches. Although our children knew I volunteered at crisis pregnancy centers, Bob and I had not shared our story with them, even though they were now almost adults.

Within a couple of weeks of Phil and Priscilla sharing their story with us, we had met with our three children and shared our story. Several weeks prior, Phil and Priscilla had met with each of them and shared their confessions, so we'd known that sharing our story with them would probably make them wonder what was going on with our families.

Interestingly, only weeks after we'd shared our story with our children, our oldest son had abruptly broken up with his girlfriend, saying the relationship wasn't honoring God. And now, there we were with

Mom and an opportunity to share it again. "Mama, I'm so sorry that happened to you. I can relate to everything you said because, when Bob and I were dating, I also had an abortion." Mama's mouth opened as she tried to form words that wouldn't come, so I continued. "I've shared this in the past with many people, and God has used my story to help me counsel women at crisis pregnancy centers. I'm so glad you shared your story with us because no one should keep secrets like this; they're poison to our hearts." Mama remained quiet, and Bob jumped in.

"Do you feel like God has forgiven you?" he asked.

"Yes, I've asked Him to forgive me, and I believe He has."

I asked, "Mama, why did you decide to share your story?"

She paused, her eyes moving alternately down, then up, and then back to Bob and me. "When Phillip told me his story, I could see how much pain he felt. Everybody sins, and I wanted him to know that I'd sinned too so he wouldn't feel so bad." Interestingly, that was the same reason I had shared my story with her.

As I'd witnessed her painful retelling, my instinct had been to empathize by letting her know we weren't all that different. Transparency has the power to create more transparency, and I was glad Mama and I could be open with one another after so many years.

Throughout our conversation, her unconditional love as a mother persisted. She showed no shame toward my secret or Phil's. She didn't say, "Let's just keep this quiet between us" (as I had anticipated).

We ended the conversation with hugs and a closer relationship. In fact, the entire situation, beginning with Phil's and Priscilla's transparency, created a new openness in our family that felt refreshing, like a family's love should feel.

In the months that followed, Mama decided to write a book telling her life story, including her abortion and other things she wasn't proud of. Although copies went only to her family, I was so proud of her. Even in her eighties, she'd let go of her shame and discovered the freedom of no longer keeping secrets. What a great blessing for her and us.

PHIL

Cindy and Bob's conversation with Mom created another positive ripple, one more ricochet of our freedom from shame.

I had been so scared to let anyone see the real me. I had never imagined the impact vulnerability could have on others. I considered my initial confessions to Priscilla and our children, their confessions to us, our confessions of our take-it-to-the-grave lists, Bob and Cindy's confessions to their children, Mom's and Cindy's confessions of abortions, my mom writing her book, and the subsequent breakups of my son's and nephew's relationships with their girlfriends. I reflected on all that God had done—"far more abundantly beyond all that we ask or think, according to the power that works within us" (Eph. 3:20).

Just a few months prior, I had cried out to God for freedom from my past, having no idea He wanted to do much more than free me. He wanted to free our entire family! With everything I'd done and gone through, and all that I'd since witnessed in our families, I understood why I'd had to come to utter despair and brokenness: to become one of "the weak things of the world" (Eph. 3:27) to show God's redemptive love and grace, because "when I am weak, then I am strong" (2 Cor. 12:10). God's plan has always been to use one person's freedom to cultivate freedom in others.

> God's plan has always been to use one person's freedom to cultivate freedom in others.

Later that week, after Cindy and Bob's visit, Priscilla and I received our STD results. Both were negative. Only a few months earlier, I had been gasping for air at the thought of what an STD would do to my life, marriage, and family. Now I was seeing the greater picture—why God had allowed me to push myself to the edge. I had hated myself and who I'd become but hadn't known how to be free. In God's amazing providence, He'd known what it would take to break my pride. Sin, secrecy, and pride had pushed me not only over the edge but down into the lowest pit, where the Holy Spirit had received my full attention. He'd shown how only He "redeems your life from the pit" (Ps. 103:3). That's what He had done for me.

For the first time in my life, I felt fully known and fully loved. It was an amazing place to be, and I saw that confessing my sin had produced an earnestness in my prayers that I'd never before known, and had created deep healing in my soul. God had led our families to experience healing as well. Amazing. God had allowed Priscilla and me to participate in not only each other's healing but our entire family's.

As family members' confessions drew to a close, we didn't know God was still just getting started with all He wanted to do in our lives. A test was right around the corner.

| Savage Questions for Reflection |

1. How have you personally experienced the positive effects of vulnerability? What happened?

2. What's on your take-it-to-the-grave list? How do you feel when you're reminded of something on your list? Are you willing to share the list with your spouse?

3. How would you describe your story? How much of your story do your spouse and family know? How do you feel about sharing your story with them and believing God will use it in their lives for freedom? Are you willing to trust Him and step out in faith to free yourself and those you love?

Chapter 8

UNSEEN FORCES
IN OUR MINDS

We are taking every thought captive to the obedience of
Christ.

—2 Corinthians 10:5

I've had more trouble with myself than any other man.

—Dwight L. Moody

PHIL

Elbows bumped as people jostled for position to get the best view of the
solar eclipse. I stood outside my office building, put on the paper eclipse
glasses, and stared up at the sky.

Out of the corner of my eye, I glimpsed a young woman wearing a
backless flowy blouse. It was certainly not the type of blouse someone
would wear to our office or any office. She was sixty feet away, and as
the slight breeze ruffled her blouse, I could see she wasn't wearing a bra

and I caught a glimpse of the side of her breast.

Four months prior, I'd come clean with Priscilla about my sexual sin; but this backless-top woman could quickly pull my mind into the dark place of secret lust. I had a dilemma and turned to God. *Should I stay here with my team or turn and walk inside?* I was not confident in my ability to stand there without stealing more glances at the woman, and I had committed to being HOT with Priscilla. I would need to share this experience with her.

God's still, quiet voice said, "Get out of here." I turned on my heel, mumbled something about having a lot of work to do, and ambled through the crowd toward the now-vacant elevators. I felt a sense of satisfaction, having turned from temptation. Although the backless-top woman's appearance had presented an attraction, I had not allowed my mind to create a sexual fantasy.

I decided to share the incident with Priscilla that evening. I knew she'd be pleased about my conversation with God and how I'd chosen to turn and leave the situation. I looked forward to her warm embrace and encouragement.

PRISCILLA

After a nice family dinner, Phil and I walked outside. Standing there, gazing at the sunset from our front yard, I heard those dreaded words from him: "I have something I need to tell you." These were the same words he'd used repeatedly after coming clean to share something that would be hard for me to hear. My heart sank. *Please, not right now. I don't want to hear it!* But I knew I needed to listen. We were committed to being HOT with each other, no matter what.

PHIL

While I was a little apprehensive about sharing, I was thankful I had successfully overcome the temptation and done the right thing. I was looking forward to our leisurely sunset stroll and sharing, which had become part of our new evening routine since I'd come clean. Our walk and talk was a time of intimacy and reflection on our day that provided salve to our charred and healing souls. We were four months into our marriage recovery, and all the details of my secret life had been confessed to my wife and family. I felt free. Priscilla and my family had forgiven me, Priscilla had confessed her shortcomings, and we had reengaged emotionally. We still had a lot of work to do, but I sensed we were past the worst part and on an upward journey together. Having climbed out of the near-fatal wreckage, we were now headed toward marital success.

PRISCILLA

As Phil shared his experience of the backless-top woman, a tidal wave of emotions crashed over me. I was suddenly drowning and couldn't reach the surface to take in a breath. I was engulfed in an emotional battle, fighting to move through the sea of past pain pushing me under again.

Listening to the details of his experience with the backless-top woman, I became angry and confused. I should have stopped, right then and there, and asked questions, but words eluded me as I let hostility take over. It led me down the path of making assumptions and creating not-so-appealing fantasies in my mind: Phil standing five feet from a beautiful, thin woman. She had long curly hair and was wearing tight jeans and high heels. She was laughing like she was looking for a party, and she was young, sexy, and fun—all the things I wanted to be.

As he talked, my fearful fantasy took on a life of its own, looking very real in the cinema of my mind. Phil was moving nearer her, around her, leering and positioning himself to better see her breasts. His mind was consumed with her as he lusted after her, wanting her sexually more than he wanted me. These thoughts and inner voices shut down my ability to hear Phil (and the Holy Spirit) and fueled the animosity welling up inside me.

PHIL

Priscilla was quiet as I shared about the backless-top woman. As she listened to the details, I could see her countenance changing. Her lips tightened, and her body language closed up. Then, suddenly, she began to fire questions at me. "Why were you looking at her? How many times did you look at her? Why didn't you walk away sooner?" Her eyes were narrowed on me.

Confusion washed over me. Her response was not the one I had anticipated. "I wasn't staring at her," I protested. "I *did* walk away!"

Priscilla snapped, "You did not! You were staring and lusting for her!" And the final jab: "You enjoyed it!"

I felt backed into a corner, searching for words to soothe the tempest. "I wasn't focused on her! I saw her, but I wasn't fantasizing about her or lusting after her. I did the right thing—I walked away! I thought you would be pleased with how I handled it!"

"I just don't understand how you could say you only have eyes for me and then obviously have eyes for her," Priscilla insisted. "You probably wished I looked like her!"

No matter how much I maintained I'd done the right thing, which I had, I was caught in Hurricane Priscilla.

Is this the way our life is going to be from here on out? Where's the warm embrace and encouragement? What happened to our decision to be HOT with each other?

PRISCILLA

Our conflict was left unresolved that night. We were distant, each of us feeling the pain of our struggles. There was hardly any conversation other than getting our girls squared away for bedtime.

The feature film of lies repeatedly played in my head, over and over. Phil's posturing, leering, and lusting for the backless-top woman grew more vivid. I had a long, restless, and sleepless night, fighting the enemy of my soul, who, in the nightmare, looked a lot like Phil.

The next day, he went to work without saying anything.

PHIL

I woke up early and decided to head to the office, though my mind was preoccupied. *This won't get any better.*

I was losing hope, and my thoughts grew increasingly confused. *We've conquered a lot, but she's a crazy woman! She's mentally unstable and emotionally driven by everything. She wants me to be open and honest, but she can't handle it. Just when I let her into my thoughts and struggles, she clobbers me! She doesn't really want to help me at all or truly be HOT. I shouldn't have told her anything!*

As I pushed through the day, I let the confusion take me down into a darker place.

I can't live like this anymore.

Overcome with weariness, I resolved to confront Priscilla when I got home.

PRISCILLA

After dinner, Phil suggested we talk outside on the back porch. I knew we needed to talk, but I was exhausted and angry from the drama churning in my head.

We pulled up chairs, and he immediately put his head down on his crossed arms on the table. I could tell he was drained, just as tired as me. He looked up and, after a sigh of defeat, exhaled, "I can't live like this anymore. If this is what it's going to look like from now on when I'm transparent, it's just too hard. I can't live this way."

I understood how he felt. The entire circumstance he'd pulled me into four months prior felt too hard for me as well. We'd been through a lot and taken mountain-high steps, but we both felt warworn in the aftermath. This was not the way I had envisioned our future either.

When we'd married twenty-nine years earlier, we had committed to never use the D-word. Although Phil had not said the word, I knew what he meant by "I can't live this way." It appeared we had reached the end of our well-intentioned marriage revival. In defeat and off course from the intended road and all the strides we'd made, we were getting a divorce.

PHIL

My words hung in the air like stench around a garbage dump. I immediately knew why I'd never used the D-word. Even in this instance, I'd chosen to suggest it rather than say it. Unspoken, the term was just too final, stark, and lonely.

Prior, as we'd navigated the swells of my coming clean, neither of us had suggested a divorce. But the tide had suddenly turned. We were both worn out. It was time to surrender and move our separate ways. There was just too much hurt, and Priscilla was never going to get over the pain.

PRISCILLA

We sat still in silence for a few minutes. I was at a loss for words and trying to digest what our marriage had gone through and had now come to.

Phil jarred me from my thoughts as he mumbled, "I think we should pray."

Pray? Now you want to pray? After telling me you're done? Why didn't you pray instead of lusting after that backless-top woman? Why didn't you pray before you told me we're getting a divorce?

I didn't feel like praying with Phil. I didn't even want to be around him. My emotions were reeling, but I knew God always pointed me toward a place of peace, so my heart moved toward Him. My heavenly Father would know what we should do, even if we'd given up. We had leaned heavily on Him since Phil's initial confessions, and I knew He would take care of me and my kids even if Phil and I were done. Phil might walk away from me, but my Father would never leave or forsake me.

"I agree."

Phil began to pray. "Father, we're in the middle of a mess," he admitted, "and I don't know what to do. I just want to give up. We need Your help. *Please*, Lord Jesus, help us. Help us to see and know what You want us to do."

Immediately, I felt the atmosphere change. The heaviness evaporated, and suddenly I felt peace and calm.

When Phil looked up, his eyes were moist but brighter. He looked me in the eye, and his lips curved into a sly smile like he was going to say something funny. "You know, I was thinking, if we were standing before a judge and stating that we want a divorce, we'd have to give a reason. So I'd probably tell the judge I had lived an immoral lifestyle; I betrayed my wife and children, and I did a whole bunch of other misdeeds. Then the judge would ask, 'That's why you want a divorce?' And I'd answer, 'No, Your Honor, my wife has forgiven me for all of that.' Then the judge would ask, 'So why do you want a divorce?' And I'd say, 'Well, Your Honor, you see, the reason for the divorce is not the adultery, immorality, or betrayal—it's because of a woman with a backless top.'"

Phil grinned, and so did I.

Yes, it was pretty ridiculous in the context of everything God had brought us through.

Although we had wrestled for twenty-four hours and entertained the D-word, it took only sixty seconds to look to God for help, and that decision immediately changed everything—like Jesus speaking to the angry sea in Mark 4:39. "He got up and rebuked the wind and said to the sea, 'Hush, be still.' And the wind died down and it became perfectly calm."

God had once again rescued our thoughts and marriage by providing clarity, perspective, and His remarkable, supernatural peace.

"Well, I guess if I've forgiven you for adultery, living a double life, betraying my trust, and lying, I can forgive you for looking at that backless-top woman." Phil's face relaxed, and his now-soft eyes brimmed with tears.

We held hands and resolved that we weren't getting a divorce. Ever. The only D-word we'd allow in our marriage would be *delivered*—by God, from the enemy who is always seeking to destroy us.

PHIL

After the emotion of the backless-top woman had passed, we calmly reflected on what had happened in the past tumultuous twenty-four hours. Although that wasn't our first speed bump and certainly wouldn't be our last, we now saw each bump as an opportunity to learn what we could have done differently.

One morning Priscilla asked, "How far away from you was the backless-top woman?"

"About sixty feet."

"No way!" she exclaimed. "I thought she was five feet from you! Are you telling me she was really *sixty* feet away? You couldn't have seen *anything* at sixty feet! You must have had eagle eyes!"

"I know how far sixty feet is, and the backless-top woman was at least sixty feet away!" I retorted. "And maybe I couldn't see much, but I could certainly imagine a lot. That's how the mind of a man works, you know."

Priscilla pointed to trees in the yard for me to prove I knew how far sixty feet was, and we began to laugh over how we'd both missed the importance of this crucial detail.

PRISCILLA

It was hard to believe, but one key detail, the sixty-foot distance, could have changed my initial response—as it had almost cost us our marriage and all the work we'd put into it. I had been absorbed in emotion hearing Phil's account and had failed to ask questions that could have helped me better understand what he was sharing. I had let my emotions spin me out of control, and God showed me that understanding details are key to any confession.

Details are contrary to our typical thinking, especially in highly sensitive circumstances. Most people would rather be vague in their confessions, leaving out details, worrying that too many details would be self-incriminating or embarrassing and cost them even more emotionally. But the problem with missing or withholding details is that the offended person is left with their imagination to fill in the gaps.

Many times, those conjured details are much worse than what actually occurred.

If I had paused to ask God for help to listen and hear the details of Phil's experience, it could have saved us both so much heartache.

For the future, I prayed for God to help me ask the right questions to fill the gaps with facts. We also agreed that Phil would supply all the details prompted by God to help me work through my feelings when I failed to ask the right questions.

God also showed me that forgiveness isn't a onetime event. Forgiveness is a continual walk.

> Forgiveness isn't a onetime event.
> Forgiveness is a continual walk.

At the 4 Days 2 Hope women's retreat, I had learned about forgiveness, but I needed to revisit forgiveness to grasp how much Christ had forgiven me. And I needed to allow God to continually work forgiveness in my life, especially in situations like the one with the backless-top woman.

I recalled what Jesus had said about forgiving—to forgive our brother "seventy times seven" (Matt. 18:22 NLT). In other words, repeatedly forgive. With this reminder, I was able to forgive Phil for whatever he had thought, seen, and felt regarding the backless-top woman.

We also should have prayed before Phil shared the experience. While confessing sinful desires and behaviors is necessary, confession to your spouse can be dangerous ground, ripe for confusion, frustration, and anger. The Holy Spirit had known what Phil was going to confess, and before Phil shared, my prayer could have been as simple as, *Lord, please help me in what I'm about to hear from Phil. Prepare my heart and mind to hear my spouse. Don't let my emotions go into a whirlwind.*

God was inviting me to receive His clarity, wisdom, and protection and to see Phil as Jesus saw him: a son who had left his past life behind and was walking a new road of healing and wholeness. Phil's confession about the backless-top woman was another step along our healing journey.

PHIL

I couldn't believe how our thoughts over the backless-top woman had spun out of control so fast. In twenty-four hours, we had gone from having remarkable restoration in our marriage to heading for divorce court. The battle had formed and engaged in our minds first and erupted toward destruction. In this particular confession, Priscilla and I had both heard and believed lies. I had believed she was a crazy woman who would never be able to let go of her hurt. Priscilla had believed I was lusting, leering, and secretly wishing she looked more like the back-less-top woman. We had both gotten emotionally stuck and spiraled toward divorce as the lies had seized our thoughts and led us to believe our marriage was over.

I considered where those lies had come from. Had they simply been our own generated thoughts, or had some thoughts been planted in our minds to distort the truth? In other words, were we solely deceiving ourselves, or were unseen spiritual forces also at work to deceive us?

Again, I needed to turn to God's Word for the truth and read 1 Corinthians 3:18. "Let no man deceive himself."

I reasoned that it was therefore possible for us to become deceived by our own internal thoughts, which took me back to Romans 12:2 and why it says, "Be transformed by the renewing of your mind."

The Bible also gives examples of people deceived by outside, unseen spiritual forces—such as the experiences of Ananias and King David. Two instances recount that the thoughts and actions of these two men were influenced by Satan:

- The apostle Peter sharply rebuked Ananias for secretly withholding some proceeds from the sale of land. He said, "Ananias, why has Satan filled your heart to lie to the Holy Spirit and to keep back some of the proceeds of the land?" (Acts 5:3)

- In King David's situation, the Bible says, "Satan stood up against Israel, and incited David to count Israel." (1 Chron. 21:1)

I'm not sure how Satan "filled the heart" of Ananias or "incited" King David, but the Bible shows that Satan was able to influence human thoughts, which in turn influenced human decisions and actions.

I revisited John 8:44, about Satan.

> He was a murderer from the beginning, and does not stand in the truth because there is no truth in him. Whenever he tells a lie, he speaks from his own nature, because he is a liar and the father of lies.

Since Satan is a liar, he must still be lying to *somebody* (otherwise, he wouldn't be called a liar), and that somebody, as shown in the Bible, is us!

In the middle of our struggle over the backless-top woman, a simple prayer had allowed Priscilla and me to exchange the lies we were hearing for truth. We saw the absurdity of what we had believed, and we felt God's promise for life in our marriage, not death.

Priscilla wasn't a crazy woman after all. God had brought her into my life, in part for healing, blessing, and favor. He had already supplied us with truth in His Word: "He who finds a wife finds a good thing and obtains favor from the Lord" (Prov. 18:22).

As we looked to God for help, His Holy Spirit guided us "into all the truth" (John 16:13), and we experienced how "the truth shall set you free" (John 8:32). We added another key tool to our communication that we would use from that point forward. In the middle of any argument, we ask each other a question that rescues us from numerous disagreements, struggles, and conflicts: "What are you hearing?"

That simple question immediately takes our attention away from our emotions and arguments to help us discern whether intruding thoughts are from Satan, designed to deceive us, pull us off track, and take our eyes off God.

Not bringing God into my confession about the backless-top woman had caused us to take a needless twenty-four-hour detour that had threatened to derail our entire restoration. But God had prevailed and helped us win the battle against our fallible minds—and the battle against the enemy of our souls.

The issue of the backless-top woman was dead.

PRISCILLA

Shortly after Phil came clean about visiting massage parlors, I began to notice such places all over town. I'd never paid much attention to them in the past, thinking they were just small spas. But Phil's confession had told me otherwise.

Like flashing neon signs, the storefronts pushed their way into my mind, forcing me to consider their presence. They seemed to be everywhere. Questions began popping into my mind. *Has Phil been there? What about that one?* Every time we drove by one of those places, I wondered whether he had been there and if he was also seeing and thinking about them.

I became angry at the businesses, wanting them all to be thrown into the pit of hell where they belonged. I knew that sounded pretty "un-Christian," but that was the way I felt.

One day, while running errands together, we passed a nondescript sign posted in a small plaza: **Massage**. Immediately, questions flashed in my mind, sending my emotions into a tizzy. The more I tried to ignore the hideous places, the bigger they seemed to get, and the more I imagined Phil being pulled toward them. Then my thoughts became clear. I needed to bring the questions into the light. "Phil, have you ever been to that massage place?"

"No, not that one," he answered with a sincere, unbothered tone. "I've been to other ones, but not that one. If you ever want to know, just ask me."

Immediately, I felt better. When I asked Phil questions, he was very HOT, letting me see how his emotions, mind, and will operated. He didn't respond defensively or otherwise seem bothered by my questions. Asking questions stopped the signs from flashing. I realized my questions existed in darkness, the place where all sin originates and grows. All I needed to do was share them openly with Phil.

That wasn't the last time I'd bring up that question, and I no longer felt the need to look for massage parlors every time we got into the car, nor the need to question him every time we passed one. On the occasions when I did feel impressed to question him, the answer was a simple "Yes, I did go to that one" or "No, not that one." Sometimes I had follow-up questions such as, "How many times?" or "Do you remember when?" or "Did you ever go back to see the same woman?" Phil always gave me straightforward answers of truth without hesitation.

As the months passed, my need to ask such questions diminished, primarily because Phil's transparency increased my confidence that he had nothing to hide. His willingness to revisit his earlier confessions helped me get over my fears.

Some wives have told me their husbands demand they never ask them another question about their coming clean. Any time the women's fears and questions resurfaced, their husbands became angry and frustrated, backed with remarks such as, "Why do we have to talk about that again? I've already told you everything, and the answer hasn't changed."

I'd heard Phil respond to men who deflected their wives' questions. He'd share with them from his heart of understanding his own shortcomings. "Priscilla and I certainly didn't do everything right in our recovery, but one tool really helped us progress more quickly toward reconciliation: me taking personal responsibility for causing her to feel as she does. The truth is it's your fault your wife feels so insecure. If she asks the same question a thousand times, you have to humbly answer her question, every single time, without frustration."

Our foundation of transparency was now paying deeper dividends. I could see how being HOT was working in our everyday lives, allowing us both to come clean when our imaginations were fighting unseen forces.

PHIL

I finished lunch downtown and was walking back to the office when I saw two attractive young women walking toward me. Although they were over a block away, their presence caught my attention. Tall, blonde, slender, and dressed in shorts and sandals, they looked like tourists. They bounced as they walked, laughing and joking with each other. We see a lot of tourists in Orlando, so nothing was particularly surprising about them. But as they got closer, they were looking at me, and I momentarily caught their gaze and looked away. Another glance at them revealed they were still watching me as they smiled and laughed. Questions popped into my head. *Why are they staring at me? What do they want? Do they need help?*

As they got within earshot, I heard their accents and imagined they were from Sweden or another country famous for beautiful women. Within steps of me, they slowed, as if they wanted to talk to me. The taller of the two, probably in her early twenties, started the conversation. "Excuse me; we're just wondering whether there are any good bars or places to party downtown? Do you know?"

I knew downtown pretty well since I had worked there for over twenty years. I quickly rattled off some places, joking and laughing with them as we talked. But what was happening on the outside was not as important as what was occurring inside me. I imagined they weren't seeing me as a man in his late fifties but maybe twenty years younger. *Do they possibly prefer older men? Maybe these women are giving me a line about locations when they really want to party with me.*

As ridiculous as that now sounds, my feelings at that time weren't controlled by logic. They were controlled by my fertile imagination, along with some intruding thoughts and lies thrown in for good measure (by unseen forces).

The Swedish bikini models eventually said thanks and walked off. But my imagination continued to run toward them as I created all sorts of crazy scenarios of how this chance encounter could have played out. Two beautiful young women wanting to talk with an old guy like me did quite a lot for my ego, which positioned me to continue conceiving thoughts of what could have happened.

When I got back to my office, I sent Priscilla a praying-hands emoji—the code we'd agreed I would use whenever a battle was forming in my mind that threatened to lead me down the dark and well-trodden path. In other words, not just momentary thoughts that came and went but thoughts that seemed impossible to get rid of, that stuck like Gorilla Glue, threatening to take me captive and pull me back into the sin that had dominated my life.

Ever since the backless-top woman, I'd experimented with sending Priscilla the praying hands each time temptation confronted me. I was amazed how fast the thoughts would evaporate as soon as I hit the Send button. Moving my imagination out of darkness into the light positioned me to take "every thought captive to the obedience of Christ" (2 Cor. 10:5). Otherwise, when I allowed thoughts to simmer in secrecy, they took me captive.

The praying-hands code became a powerful tool God used to free me from temptations that continued to plague my life. Hitting the Send button would immediately open the door to my secret thoughts and remove their power. By alerting Priscilla to my desires, I invited her to be a battle partner with me rather than merely a confession partner I used to unload the guilt of my sin. She always quickly texted back with emojis of hearts, googly eyes, or a kiss and texted that God was with me and had the power to help me overcome every temptation. Her words were powerful, letting me know she loved me and was praying for me. My texts helped her learn how I thought and prompted her to come to my aid in situations that wouldn't be good for me.

As thoughts of the two women teased my imagination, the praying hands to Priscilla tipped the battle in my favor. Unseen forces threatening to control my mind simply couldn't exist without secrecy.

By the time I arrived home that evening, I had forgotten about the incident. But Priscilla hadn't. "What was the praying hands about today?"

"Oh, it was related to two young women I saw on the way back from lunch."

"What happened?" Priscilla wanted to understand the details to avoid repeating the backless-top woman debacle.

"After lunch with a client downtown, I was walking back to the office when I saw two attractive young women walking toward me, laughing, joking, and looking like they wanted to talk to me. They were foreigners and kept staring at me, and as they drew closer, they stopped to ask me about bars and places to party downtown. So I thought maybe they were interested in me and wanted more than just information. They kept talking and joking with me, and my imagination started going haywire, thinking maybe they wanted to have sex with me. Well, they eventually left, and as I went up to the office, my thoughts about their interest in me were still spinning. That's when I decided to send you the code."

Priscilla had been watching me intently, and when I told her I had imagined the girls wanted to have sex with me, her mouth curled up like she was trying not to laugh. As I finished my heartfelt confession, she couldn't contain herself anymore. She doubled over, holding her stomach as she laughed. "Phil, do you really think those girls wanted to have sex with you? I don't think so! Do you know what they were actually thinking? That you looked like a safe guy to ask for help, like someone who could've been their father!"

Although I was a bit offended Priscilla was laughing so hard at the thought of those girls wanting to have sex with me, the truth of what she'd said quickly sank in. "Well, I guess you're right. Those women probably weren't thinking about having sex with an old guy like me, but my ego and imagination said otherwise. That's why I sent the praying hands to you. It's interesting; right after I sent it, the thoughts just vanished."

Priscilla kept laughing, and I sheepishly forgot the whole episode. Whatever subconscious thoughts may have been lingering were now completely gone in light of the truth Priscilla had shown me. She helped me cast down the vain imaginations that had dominated my mind only a few hours earlier.

PRISCILLA

Phil's confession about the women downtown gave me another glimpse into the battles taking place inside his head, but they also created insecurities in me. Yes, Phil's imagination could run wild, but so could mine.

I sometimes became the "police" or the Holy Spirit, wanting to protect Phil and me from beautiful women I imagined he was lusting after—women I could never match up to. It was the prison of my mind, and I hated thinking such thoughts. Because of my fears, I became trapped in situation after situation. I asked God to help me break out of my self-imposed prison.

One morning, the answer came: *No matter how much I try, I cannot control, protect, or limit what's going on with Phil. He isn't my problem; he's God's problem.*

I had been relying on my own strategies, strength, and diligence to make sure I wouldn't be hurt again. In my frustration, I had become the author and perfector of Phil's faith and mine. I had placed myself in a position that only Jesus should have occupied. Once again, I recognized Phil was in God's care, and He was the shield and protector of our lives, not me. God loved Phil more than I ever could in my humanness, and He wanted me to get out of the way and rest in what Jesus was doing as the "champion who initiates and perfects our faith" (Heb. 12:2 NLT). God wanted me to simply fix my eyes on Jesus while He took care of Phil.

Going forward, anytime I heard the enemy's voice telling me to pick up my police badge, I told the unseen forces, "Go talk to Jesus!"

Embracing the spiritual authority that God had given me allowed me to escape from the prison of my mind.

PHIL

Our experience with radical transparency produced more victory over my thought life than I had ever thought possible. When meeting with my accountability partner for over ten years and several men's accountability groups, I'd merely used them as pressure-relief valves. I'd confess just enough sin to feel better while hoping the other men were admiring me for being a great Christian guy. It was all hypocrisy and self-righteousness on my part.

One day I met with a man named John, who was helping lead a men's accountability group. I shared my story with him and eventually got to the punch line. "You know, John, Priscilla is now my accountability partner." His eyebrows arched, and his jaw dropped as his back straightened.

"Priscilla?" His brow furrowed. "I don't think that's a good idea. While it may feel good for you to unload your guilt on her, just think how that must make her feel. Are you really going to tell her there's other women you think want to have sex with you?"

"I've already told her things like that," I said, thinking back to the Swedish bikini models.

"Really? How did she react?"

"She laughed and assured me the women didn't want to have sex with me." John pondered my response.

"So you don't think men's accountability groups are any good?"

"Accountability groups can be good, but they allowed me to share more intimate details of my life than I'd shared with Priscilla. God wanted me to be as intimate with her, as my wife, as I am with Him. I had let my accountability partners take a place that only Priscilla should have occupied."

"What do you think needs to change?" John asked.

"I think many men let each other off too easy, without asking hard questions because they don't want to answer any themselves. For example, someone typically asks, 'How did everyone's week go?' which is the code phrase for 'Did anyone act out sexually?' Usually, some guy looks up and sheepishly says, 'I was on the internet checking on travel and got sidetracked from one website to another, and I found myself on some inappropriate sites that just popped up.' The other men listen, nodding to show empathy and understanding, and usually, another man then shares he had a similar experience, maybe with a slight variation. As the meeting wraps up, the leader thanks everyone for being open and honest, saying it's so good to know that we're forgiven, and assures everyone that next week will be better. Everyone agrees to pray for each other, and then, with fist bumps and shoulder hugs, everyone leaves, feeling better about what happened in their past week but still a bit unsure they have what it takes to make it through the following week."

John nodded, and I continued. "I think we've got to be more transparent about the details of what really happened. For example, when someone says, 'I looked at some inappropriate websites,' we should ask tougher questions—like, 'Which ones? What genre of porn was it? How long did you look at it? Did you masturbate? Did you go back to the websites later and masturbate again? Did you have sex with your wife later while thinking about the porn you just looked at? Have you told your wife?' These details are where the shame resides, and shame demands secrecy. When we pull all these details out of the darkness and expose them to the light, their power over us just dissipates."

"You tell Priscilla details like this?" John was clearly curious about how far I was taking this line of thinking.

"Yes, although I've not had anything like that to tell her since coming clean. And you know what? She's ended up sharing some things with me from her past that she'd never told anyone. So God used my freedom to encourage her to be transparent as well. We've learned we're both broken in our human nature, and through our brokenness, we've seen God use us as instruments of healing with each other. That never happened in our previous twenty-eight years of marriage."

John agreed. "Yes, I do believe we have to be transparent with our wives. I've seen that in my marriage and know that transparency really brings a couple closer. But how are you doing with acting out sexually?"

"I've not looked at porn or masturbated since I came clean with Priscilla. In the past, I thought my porn addiction needed to be controlled by the fences, curbs, and bumpers—accountability groups and partners, phone apps, and counselors. Although these tools reduced the acting out, they were ineffective in helping me walk away from my sexual desires. I've seen that being honest, open, and transparent with

Priscilla about everything from my past and present removes the shame and secrecy that kept pulling me back to porn. Although I still regularly meet with my accountability partner, our conversations are now more spiritually wide ranging. While we still discuss potential sexual temptations and traps, I haven't needed to discuss sexual acting out since coming clean and battle-partnering with Priscilla. "

Although I'm not sure my conversation with John changed his thinking about men's accountability groups, it further grounded me in my conclusions. Priscilla had become the best accountability partner I'd ever had because she was my most intimate relationship and the person most directly impacted by my actions (in addition to me). She was there when I needed her; she loved me more than anyone else and had much more at stake in our relationship than any other accountability partner. When God said it wasn't good for Adam to be alone, he created Eve. If Adam needed Jack as his accountability partner, God did a huge disservice to Adam by giving him a wife. But that wasn't the case.

> There's no true freedom in the darkness
> of shame.

I'm not suggesting men's accountability groups are ineffective. The Bible says, "Iron sharpens iron" (Prov. 27:17), and I've experienced that truth. I'm merely suggesting that when another person takes the spouse's place in intimate accountability, they're out of bounds. Accountability groups and partners need to push men harder to disclose everything to their wives rather than being a relief valve that enables shame to remain hidden and unresolved. There's no true freedom in the darkness of shame. In that context, I believe the accountability groups and partners can be very beneficial.

PRISCILLA

Six months had passed since Phil came clean, and we attended a Couples Weekend Intensive with Whatever It Takes Ministries. At one point, Jenny Speed asked couples to face their spouses and say, "You're not my enemy." As Phil and I did that, there was a glimmer in our eyes as we embraced, feeling new emotions of togetherness, realizing that in six months, we had come a long way. Gone was the fear that we would have to live in this mess for five to ten years before God would heal us. Gone was our old life of hypocrisy, chasing a pretend Christianity while wallowing in depression and anxiety that was sucking the life out of us. Gone were the anger and bitterness that had dominated my life. And gone was the unforgiveness that had demanded revenge on Phil.

We were not enemies; we were battle partners. For the first time in our marriage, we were engaging in an epic quest for life together—a new season, a new chapter without secrets. The shame and wounds of our past were behind us, and it was time to rebuild, to create a new relationship.

Although being HOT had given us new power to break free from our past, it had not been the foremost key. Something even more beautiful had created the foundation for healing--the part of relationships that Christian couples long for but find elusive until something goes terribly wrong. It started within weeks of us coming clean. Without this key change, we wouldn't have been equipped to write this book, and we probably wouldn't still be married. And we're about to share this pivotal point with you.

| Savage Questions for Reflection |

1. Have you ever wondered if intruding thoughts are your own or the work of an unseen force? If so, describe what happened and how those affected you.

2. Do you struggle to overcome thoughts you wish you didn't have? What can you do to have more power over your thought life?

3. What's been your experience with accountability groups? What can be improved?

4. How open are you and your spouse in sharing the battles going on in your minds? Do you see yourselves as battle partners? What can you do to improve?

Chapter 9

SPIRITUAL FUEL

I want all of them to be one with each other, just as I am one with you and you are one with me. I also want them to be one with us. Then the people of this world will believe that you sent me.

—John 17:21 (CEV)

Spiritual intimacy is the fuel; emotional intimacy is the gauge; and physical intimacy is the expression of both.

—Phil and Priscilla Fretwell

PRISCILLA

"Hey, Priscilla. Are you ready to go?" Phil asked as I sat on the stairs, lacing my shoes for our morning walk.

"Sure, just a minute." Even before coming clean, we had started most mornings cycling, running, or walking around our neighborhood. We had always heard that emotional intimacy was the glue of marriage, and we'd thought our morning routine would give us a chance to discuss our day ahead, our kids, and our feelings. We'd even regularly had date nights, thinking they would make our marriage bulletproof. But our relationship had still felt mediocre. Not bad but not remarkable. Based on my interactions with other women, they experienced the same feelings, so I had thought this was just what most "good Christian wives" could expect.

When Phil had disclosed his double life and our marriage had crumbled, there had seemed to be nothing left. No matter how well intentioned we'd been to create emotional intimacy, our efforts hadn't provided the fuel we'd needed to save our marriage. Even though magazines and self-help books proclaimed that emotional and sexual intimacy were the keys to a good marriage, they were powerless in the face of real problems.

In the months that followed our repentance from infidelity, apathy, pride, and the like, God showed us what was missing: *spiritual intimacy* with Him and each other. We had been like many couples; we knew each other emotionally and sexually but not spiritually. If someone had asked me to describe my spiritual relationship with Phil, I would have described our religious activities—going to church, attending and teaching Bible studies, etc. I hadn't understood what *spiritual intimacy* meant or looked like as husband and wife. When I attended the 4 Days 2 Hope conference, a key verse came into focus for me:

> I want all of them to be one with each other, just as I am one with you and you are one with me. I also want them to be one with us. Then the people of this world will believe that you sent me. (John 17:21 CEV)

I saw for the first time that God wanted my horizontal relationship with Phil to be the same spiritual intimacy as my vertical relationship with Christ. I wasn't sure what this meant, but the Bible promised that spiritual intimacy with each other would be so amazing that it would cause others to believe in Jesus. In the forefront of my mind, *others* meant my children. I'd desperately wanted our children to know Jesus intimately, and I had been concerned that our mess of a marriage was going to turn them off. God's promise in John 17:21 gave me hope for a better outcome.

After Phil came clean, I'd see him sitting at the kitchen table, morning after morning, reading his Bible with his journal open. I hesitated to join him, remembering his previous preachy attitude and my apathy toward reading the Bible. Although I knew a lot about the Bible from being forced to read it as a child and as a student attending a Christian college, I had not included daily devotions in my adult life. I'd sometimes joined small-group Bible studies simply to meet other women, and I'd read just enough before each meeting to come across as prepared. But my heart hadn't been in it. Even when we'd had sporadic family devotions, it had been Phil's idea. He would typically announce to me, "Hey, we should have some family Bible time with the kids. It's been a while." We'd gather the kids with their Bibles, sit around the kitchen table, and read a passage. Phil, somewhat preachy, would add insightful teaching points and ask the kids questions to see if they had listened. Then he'd make sure we all saw how the Scripture applied to our lives, and he'd end the family devotion with a prayer. The only thing he hadn't done was collect an offering.

> Spiritual intimacy with each other would be so amazing that it would cause others to believe in Jesus.

I had followed Phil's lead out of a sense of duty, believing family devotions were part of the prescribed homeschool family mantra and important to raising well-rounded children. I'd had no real desire or delight for God's Word. I had merely been checking off the list of religious things I was supposed to do as a good Christian mother.

"Okay, I'm ready to go." I rose from the stairstep, looking forward to our time outdoors in the early-morning darkness.

As we began our walk, Phil started sharing, and again I felt the newness of his openness with me and having so much to say. The experience was almost like he'd been taken over by an alien. I'd think, *What's happened to my husband? Where's the real Phil?* Our walks consisted of him talking almost nonstop and me listening, trying to piece together what was going on inside him. He had so much to share—what God was showing him, bits and pieces of his past life that I hadn't known, and how we should continue to process our journey with our kids. He would keep talking, and I'd occasionally ask a question, agree, or simply affirm what he'd said.

As we'd make our way back home, Phil would ask, "Do you want to pray?" In the beginning, I had wanted to remain a silent spectator. I hadn't been so sure about this new Phil and had wanted to wait and see how my relationship with the new Phil would unfold.

"I'm okay," I'd typically respond. "I'll just pray silently and agree with you." This had been our routine for the first couple of weeks.

One morning, I'd gotten up extra early and sat beside Phil at the kitchen table. He had been following a daily Bible reading plan since the beginning of the year (four months before coming clean). As I approached and sat down, he said, "Good morning."

"Good morning," I replied.

"I'm reading in First Samuel. Want to join me?"

I found one of the kid's Bibles, opened it to 1 Samuel, and began to read. For the first time in my life, the Word of God came alive to me. It was remarkable to see His hand, His graciousness, and His plan for me in Old Testament passages. I had never before had that experience. Unlike my childhood and college days, I was not being forced and was under no obligation to read the Bible; I just wanted to be part of the changes I was witnessing in Phil's life since he had come clean and given himself fully to Christ three weeks prior. If the Word of God could change Phil—from a narcissistic, self-centered, prideful know-it-all into someone who shared his feelings and shortcomings and walked in humility before his family and friends—I wanted to experience that supernatural power.

That morning, reading our Bibles together, we shared what we saw in the passages. Not in a preachy way; we simply exposed what we were feeling and hearing from the Holy Spirit. God's Word illuminated our thoughts, and we shared everything He put His finger on.

After that, our early mornings together in God's Word sometimes stretched into hours of sharing and discussion, and the Word of God became a delight to me. Phil frequently said our morning sharing was his favorite time of day. We developed true spiritual intimacy with God and each other as we learned how we each saw God and shared what we were hearing from Him and how He was changing us and helping us process our grief. Every morning, we gained more healing of our souls, the most beautiful experiences I'd ever had in our marriage.

PHIL

During the first twenty-eight years of our marriage, I had known it was important for Priscilla and me to do spiritual things together. But I had mistakenly thought attending church, joining Bible studies, and having individual quiet times and occasional family devotions would somehow make our marriage radically different. Although these were important activities, they had become part of our religious checklist that created our attitudes of self-righteousness and spiritual pride.

When anyone else had shared their struggles, I'd told them they needed to do more religious stuff. Then I'd succinctly described all the "spiritual" stuff I was doing. Such conversations had stroked my ego, making me feel smug in my religiosity, but had done little to help the individual. I had been full of self-righteous pride and hypocrisy, as if I had my heart and life perfectly together. In reality, I had been a Pharisee, full of "dead men's bones" (Matt. 23:27). I had been a limited, fallible human being pursuing my spiritual superiority like I'd pursued my career: with human intellect, vim, and vigor. I had limited my spiritual experiences to what my human talents, abilities, and finesse could produce rather than what God's supernatural power could work in me.

The religious circles I had participated in had always encouraged men to be the spiritual leaders of their families. I had readily embraced this concept since my narcissistic tendencies had caused me to love being the leader and center of attention. I'd also rationalized that men were to take the lead in just about everything because the Bible described wives as the *weaker vessel* (1 Pet. 3:7 ESV). But after Priscilla joined me that first morning of Bible reading and sharing, something fundamental changed in my attitude toward her.

I had interpreted *weaker vessel* to mean spiritually weaker, but that morning with Priscilla, I realized her spiritual insights and words were breathing life into me. God led me to look more closely at 1 Peter 3:7, and I realized what I'd believed about women was not at all true.

> Likewise, husbands, live with your wives in an understanding way, showing honor to the woman as the weaker vessel, since they are heirs with you of the grace of life, so that your prayers may not be hindered. (ESV)

It became clear to me that *weaker vessel* meant physically weaker and that I should seek to deeply understand Priscilla and treat her like she was precious—with care, tenderness, and concern. God also wanted me to honor and respect Priscilla as my spiritual equal, a fellow heir of "the grace of life," honoring God and His intention for our marriage. I wasn't completely sure what the verse would look like in daily life, but I knew I needed the blessing of effective prayers!

God also showed me I had failed to understand how Priscilla thought and felt about her life with me and her relationship with God. I realized that 1 Peter 3:7 instructed me to be a *student* of Priscilla and seek to understand her true thoughts and feelings.

As we spent time together each morning, I saw that God's Word was the key to opening the "thoughts and intentions" (Heb. 4:12) of her heart, and I reveled in sharing with her at a much deeper level than we ever had in the past. I was learning how she thought and felt about our life together and her life with God. She saw my enthusiasm to know her deeply and opened up to me like never before.

As I affirmed Priscilla spiritually, I saw God doing amazing things through her. I became more open to hearing her opinions and believing God was speaking to me through her. I committed to God and Priscilla to refocus our relationship on spiritual intimacy, the fuel for marriage.

After twenty-eight years of being married, teaching numerous Bible studies, and holding church leadership positions, I had finally discovered the joy of spiritual intimacy with my wife. It felt marvelous! When I embraced Priscilla as a spiritual equal, she blossomed. I could see her spiritual boldness growing and God using her in unimaginable ways in our relationship. For example, God put His finger on something else in my life that had pulled me away from Him and my family: my Prized Possession.

Many people have a prized possession that consumes their thoughts and makes them appear significant, important, or admirable. Mine made me feel wonderful and looked something like this: When I'd meet someone, I'd subtly disclose sooner or later how precious my prized possession was to me. I'd even occasionally invite a friend to enjoy my prized possession with me, hoping they, too, would feel how special it was and maybe envy me.

Having breakfast with my friend Jay (whom I'd called from the plane before coming clean), I confessed, "I've been thinking about my prized possession, and I believe it's pulling me away from God and my family."

He immediately put down his fork and looked me in the eye. "Phil, I think you need to sell it and give all the money away. Turn your prized possession into a blessing for someone else." He was blunt but full of care and concern.

I glanced down and asked God to confirm whether Jay's instruction was indeed the right path. "I think you're right," I replied slowly, meeting his eyes again. "I'm going to sell it."

That evening I told Priscilla I planned to sell my prized possession and give all the money away. Without hesitation, she nodded her agreement. "I think that's a good idea."

I quickly placed an online ad. Over the next few weeks, I received a few inquiries but no sale.

One morning Priscilla asked, "How's the sale of your prized possession going?"

"I've received a couple of calls but no real bites. God knows I'm going to give the money away," I reasoned, "so when He's ready to sell it, I think He'll sell it." Priscilla looked down in thought, rolling her pen against her Bible.

"Phil, I don't think it takes any faith to wait until your prized possession sells to give the money away. I think you should give the money away first, right now—then it will sell. That takes faith." Priscilla's thoughts were sometimes very black and white, coming across like an Old Testament prophet. Prior to coming clean, I would have pushed back by saying I didn't know how much the prized possession would sell for, it could take months to sell, etc. However, I had learned that God sometimes spoke to me through Priscilla, so I'd better listen.

"Okay, I think you're right." I estimated the proceeds, split that figure in half, and immediately processed online checks to two nonprofit organizations. "There—it's done."

"Good," she said. In faith, we thanked God together for an impending sale.

The next day I sold my prized possession—to someone who had not even known I'd listed it for sale! It was a blessing to have sold my prized possession, but the bigger blessing was seeing God affirm how He had used Priscilla to speak to me through the precise timing and means.

PRISCILLA

For Phil to take my advice without arguing was a miracle. Although my suggestion to give away the money in faith before selling made no sense in the natural world, it made complete sense in the spiritual world. He had needed to plant that seed of faith to reap the results, and afterwards he seemed to have newfound spiritual respect, frequently telling me, "You have an anointing."

As we grew spiritually with God and each other, Phil and I felt deeply intertwined, as if our innermost beings were operating as one. All our past focus on emotional and sexual intimacy had never brought us this close, and we began to understand what God meant about two becoming one (Gen. 2:24; Mark 10:8). We also began to believe God would show us more amazing things that our natural, intellectual minds would struggle to believe.

On a Sunday morning after church, as we corralled the girls and headed to our car, I remarked, "Well, that was interesting."

Phil glanced at me as we walked. "What was interesting?"

"The woman who's coming to speak in a few weeks. They say she has a prophetic gift. What do you think about that?"

Phil arched his eyebrows and rolled his eyes. "I don't know what to think. I know the Bible talks about gifts of prophecy, but I've never heard someone described like that."

"Me either. This is exciting, don't you think?" Phil shrugged and murmured something about *prophetess* and *snake oil*. Typical Phil, trained as an auditor and thereby groomed to be skeptical, always looking for fraud and lies. I relied more on my intuition and feelings, and God had been showing me spiritual truths that sometimes contradicted natural human logic.

For the next few weeks, as I heard the repeated announcements about the upcoming guest speaker, I was filled with the expectation that something was going to happen . . . and I was going to be part of it. I didn't know what, but I was ready to receive whatever God had for me.

The Sunday finally arrived, and I woke that morning with a spirit of expectancy. Phil was out of town, so the girls and I went to church without him. I thought there might be a big crowd, so we arrived early.

I checked the girls into their programs and headed to the sanctuary, where I was greeted at the doors by ushers. To my surprise, the sanctuary was mostly empty. *Wow, I must really be early. Where is everybody?*

I picked a seat about midway down the center aisle and was about to sit when an usher walked up and motioned toward the stage. "Why don't you move closer to the front?" he asked.

I glanced at the stage. "Why does it matter where I sit?"

"Because you'll experience more of the anointing up there." He pointed to the front.

After what I've been through the past six months, if that's where the anointing will be, that's where I want to be! "Okay, I can't argue with that!" I moved to the sixth row and took the first seat beside the center aisle.

People filtered in and slowly filled the sanctuary as the usual welcome video played with its five-minute countdown. The worship team took the stage as I eagerly anticipated what was ahead.

Finally, the moment I'd been waiting for arrived.

Our pastor introduced the special speaker, who walked toward the front but not onto the stage. She stood on the floor, where everyone was seated, and asked for instrumental music. Then she headed back down the aisle, right past me. Her long black sweater over her pants and blouse flowed as she walked.

About halfway down the aisle, she turned around and passed me again, her soft, calm voice speaking encouraging words to the group, sharing thoughts about God and what He was doing.

Before reaching the stage, she turned back again, paced down the center aisle, and stopped right beside me. Turning to me, she rested her hand on my shoulder and met my eyes. She spoke directly to me through her microphone, allowing the entire congregation to hear.

She's talking to me!

Although I had anticipated something would happen, I was honestly shocked that she'd chosen to speak to me out of the almost-full sanctuary—and no one in my family was there to witness it! *Phil! You should be here to help me remember what she's saying!* Her words were soft and comforting.

I was looking directly at her to let her know I was receiving what she was saying.

She spoke for only a brief time, but one phrase stopped my heart. "You will fight valiantly like Deborah to see the goodness of God restored in your family's lives."

I was stunned because those were the exact words I had written six months prior in my identity statement at the 4 Days 2 Hope retreat! I had framed those very words and hung my statement on our kitchen wall, but I had never made the statement public. *How could she have possibly known the exact words I'd written referencing Deborah?*

Deborah's story is an obscure Bible passage, and God had privately impressed me to write that battle statement. Now, here was a woman I'd never met or talked with who'd just spoken the very words I'd written!

Oh, how my heavenly Father knows and loves me so intimately that He would again confirm His Word to me!

The speaker lifted her hand from my shoulder and continued walking back and forth, but my mind remained on what she'd said to me. Through the ministry of a stranger, in front of the whole church, God had encouraged me by putting an exclamation point on what He'd told me six months earlier—His battle plan for me. Indeed, I was a warrior—just like Deborah! And I was fighting valiantly for my family's restoration.

I had just experienced a supernatural encounter with God that blew me away. I couldn't wait to tell Phil.

PHIL

"Can you say that again?" I said to Priscilla, not sure I completely understood what she'd just shared with me.

"She told me what I'd written on my identity statement—you know, the part about fighting valiantly like Deborah!"

Priscilla had waited to share her experience with me until I'd returned from my business trip. She'd said over the phone that she wanted to see my expression when she shared what had happened five days earlier.

Her excitement convinced me she had indeed had an encounter with God, and her testimony made me reevaluate my previous doubts about the speaker. "Priscilla, that's amazing! I don't really know what to think. I've had God in a theological box my entire life, and now He's thrusting His arms right through the walls of the box and waving them in front of me."

Experiencing prophecy was new for us. I had always questioned such incidents, thinking some shyster was fooling a bunch of people into believing something that didn't make logical sense. I generally struggled when it came to believing things I couldn't understand intellectually. But as Priscilla and I continued developing our spiritual intimacy and seeing more God instances in our life, I let go of my natural human logic to have my spiritual eyes and ears opened. Another example was the dreams Priscilla used to have of my infidelity—I'd never considered that the Holy Spirit was possibly disclosing the truth to her. I had brushed her dreams aside, believing she was just living in fear and insecurity about our relationship that consequently disturbed her sleep. Once I came clean, her dreams stopped—until a particular business trip.

Two male colleagues and I had an important meeting scheduled with a female executive in another city. Upon our arrival, she greeted us warmly, not only with traditional air-kisses but also with tight, lingering embraces. As she hugged us, I knew her greeting was intended simply as a welcome. But my mind raced with other thoughts, provoked by her appealing look and close contact. She was wearing a fitted outfit, show-ing her trim, athletic build.

After our meeting, I took a late-afternoon flight to another destina-tion, preparing to return home the next morning. I arrived at my hotel around midnight, and my mind returned to the memories from earlier in the day, threatening to turn into fantasy.

I called Priscilla the next morning. Although it was six o'clock, I knew she would be up. We had established a pattern of rising early to pray and read our Bibles together. She picked up with a quick "Hi, Phil."

"Hi!" I tried to sound chipper. "How are you doing?"

"I'm doing pretty good," she said, the words slowly rolling off as though she had something else to say. "How are you doing?"

"I'm doing okay, but something happened yesterday that I want to share with you."

"That's good—because I had a dream about you last night."

"Oh, what was it about?"

"No, you go first," she said.

I paused, collecting my thoughts, thinking through the details I could provide so Priscilla's imagination wouldn't take off running before I could explain. Then I dove in. I told her not only about the woman's embrace but how her physical contact had made me feel, including the desires that had crept into my mind. "So that's what hap-pened," I concluded. "You know secrecy creates fertile ground in my imagination, but once I decided to call you this morning, the hold on my thoughts just let go."

"That's very interesting," she pondered. "My dream was about your experience. It had all the same elements: an attractive woman, you staring at her body, and her confirming you two were only friends and that her close contact with you meant nothing to her."

Priscilla then provided more details of her dream, eerily consistent with my experience.

"Priscilla, do you remember all those dreams you had about me before I came clean—that caused you to wake up agitated, wondering what was going on with me?"

"Yeah, I do."

"Aside from last night, have you had any more of those dreams?"

"Nothing significant; this is the first one."

"Okay. So you were having these dreams on and off for twenty-plus years, and after I came clean, they stopped, right?" Although I anticipated her answer, I wanted to make sure I wasn't overlooking something.

"Yes, that's right."

"And now, six months after I came clean, and at the same time something was happening with me, you had another dream?"

"Right," she said.

Is this really how spiritually connected we are as husband and wife? I briefly contemplated what such a connection meant and realized, *I can't do anything without Priscilla knowing about it!* I was incredulous. *We are really "one flesh," experiencing intimacy that's more than sexual and emotional. It's spiritual intimacy!*

Priscilla and I marveled at how God had revealed truth to her that she could not have known in the natural realm. The Holy Spirit had repeatedly shown her truth in dreams through the years, which now emphasized His power available inside us.

I reflected on the apostle Paul's prayer in Ephesians 1:19–20.

I want you to know about the great and mighty power that God has for us followers. It is the same wonderful power he used when he raised Christ from death and let him sit at his right side in heaven. (CEV)

In the past, I had thought the Holy Spirit worked primarily in my mind through my academic approach to discovering God's promises. However, I was seeing something greater and spiritually intimate. *Can it be that the power of the Holy Spirit can be sensed in more than just my mind?*

When I had received Jesus Christ into my life at twenty-one, I had known it was God's power that saved me. Like electricity turns on a light bulb, God's power had "turned on" my spirit and made me spiritually *alive*. Now I was considering that God's supernatural power did more than just make my spirit alive. *Can His power also affect my entire person—spirit, soul, and body?* Intellectually, I knew the answer, but experientially, I had understood God's power only as a somewhat distant helper to my natural intellectual strengths and emotional zeal. *Have I confused the power of God with my natural power?* I had taught the Bible for over thirty years, but I'd had very few experiences I would call *supernatural*—until now. Priscilla and I were encountering situations that had no earthly explanation, and I became convinced that the Holy Spirit wanted to be more than a distant helper. He wanted to lead my spirit and transform my soul and body.

> The Holy Spirit wanted to be more than a distant helper. He wanted to lead my spirit and transform my soul and body.

PRISCILLA

As the months went by, I felt God healing and restoring our broken marriage. Phil and I were enjoying each other in a new way, and I believed our deeper connection resulted from us engaging spiritually.

With the Holy Spirit as our guide, we had made it through a wall in our marriage and cherished our mornings together as we included God, discussed His Word, and enjoyed His presence. We began to see what He, the living Word (Heb. 4:12), was doing inside us.

In the past, our home Bible studies had meant a carefully crafted, scheduled time of Bible teaching (with Phil in charge), followed by prayer. Now our mornings together were completely unscripted, and I had just as much to say as Phil. The spiritual intimacy I enjoyed with God and Phil was a time of further healing and restoring our marriage. Although we still experienced our ups and downs, I was full of hope. Also, due to spiritual intimacy, Phil and I resolved normal day-to-day conflicts much faster than in the past. The whole experience of us each coming clean had allowed me to see my sin before a Holy God, which positioned my heart and mind to surrender everything to Him.

God had given me a new identity, rooted in and formed by who He said I was as His child, described in His Word. I saw more fully how He had designed me as an individual with a purpose. Like Eve, I was constructed out of bone and made strong spiritually, emotionally, and mentally by my Creator. My trust was now completely in Him.

About a year after coming clean, Phil and I began receiving opportunities to share our savage marriage story with others. Although we had shared our story many times with individuals, sharing in front of groups was an entirely different situation for me. I'd always feared speaking to groups and taking the lead in anything, including praying in a group setting. Being in front had always been Phil's job. He loved to be the center of attention. Not me.

I was in third grade when I got my first-ever speaking part. It was for the Christmas production at our church. Never before had I been in front of an audience. But I worked on my lines, practicing to say the few sentences without stumbling.

When the day of the Christmas performance arrived, I walked onto the stage with another little girl, and I looked at the congregation and completely froze. I couldn't remember a single word. The other girl said her lines, and it was my turn.

Silence.

She waited, then nudged me with her elbow, but I was looking at the audience like a deer in the headlights, terrified and unable to speak. She whispered to me, "Your turn."

"No," I whispered, "it's your turn. You go." She gave me a puzzled look, as if to say, *What are you talking about?* Still, I stood there, unable to remember the script. Thank God she had memorized my lines too and went on to recite the whole thing.

As I stood in terrified silence beside her, fear told me, *You're incapable and stupid!* With the entire audience staring at me, I felt so humiliated. That incident was the moment the enemy of my soul took my voice from me, and his taunts were all I heard: *Don't ever speak again in front of groups; you have nothing worthy to say. Stay silent.* I shook hands with that lie and agreed to never again speak in front of a group.

Even later, in high school and college, I did everything possible to get out of speaking to an audience. In the few unavoidable times, I felt like a complete failure and an embarrassment to myself.

About a year after Phil came clean was my first opportunity to share our story with a group. Paul and Jenny Speed, founders of Whatever It Takes Ministries, asked us to serve as coaches at a weekend marriage intensive. Only six months earlier, we had attended the same marriage intensive as participants, listening to table coaches give their testimonies. Asked to serve as a table coach, I felt completely inadequate. Phil and I had just come through our living hell and had walked through our valley of the shadow of death. But Paul and Jenny encouraged us, pointing to the work God had done in our marriage. They said we were credible messengers, and we agreed to serve.

At the retreat, as the time approached for us to share, Paul said to me, "You're on after the next breakout session." I was no longer ruled by fear because God had done so much in me, including giving me a new boldness. I had a story to share of His work in my life, and Christ, my King and Friend, would speak through me. I would not be silent; I would set a trumpet to my mouth and testify of His work, His goodness, and the restoration He had made in my life.

As Paul kicked off the session, Phil and I stood behind one of the banners at the front of the room, and I prayed, *Lord, help me. I can't do this without You. I need You. Speak through me. Thank You for Your peace and calmness and, most of all, Your presence.* I thought of the verse on the back of my T-shirt, Revelations 12:11. "They overcame him by the blood of the Lamb and because of the word of their testimony."

Phil and I walked to the podium and began to share.

I can't recall exactly what I said, but I remember telling my story and feeling God's hand of peace on me. As I spoke about what He had done in my heart and life, I felt His joy come over me, and I was ecstatic in His love.

Over and over in my life, speaking in front of groups had been a battle I'd lost. But not this time. I felt like a victorious warrior, like Deborah. God had returned to me what the enemy had long before stolen: my voice. Using my voice was an amazing, glorious experience, walking through a battle on the winning side with Jesus—God's side.

PHIL

Seeing Priscilla talk in front of groups was amazing. Even more amazing was how in tune she seemed to be with the Holy Spirit. God opened up more opportunities for us to share with people who were struggling in their marriages. He also gave us insight into their problems, which allowed us to speak to their hearts. We encountered some situations where God told us things we had no human way of knowing.

One day, my friend John shared with me that his marriage was in trouble and heading toward divorce. "John, what's the root problem?"

"I can't tell you." He shook his head, his eyes tinged with fear. "If it got out, it would be devastating to our family." My thoughts immediately went to my sin and its gripping fear. "It would really blow things up. I just can't say, but let me tell you—it's bad."

I tried to assure him with truth: "God can rescue your marriage out of the deepest pit, no matter what it is."

When I got home, I told Priscilla about the conversation and that

John was too fearful to disclose the real issue. "What do you think about that?" I asked. Priscilla was busy in the kitchen and said nothing. But I could see she was contemplating John's circumstance.

After a couple of minutes, she looked up and said what she believed John was thinking, and she went on to describe his fear.

"Wow," I replied. "Do you really think that's the issue? I would have never thought of that."

"Yes," she replied confidently. "That's it. I'm sure of it."

I called John the next day. After brief chitchat to learn how he was doing, I cautiously said, "John, you know how you said you couldn't disclose the real issue to me?"

"Yeah, that's right."

"Do you believe . . ." I repeated Priscilla's thoughts.

"Who told you that!" he exclaimed. "No one knows that!"

"Priscilla told me."

"Who's she been talking to?"

"Priscilla talks to God. She sometimes knows things from Him that she would otherwise not know. That may sound weird, but it's not the first time." I realized I had dropped a lot on John, but that was the truth.

"Well, she can't tell anyone!"

"Okay," I assured him.

As I shared with Priscilla what John had said, she didn't appear surprised; but I was astounded at what the Holy Spirit had shown her. Indeed, Priscilla was hearing truth from the Holy Spirit, which encouraged me to listen to what she had to say.

PRISCILLA

Today, whenever Phil and I describe what happened in our life, many listeners ask how they, too, can experience this type of grace. We wish we had a formula, but there isn't one.

We can't tell you how to become broken over your sin, but we can tell you how to position yourself to receive brokenness and grace from the Father: through humility. Humility will always point you toward being HOT (honest, open, and transparent), removing your mask, and allowing others to see you as God sees you: "open and laid bare" (Heb. 4:13). Humble and HOT is where God will help you experience spiritual intimacy with Him and your spouse.

In the years after coming clean, our spiritual intimacy deepened to entirely different levels of faith, trust, hope, insight, and awe. Our relationship felt more whole and complete than we had imagined possible. And God had more abundance in store for us . . .

| Savage Questions for Reflection |

1. How satisfied are you and your spouse with your spiritual intimacy, both with God and each other?

2. What obstacles are you encountering toward spending more time—together—with God? Consider practical obstacles such as time, spiritual obstacles such as pride, emotional obstacles such as past wounds, lies you've believed, and your family background.

3. What steps are you willing to take to create more spiritual intimacy in your marriage?

Chapter 10

EMBRACING OUR EMOTIONS

If the Son sets you free, you really will be free.

—John 8:36

Empathy and compassion are the gateways to emotional intimacy.

—Phil and Priscilla Fretwell

PHIL

"Daddy, how much longer till we get there?"

"About thirty minutes," our dad answered as we headed toward our grandmother's house in South Carolina. He had moved from our home in Florida to South Carolina a year earlier when he and Mom had separated, and he'd taken a new job as an elementary school principal. My sister, Cindy, and I had spent the summer with him and his new family, and our grandmother's house was a convenient rendezvous point from Florida for our mom.

Cindy was four and a half years younger than me and years later told me she didn't remember when Daddy lived with us. But I remembered and missed him terribly. Aside from the summer visit, our communication was limited to infrequent long-distance phone calls (as they were expensive) and to letters.

Our parents' divorce had become final only a few months prior, and on that drive from Florida to South Carolina, we learned of his quick remarriage, which had occurred just a few days after the divorce. My ten-year-old mind struggled to absorb all the changes in our family, but despite my dad leaving our family, I loved him and tried to adjust.

I'd grown up admiring my dad and loving the summers our family had spent camping in North Carolina. He'd taught me how to hike, build campfires, and roast hot dogs and marshmallows. While Mom preferred a hotel to camping, Dad loved being outdoors. I admired how smart he was and how he could instantly get people's attention with his commanding voice. I proudly told people he had even gone to seminary (though for a short time). Even with all his marital shortcomings, I wanted to be like him.

As we drove down the long dirt road, I caught sight of my mom standing on the back porch of our grandmother's two-story country home, waiting for us.

Dad parked in the large dirt area between the house and barn and helped us with our bags. Across the distance between the car and back porch, Dad and Mom exchanged a few awkward words while Cindy and I ran to hug her. Dad watched from beside the car. After a few minutes, Cindy and I returned to him to say goodbye. I lingered in his embrace, wanting to feel close to him and not wanting to say goodbye.

"I love you, son. Take care, and I'll try to see you soon."

"I love you too, Daddy." We reluctantly let go, and he turned to get in the car, shaking the dirt from his shoes.

He rolled down the window, and I walked over to him and put my face and arms on the edge of the car door. Our eyes met, and I wanted to cry but resisted, stuffing down my emotions. I didn't want my tears to make him think I was weak. I had seen my dad cry only once—when my grandpa had died.

He started the car, and I pulled back from the window and watched as he slowly drove away, making a wide circle and heading down the drive. Six weeks together had renewed our relationship and reminded me what it felt like to have my dad in the house. I stood there longing, watching him leave, and not wanting him to go. It was a painful departure. I didn't know when I'd see him next, but one thing was certain: I didn't want to feel pain like that again. Something inside me died at that moment.

Although I went through many similar departures in the years ahead, I never again felt the same sadness and longing. Somehow on that summer day as a boy, watching my dad leave, my emotions turned off, a means of coping with the pain.

Over the ensuing years, Priscilla encouraged me to press into my relationship with my father. So periodically, I asked him questions about his life and eventually learned he had never heard his father say "I love you." Nor had he ever felt his father's embrace. Reconciling this news with my memories of my grandfather, who'd died when I was eight, was difficult. I had good memories of him, such as riding in the bed of his truck to the orange groves, learning to drive the tractor, and looking through his cigar box full of rattlesnake rattles on the dashboard of his truck. But my dad's description of his relationship with his father was different. The pain I saw in my dad stirred my empathy and compassion for him. His parents had sent him away to a military school because he had been too hard to handle. He'd later joined the navy, and before he had met my mom, he'd had two brief failed marriages. In his eighties, he told me he had just lived with the women. I hadn't been sure until he told me. Back in the 1950s, it had been more acceptable to say they were married. In any event, his past life was murky and had undoubtedly affected his life choices.

I loved my father and wanted a relationship with him, but I knew I wouldn't pursue him if I felt any sort of unforgiveness. Discovering my father's story allowed me to embrace compassion, empathy, and finally forgiveness toward him.

As a kid, several months after my first summer with my dad, I'd found pornographic magazines in my neighbor's trash. The thrill of those pictures had jolted my emotions and made me feel alive. I hadn't been mature enough to see that my feelings were based on fake, imaginary women. I had loved those feelings, and they'd helped me cope with my pain, which had quickly created all the components to fuel a burgeoning addiction.

Decades later, God helped me understand what happened to that ten-year-old boy.

My dad had always been a cheerleader for me, and after his departure, I'd struggled to find significance. In fact, I couldn't remember any man taking a real fatherly interest in me after my dad moved to South Carolina. In my search for significance and the desire to feel alive, I had turned to two things: porn and achievement. Porn (heightened by masturbation) artificially and temporarily numbed my pain and satiated my natural God-given desire for feelings of emotional intimacy. Unknown to me at that age, porn was a substitute for emotional intimacy with real people. I wasn't so much addicted to the porn as to the feelings porn (combined with masturbation) gave me—feelings that I was significant, even if only to imaginary women on magazine pages. Porn and masturbation became an addiction I wasn't willing to give up, even after marrying Priscilla.

The other thrill I'd pursued was achievement. I had worked hard in college, secured my first job with a prominent accounting firm, and quickly become a partner. Porn and recognition by others made me feel alive and significant, and I had pursued them with vigor.

PRISCILLA

Ten years into our marriage, my discovery of Phil's porn use (not called an addiction back then) propelled me into a pool of anger, disbelief, and fear. Inner voices told me I wasn't good enough, sexy enough, or smart enough to keep my husband's attention. My insecurities and pain told me to smother my emotions, put them away, and never go back to look at them. I tried to forget Phil's porn use, but my anger was always close to the surface. Fear that Phil would fall back into porn was my constant companion.

Hoping my pain, fear, and disbelief would go away, I made a silent agreement with the enemy to keep things quiet and never ask Phil questions. To keep that pact, I focused on what had happened to me after Phil's betrayal rather than what had happened to him. When he shared his childhood experience with me, I should have asked him questions like, "What happened to you? How did this start? When did you first look at porn? What were you feeling? What was the pain in your life that porn medicated? Did you have anyone to talk with about your problems as a kid?"

I couldn't ask Phil questions because I lived in fear of his answers that might prompt him to ask me about my childhood. After all, I lived with secrets and shame of my own.

After Phil came clean, twenty-eight years into our marriage, God softened my hard, self-centered heart. I then saw Phil differently and asked those hard questions to bring everything into the light. God used my questions to help us discover together what had happened to Phil in his childhood, rooting him in sin and despair. We moved from the fruit of *what* he had done to the root of *why* he had entered into those sabotaging behaviors. God made very clear to me that I had to ask Phil the hard *why* questions to unearth his rooted, innermost feelings and the hooks that caused him to continue to embrace porn as a way to make himself feel good emotionally. We examined his past with new spiritual lenses to see how his childhood experiences had contributed to the brokenness in our marriage.

When Phil shared his feelings about being dropped off at his grandmother's house, the Holy Spirit enabled me to empathize with his pain of abandonment and rejection. I felt compassion for him, understanding why he had struggled to be vulnerable in our family relationships.

To protect himself, Phil had subconsciously decided emotional intimacy with real people would be only at a distance. In the fantasy world of porn, he'd felt safe and intimate with imaginary women who always chose him and made him feel significant. He had traded the opportunity to experience intimacy with a real person for the emotional safety of imaginary playmates who promised everything but delivered only emptiness. I was saddened that this blockade had formed in Phil's young heart, when what he had wanted and needed was to feel real, true, and lasting emotional connection with his family.

As I showed empathy and compassion to Phil, he felt encouraged and safe to become vulnerable and unpack his past. His vulnerability then encouraged me to unpack my past, and he showed me empathy and compassion for the pain I still carried.

Throughout our journey of reconciliation, empathy and compassion were the keys to showing God's grace to each other and experiencing healing. Pain in both our lives needed a special touch from Jesus to heal our broken hearts. During this time of painful exploration, God enabled us to join in each other's pain, bringing healing to our souls.

> Throughout our journey of reconciliation, empathy and compassion were the keys to showing God's grace to each other and experiencing healing.

PHIL

"Hey, Priscilla, we need to get going. Our flight is leaving in about ninety minutes." We were getting ready to go to Guatemala with several other couples from our church for a mission trip. I was excited about getting to know people from our new church, and the trip represented a return to normalcy. We had shared our story with our pastor, who was traveling with us. His invitation to us meant he wasn't ashamed of our story. His care made us feel accepted, and we really appreciated the chance to connect with others on the trip.

"Yes, let's go. I'm ready," Priscilla said as she wheeled her luggage to the car.

Our first mission task was to build two simple houses for needy families. Our group split in half, and Priscilla and I went to the city outskirts beside a garbage dump to meet a very poor family living in a lean-to with curtains for walls and no plumbing or running water.

As we got out of the van, we saw Rosa, the mom, heading toward us, nursing her newborn. Rosa was weathered and looked beyond middle age. We recognized her from the photograph we'd received before the trip. She, her husband, and their five children were all wearing the same clothes they'd worn in the photo. The clothes now looked dirty and the family disheveled. Rosa's hair was in a tousled bun like she had slept with it tied up. Many of her teeth were missing, making her swollen gums stick out. I'm embarrassed to admit I didn't want to get close to her. I had been on other mission trips but had never been so up close and personal to such poverty. I was ashamed of my thoughts but couldn't shake the way I felt.

By the second day, our team had completed two simple one-room houses—one for Rosa's family by the dump and the other closer to the city.

Isabella, a Guatemalan woman in charge of the local home-building ministry, suggested we have home-dedication ceremonies. She met us at the city house first. She looked like a business professional, dressed in dark slacks and a nice blouse. Her hair and makeup reflected a conservative style, and she seemed "all business." I rationalized our mission trip was just a job to her. Getting all these people to travel from the United States for mission labor was probably a lot of work.

We prayed with the family moving into the city house and then left for Rosa's newly constructed home.

After we arrived at Rosa's, Isabella led us up the path to the new house. To my surprise, she exchanged pleasantries with Rosa, as though she knew her. They talked privately for several minutes as our group gathered to pray for Rosa's family and dedicate their new home.

Isabella then addressed us in English. "Rosa asked us to pray for her oldest son. He left home several months ago, and she's very sad. She has no idea where he is. She doesn't know if he's dead or in jail or simply disappeared. Will you join me in praying with her?" We all nodded, and Isabella opened the prayer.

Although she prayed in Spanish, I could tell by her tone and voice breaking with emotion that her prayer was not perfunctory. She embraced Rosa and then held Rosa's face and kissed her cheeks, wet with tears. As Rosa clung to her, Isabella's tears flowed too. I could see her vulnerability and true care and that her prayer had touched Rosa's heart. Their emotional exchange created an intimate, compassionate moment of shared vulnerability that changed my assumption about Isabella.

After we all finished praying, I couldn't forget Isabella's authentic empathy and compassion. I had judged her harshly only a few hours earlier, thinking she was simply doing her job without feeling any real care or concern. I saw how wrong I had been and remembered that as Jesus performed miracles and shared life with people, He had shown empathy and compassion for those who were hurting. Jesus had understood how important it was for individuals and families to receive both physical and emotional healing.

I'm sure Rosa appreciated her new house, but I also believe she appreciated Isabella's hug, kiss, and tenderness. God speaking through Isabella's prayer had unlocked Rosa's emotional healing and let Rosa know she was loved. Rosa had felt Isabella's empathy and compassion. Neither woman had been afraid to lose their dignity in front of the group. They had openly embraced their tears and experienced emotional intimacy that could come only from the Holy Spirit. The empathy and compassion Isabella had shared had created the path to emotional intimacy with Rosa. It had been beautiful.

After returning home to Orlando, I continued to think about the intimate spiritual experience at Rosa's home. The words Isabella had expressed to her had contained power that had been obvious to our group despite the language barrier. Her words hadn't been any old words but had been spiritual words breathed by God. I wanted God-breathed words that would truly convey to others my empathy and care for them because I had never been very good at vocalizing my feelings. In business, I had always been unflappable in the face of adversity, easily managing my feelings and containing my emotions since the day I turned them off as a child. As an adult, my words had been carefully cultivated over a business career to be direct, clear, and unemotional. I needed a new vocabulary of beautiful words from the Holy Spirit to help me express what was in my heart—the heart of God. I asked God to give me loving words that would reflect His thoughts for the people around me.

One day, God impressed me to write words of life to my mother. She had sacrificed quite a lot for my sister and me after our father left. She'd remained single for twelve years and struggled to raise two children by herself. I knew the Bible said to honor your mother and father, so I asked God for beautiful words to express my feelings to her. I had often marveled at how King David could write such glorious psalms as if hearing directly from God, word for word. I asked God to give me divine words that would touch my mom's heart. Almost immediately, I started hearing and writing words that felt special, like the Holy Spirit was helping me express something I couldn't put together in my natural, logical mind. I wrote:

A Psalm for My Mother

A mother knows both blessings and sorrow. Her life is freely given to her children.

She is used by God to provide His precious and magnificent promises, to mourn with them when they mourn, to cry with them when they cry, and to love them when they are unlovable.

Mothers display God's grace, and God has given them a place of honor in the hearts of their children.

Through all things, God enables them to endure pain, hardship, and suffering; and there is nothing that can ever remove mothers from their special place of honor.

For it is through their mother that God first began teaching each child about His protection and provision. A child learns to look at God the way he looks at his nursing mother—with love, satisfaction, and peace—and he rests in full contentment in his mother's arms the way our Heavenly Father wants us to rest in His.

Mom, you have provided all this in my life, and today I honor you as my mother. You have been used by God in my life, and I am forever grateful.

I mailed the psalm to my mother, and she was so appreciative, remarking over and over how special it was to her. I could tell my words touched her heart. She sent copies to her friends and family and seemed to relish in God's special words of praise.

Most of my words to Priscilla throughout our previous years of marriage had not been special, God-given words but had principally been words about family logistics, such as who needed to be where and what needed to be done. I had neglected to share beautiful words from God that would let Priscilla know I cherished her.

One morning I was thinking about 1 Corinthians 11:10. "The woman should have a symbol of authority on her head, because of the angels." This passage about head coverings for women had always seemed antiquated to me, but I knew there was purpose behind all Scripture, relevant for people today. Looking at the Greek word for *authority*, I saw that it was translated most often in the Bible as *power*. So I began telling Priscilla she had power on her head. Affirming Priscilla with God's truth had a tremendous impact on her. Many times, after she said or did something profound, I would place my hand on her head and exclaim, "You have power on your head!" She began receiving this truth and then believed she did indeed have power on her head. The influence of God's Word through me further built her up spiritually and connected us emotionally.

PRISCILLA

I had never experienced so many spiritual things happening simultaneously in our life. We were experiencing God's presence in our marriage, in our family, and in the church body where God had placed us. Our time together in the mornings was real, with God revealing His Word and showing us His heart. We were having an adventure with our heavenly Father each day, and I began to see myself the way He sees me. Every day was a supernatural experience, and His love toward me was overwhelming. I felt like I had been dropped into a sea of His love. I was His special daughter, highly favored, standing before Him in His confidence and righteousness. I was not the lowly worm I had seen before, not good enough, smart enough, or desirable enough. I was the daughter of the Eternal King, no longer a prisoner of my shame and secrets. I was totally freed and anointed by Him.

God was using Phil to plant words of life in me, which had not been the norm for us over the past twenty-eight years. His words were refreshing and real and still ring true today. I believe *I have power on my head* because the power is from my heavenly Abba, who gives so freely.

My emotional relationship with Phil grew from a molecule of almost nothingness, blossoming into a beautiful vibrant flower after he came clean. This didn't happen overnight or even within weeks. It happened over months of dedicated time through sweat and tears. It was a painstaking effort to get to know one another like never before, in the emotional sense. When dating, you think you know the person emotionally, but you see just the first layer of emotions. Everything seems great, nothing can go wrong, and you conclude this person makes you feel good. Nothing could be further from the savage reality of what lies ahead in the context of lifelong marriage. To dig in, lean into, and pull out all that encompasses a person and their emotions are not easy in one's natural strength. But in Christ, His grace, compassion, and empathy can take you on a marvelous journey. It was clear that this new emotional intimacy was a result of the spiritual fuel we were now drinking. It felt wonderful.

As the Lord became more real to me, I discovered God wanted to revive both our spiritual lives and how we experienced our lives emotionally. He wanted us to look at our past and present events and circumstances through new spiritual lenses to see how the enemy had stolen from us and deceived us. As the Bible says in Ephesians 6:12, "We are not fighting against humans. We are fighting against forces, authorities, and rulers of darkness and powers in the spiritual world" (CEV). We had always thought we were on a journey where the rules, boundaries, and outcomes were determined by what we perceived through our natural senses. But what we discovered was that our journey was influenced by spiritual forces that were beyond what we had previously contemplated. We needed spiritual eyes and ears more than our natural eyes and ears.

A particular place where my emotions could be assaulted was our neighborhood gym. Even though we were connecting better than we ever had, the gym was equipped with women wearing revealing exercise outfits that got my mind going. *Is Phil looking at them?* Their presence played on my insecurities and fears. There seemed to always be some-one I felt was a threat.

I began to give the women nicknames so I could discuss them with Phil. The long-legged lady, plastic-face lady, thong girl, tattoo girl, and so on. Initially, their presence hit me hard. While I could see all that God was doing, I felt defeated as soon as Phil and I walked into the gym. I was letting my emotions highjack me and take over.

One time, I got so mad at Phil that I left the gym fuming and sat in the car to wait for him. He stayed and finished his workout, which made me even madder because I began to think he really didn't care about me. There I sat, waiting on Phil, who I thought was probably ogling thong girl. *Ugh!* All this happening in my mind and emotions was unbe-knownst to Phil.

After he finished his workout and got to the car, he asked, "Why did you leave?"

"You don't know? Did you see that woman? Hello!"

All my emotional junk wasn't serving me or our relationship so well.

In such circumstances, Phil would apologize, emote with me, and then ask questions to understand my thoughts and feelings. We dis-cussed these situations openly, concluding they were spiritual battles. Yes, the women were real people, not ghosts, but the thoughts planted in my mind seemed almost intentionally designed to send me into a spiral of emotions. By listening to me, Phil learned how these situations were affecting my emotions, and he brought up potential problems, both for himself and me—even those I hadn't noticed. As he became consistently HOT with me about what he saw and thought, I became less sensitive about the other women.

One morning, I couldn't go to the gym but had gained enough confidence to encourage Phil to go by himself. When he returned, I asked, "How did the workout go?"

"Fine, but a woman running next to me on the treadmill pulled up her shirt and tucked it into the top of her bra. With the mirror right in front of us, it was hard to ignore her. I wanted to tell you so I'm not holding this in secret."

"Okay, thanks, and I'm glad you told me right away." With Phil's transparency, I gradually gained confidence that he was disclosing his feelings, and I gained power over my intruding thoughts that could ransack our relationship.

Over time, such situations no longer plagued my mind because I learned to ask the Holy Spirit questions whenever I felt my emotions rising. *What's really happening here? What am I feeling? What am I thinking? What am I hearing?* Our spiritual life together became real because Phil and I became battle partners. Rather than fighting against each other, we joined together to war against spiritual forces who wanted to destroy the work God had done in our marriage. I began to see Phil was there for me as much as I was there for him. Together, we followed the admonition in 1 Peter 5:8. "Stay alert! Watch out for your great enemy, the devil. He prowls around like a roaring lion, looking for someone to devour" (NLT).

Being HOT in each new circumstance allowed me to see victory over these schemes of the devil.

PHIL

One morning, I joined my brother-in-law, Bob, for a men's breakfast at his church. The speaker talked about discontentment, and the Holy Spirit spoke to me, pointing out I was not content in my relationship with my father. Although I had forgiven him, anytime someone brought up father-son relationships, it pressed on an old wound from my childhood, like it had never fully healed. As the speaker concluded, he encouraged us to take steps to deal with any areas of discontentment that had come to our minds. He then directed us to begin our table discussions.

After a few guys shared what they had learned, I motioned to speak. "Guys, I feel like God told me I'm not content with my spiritual relationship with my dad. I don't remember him ever praying for me or blessing me. I need to talk with him." The men nodded and agreed.

Bob asked me, "When do you think you can go see him?"

"Right now," I replied. "I'm going to his house as soon as we're finished." My dad lived about an hour from Orlando.

After breakfast, I quickly left and drove to his house, unannounced. He'd likely be home unless he had a doctor's appointment. He'd be surprised to see me since I'd always arranged visits in advance.

My father's health was poor. He was eighty-five years old and struggled to walk as a result of poor circulation in his legs. He used a walker and spent most of his days in his recliner, watching television.

I knocked on his door, and Nadine, my stepmother, answered. She was surprised. "Well, good morning, Phillip! I didn't know you were coming over today."

"Hi, Nadine. I decided to surprise you. How are you doing?"

"Fine. Come on in. Your dad's here, but I have to go to the store in a few minutes."

I walked in and saw my dad in his familiar chair. "Good morning, Dad! I was hoping to catch you at home."

"Hi, son! It's good to see you! Come on in and sit down. Let me turn this thing off." He fumbled for the TV remote as I bent down to hug him.

We caught up on the kids and his doctor appointments while Nadine left to run her errands.

Father, help me know what to say to my dad. Give me words of life for him.

"Dad, I was at a men's breakfast with Bob this morning, and something hit me that I want to talk with you about."

"Oh? What was it?"

"Well, the speaker encouraged us to think about relationships and identify anything we wish we had experienced. It made me think of our relationship. I don't remember ever hearing you pray for me or bless me."

My dad's eyebrows arched in surprise. It was always hard to discuss more than superficial topics, such as my kids' activities and his health, with him. But he quickly said, "Oh, son, I've prayed for you many times, and you've always had my blessing."

Although his tone was convincing, I needed clarification and pressed in. "I know, Dad, but I've never *heard* you praying for me, and I was hoping you would pray for me today and bless me. Will you do that?"

His eyes searched mine. After a few seconds, he nodded and said, "Why sure, son. I can do that."

I kneeled beside his recliner. I placed my hands on his leg and my head on my hands. My dad responded by resting his hand on my head and started praying for me. "Lord, I pray You will bless Phillip . . ." As his first words flowed over me, I started weeping. The emotions bubbled up from deep inside. "That You will bless him, bless him, bless him . . ."

The longer he prayed, the louder I wept, and the stronger his voice grew. He was no longer a frail old man with uncertain spiritual power but a spiritual man controlled by God's Spirit. His words breathed life into my soul, and I let go of all my dignity. There, kneeling by my dad's recliner, I felt a spiritual closeness to him that I'd never before experienced, created by the spiritual words he was speaking over me.

When he finished praying, I slowly stood and leaned over to give him a long hug. He hugged me hard, also realizing we had shared an intimate moment. I sat back down on the sofa and wiped away my tears. "I love you, Dad. Thanks for praying for me and blessing me."

"You're welcome, son. I love you and have always been so proud of you."

On the drive home, I was overcome again with feelings and emotions from time spent with my dad. There I was, in my fifties, having a spiritual encounter with my dad that I had longed for my entire life. I was so thankful.

Such a moment would have never been possible if God hadn't been healing the wounds of my soul in the months prior. There had been a cost for my numbed emotions, and God had enabled me to move to a deeper place. I was so happy. My emotions had needed to be freed for me to experience the richness of life with those I loved, and I was now witnessing God's fullness more completely—and for the first time with my dad.

People frequently say they grew up in a dysfunctional family and then go on to describe their parents' failures, abuse they suffered, and how they wish it had been different. The term *dysfunctional* should be dropped because *all* families are fraught with human frailties and are flawed in one way or another. While we may drag along emotional baggage from our family relationships, the real problem in marriage is that we each shut the door to our scarred past and refuse to open it to the light of God's introspection. Allowing God to open the difficult chambers of our lives can lead to emotional healing in our marital relationships because we all view our present circumstances through the lens of our pasts. For over fifty years, Priscilla and I let our pasts be in the past, and only recently did we discover that God's plan for our healing required us to be open, honest, and transparent about what had happened to us in our pasts and how those experiences were still affecting us in the present. Through that difficult self-reflection, God revealed some triggers and tendencies that were connected to our present-day struggles.

> The real problem in marriage is that we each shut the door to our scarred past and refuse to open it to the light of God's introspection.

PRISCILLA

Three months subsequent to Phil coming clean, we were living in our little cocoon in Orlando, our safe place, and Phil was not traveling for work. We were together, working on us and doing really well. Our relationship was healing, and life felt good.

Eight months prior, Phil had planned a wonderful summer vacation for our family. Spain promised to be an awesome three weeks of enjoying food, hospitality, and the sites. But upon our arrival in Barcelona, the wonderful anticipation soon turned into a nightmare for me. People milling about were dressed for the heat and showing so much skin that I thought the beach must be right around the corner. Everywhere we went seemed to reveal dresses lifting by the wind, balconies giving views up women's skirts, and women in short shorts bending over to fix their shoes—right in front of Phil. It was crazy. My mind felt like it was blown into tiny pieces. *How can this be happening, and only a couple of days into our vacation?* Instead of watching out for how the enemy was trying to steal my peace, I got so caught up in the emotions that I couldn't think spiritually.

Constantly in fear that Phil's lust was being stoked by these women who had become my imaginary adversaries, I had a meltdown. We were walking back to our apartment after a tour of Barcelona, and I was fuming about everything I had seen. Once inside, I began to sob. "I'm not ready for this! I can't do it. I want out—right now! Let's go home! I want to go where I feel safe. I want to be at home. Everywhere we go, I see scantily clad women, and wonder whether this is what the next several weeks are going to be like. I don't want to be here anymore; I want to go home!"

Phil was extremely kind and patient with me. "Priscilla, I'm so sorry you're feeling this way. It's my fault. When I booked this summer vacation eight months ago, I knew there was a possibility women would be dressed for the hot weather. If you want to go home, I'll check flights, and maybe we can go home tomorrow." We sat for a few moments in silence while Phil reviewed our travel itinerary and flight arrangements.

We had only one more day in Barcelona, and Phil said the next city should be cooler and maybe the women would be dressed differently. The first few days in Barcelona had been hard, but after my meltdown, God showed me how my thinking and emotions were being played by the enemy, who was clobbering my thoughts and pulling my chain all over the place. I hadn't stood against him or resisted him. I had done nothing but cry.

I decided I needed to stand in Christ and resist the enemy.

In the next city, there were some moments when I had to stand and resist, but my emotions were not as fragile. We continued to travel throughout Spain, and our emotional connection grew stronger. Phil frequently asked how I was feeling about the places we were visiting. I began to believe he was willing to be my battle partner and wanted to stand with me, side by side, to face whatever came *our* way. We were true battle partners, which drew me closer to Phil.

As our travels through Spain continued and I saw his genuine kindness and care for me, I felt a dramatic shift in our emotional relationship, and I was more receptive to him. I mattered to him—and not just sexually. There were tender moments as we lay in bed talking at the end of the day. They were baby steps toward a closer emotional connection. At first, it was just a squeeze of his hand to say good night, then a kiss good night, and then an embrace with a kiss good night. Little by little, each step drew me closer to letting him hold my heart again, to being vulnerable and not holding back. These moments were precious, and I knew I would always hold them dear in my heart.

As our trip drew to a close, we headed back to Barcelona for our return flight. I wasn't looking forward to revisiting where all the chaos had initially begun. But we had to spend only one night there for our 6:30 a.m. flight.

We went to sleep early, and I woke up at 2:00 a.m., somewhat startled. *Is it time to leave?* I heard Phil tossing and realized he was also awake. *Okay, it must be early. I can relax. I don't have to get up yet.* The room was quiet, and a streetlight shone dimly through the curtains. I felt Phil's foot nudge me, and a moment later, his foot was caressing my calf. *What do I do with this? Do I say no, stop? Or do I allow my feelings and vulnerability to embrace the moment?*

Let me be honest; it had been almost a hundred days since Phil and I had been sexually intimate and that long since I had physically wanted him. We were finally in a place of spiritual and emotional intimacy that would create a much different expression of sexual intimacy. Now physical feelings were stirring in me for my husband, especially the new and improved Phil. I shifted over to him, our bodies expressing the intimacy reflected in our spiritual and emotional bonding. Still, I was hesitant. Where the morning would lead, I could have never predicted . . .

| Savage Questions for Reflection |

1. How satisfied are you and your spouse with your emotional intimacy?

2. How well do you and your spouse express empathy and compassion for each other? What could be improved?

3. How can you use your words to increase emotional intimacy with your spouse?

4. What can you do to become a battle partner for your spouse? How can you encourage your spouse to become a battle partner for you?

Chapter 11

DISCOVERING TRUE SEXUAL INTIMACY

"I have come into my garden, my sister, *my* bride; I have gathered my myrrh along with my balsam. I have eaten my honeycomb with my honey; I have drunk my wine with my milk. Eat, friends; Drink and drink deeply, lovers."

—Song of Solomon 5:1

Sex is about the spiritual—a union of the soul. When you discover *that*, you'll discover great sex!

—Howard Hendricks,
from *Vertical Marriage* by Dave and Ann Wilson

PHIL

Priscilla shifted closer to me, responding to the gentle caress of my foot on her calf. I was somewhat startled. For almost a hundred days, she had established a clear boundary of no sexual touching. *What's happening?* I had accepted that our sex life could be on hold for a long time, maybe even years, so I wasn't sure where this was going.

Our time of abstinence had changed my understanding of the purpose of sex in marriage. Previously, sex had made me feel emotionally connected to Priscilla. If we didn't have sex for several days, I would wonder what was going on. *Why is Priscilla mad at me? What have I done wrong?* As a result, I'd always thought sex was the necessary and only means for me to feel connected to Priscilla emotionally.

Eliminating sex for a hundred days had helped me draw close to Priscilla spiritually and emotionally. Although it was hard for me to believe, I now felt spiritually and emotionally intimate with her, and sex was not even part of the equation. Prior, I'd thought sex was a need because I couldn't control my behaviors without it. While I desired Priscilla, I no longer believed sex was the driver of closeness in marriage. I also no longer believed I had to have sex to live since, for the past hundred days of abstinence, I hadn't died! Actually, I cherished my sexless time with Priscilla, learning how to become intimate with her spiritually and then emotionally. While I certainly wanted to be with her sexually, I was content to wait until the right time, and I didn't even know when that would be. Maybe it would be five years. I just wasn't sure. However, I was sure of God and trusting He would present the right time. I was willing to wait.

Lying in bed with Priscilla during that early morning in Barcelona, feelings of electricity shot through me. Every inch I moved toward her was tentative. With her encouragement, I allowed my feelings of desire to go beyond the boundaries she had set after I'd come clean. Slowly, our early morning turned into an amazing rebirthing, as if we were experiencing sexual feelings for the first time the way God intended. Rather than relying on sex to create feelings of emotional closeness, sex became an expression of our spiritual and emotional intimacy created over the past hundred days.

To that point of healing and restoring our relationship, I had believed sex was the glue of marriage that leads to emotional connectedness. In truth, the role of emotions in marriage is like a gauge that shows us how we feel about each other and shouts an alarm when our marriage gets out of sync. Through the past months, God had shown me that sex without spiritual and emotional intimacy is merely a natural, animalistic lust that will never create the true relational satisfaction we long for in marriage.

As Priscilla and I spent time together discovering and sharing God's Word and the intentions of our hearts, I began to see that the real glue—the true fuel of holy matrimony—was spiritual intimacy that leads to emotional intimacy. Physical intimacy then becomes an expression of what we're already practicing spiritually and emotionally. In other words, sexual intimacy is not a driver but rather a resulting physical expression of what is already being experienced in our souls.

> Sex without spiritual and emotional intimacy is merely a natural, animalistic lust that will never create the true relational satisfaction we long for in marriage.

I knew Priscilla had viewed sex for the first twenty-eight years of our marriage as the duty of a good Christian wife. After I'd come clean, she'd told me she had never really enjoyed being with me sexually. While that had been hard to hear, the truth should not have surprised me; I had been such a taker during those years. God was showing me that I needed to express my love to Priscilla the same way He demonstrated His love for us—by giving: "God so loved the world, that He gave His only Son" (John 3:16). God showed His love by *giving*, not taking. That's what I needed to do with Priscilla—become the giver in our sexual relationship.

As Priscilla looked at me, lying very close to her, she whispered, letting me know she was ready to be vulnerable.

"Priscilla, this morning is only for you. I no longer want to be the taker. I want to be a giver by putting you first."

PRISCILLA

Phil's words shocked me. *Really? Are you serious? After almost a hundred days, you aren't asking me for anything?*

Looking into his eyes, I sensed sincerity and truthfulness. He wasn't pouting like he was begrudgingly denying himself. Our past lovemaking had generally been transactional versus relational, with Phil doing nice things for me outside the bedroom so I would do sexual things for him. I was relieved and surprised to hear him forego gratification—a remarkable change to see in Phil, which helped me believe I would continue to see demonstrated change in my husband's thoughts and habits. Phil denying himself was a gift from God.

We lay close, eye to eye, nose to nose, lips near lips. Phil's hands moved up along my back to my head, and his fingertips brushed back my hair. Our lips touched. He pulled back and looked into my eyes and said, "I want God to help us remember this moment." I was captivated hearing him use gracious words to express his feelings, and those tender thoughts allowed me to open the physical boundaries I had set for him.

My husband's touch was tender and slow, and what had started inside me as a trickle gradually turned into a river that suddenly burst over the dam I had constructed three months earlier. I had never considered Phil would put me first sexually. Experiencing this convinced me that God had healed his mind. Phil was being transformed into a giver.

Although it might appear as though our early-morning rendezvous was out of the blue, it was really a harvest that had been cultivated during three months of abstinence, culminating with our recent three-week vacation.

The initial distractions of scantily clad women had triggered my insecurities of not being good enough, not being worthy of love, and not meeting Phil's expectations. From the moment we'd arrived in Barcelona, internal lies and insecurities had hammered me. But each time I had shown my frustration and anxiety to Phil, we'd faced them together. Phil had become my partner in combating the triggers. He had become more attentive and caring about what was happening in and around me. He had watched to see whether I was being affected by my surroundings and had ensured I was okay. He had always been willing to put the vacation agenda aside to talk with me in my moments of battle and work them out together. Phil had shown that he wanted to be my battle partner, and his patience and concern had made me feel safe.

As we had worked through each trigger, they'd had less and less of a hold on me. By the end of our three-week stay, I had seen how much Phil genuinely wanted to connect with me emotionally. So while our last night in Barcelona brought the surprise of physical intimacy, that connection was the result of three months of spiritual and emotional intimacy that allowed me to become sexually vulnerable again.

Several weeks before the trip to Spain, I had received a call from Sarah, our oldest daughter. After we'd caught up, Sarah had suddenly said, "Mama, can I ask you a question?"

"Sure, what is it?"

"Have you and Daddy been intimate with each other yet?"

I paused. "No, we haven't."

"Why not?"

As I thought about her question, my emotions bubbled to the top, choking off my words. Sarah was always able to get to the heart of an issue, but it was hard for me to say out loud the deepest thoughts in my heart. "I just can't let myself be vulnerable again. It's so hard to go there."

"Mama, you know Jesus was the most vulnerable person who ever lived."

"Yes, He sure was," I replied.

"Mama, I would like to pray for you and Daddy."

"Okay, sure." So right there, my daughter began to pray for her mama and daddy to be sexually intimate again and for God to work vulnerability into her mama's heart. I was sobbing by the end of her prayer. After she said amen, I said through nose blowing and with tears running down my face, "Sarah, I receive it."

I had gone directly to Phil and said, "You won't believe what just happened." I'd told him about Sarah's prayer for our sex life. To see the tables turned—my child praying for me—had been so amazing.

Our last night in Barcelona reflected God's answer to Sarah's prayers for vulnerability in my heart so I could discover God's gift.

PHIL

After Priscilla and I returned from Spain, we continued to talk and smile about our last night in Barcelona. I had loved seeing Priscilla be vulnerable again. Our time in Barcelona had been pure and strangely satisfying, even though we had not fully connected physically.

Our mornings continued to be times of spiritual and emotional connection as we got up early and read our Bibles and prayed together. There was a new openness between us, a new sense of togetherness, different from before we'd left for Spain. Priscilla embraced me differently now, looking into my eyes with a sense of closeness I had not seen before our trip. In the past, I had pushed her for sex. I didn't want her to see even a glimpse of that old man. I had decided not to bug her about when she would be willing to spend physical time together again, and I would instead wait for her to initiate, which she had seldom done.

PRISCILLA

For the first time in our marriage, I felt spiritually and emotionally intimate with Phil and wanted to be intimate with him physically as well. But I wasn't sure how to go about it. My upbringing and ignorance about sexual matters made me feel like I didn't have the know-how and capability to initiate sex. Throughout our marriage, I hadn't felt free to enjoy my sexuality. I'd been cold and resistant at the thought of talking about sex. I had even thought my lack of sexual fulfillment was because God was getting me back for the sexual images I had harbored from my past. The images had been a robber, not only stealing from my times with Phil but creating an image of sexuality that was unattainable, making me feel out of step with the norm.

I loved Phil and was committed to him, but I wanted more sexually than I'd had before. I desired to feel closeness, warmth, and togetherness with my husband, making me feel loved for who I was instead of what I could provide. I longed for the feeling of being fully known yet fully loved, in a realm of closeness with Phil in spirit, soul, and body.

After twenty-eight years of a mediocre marriage and now a new birth of sexual feelings, I yearned for all that God had for us in the union of our souls.

After a few days at home, Phil and I started talking about how to restart our intimate encounters. We didn't want them to be fast and perfunctory, Phil just rolling over and saying good night. That was in our past. We wanted our times together to be different, such as no more sex in the dark with images of other people rolling around in our heads. Yes, I wanted the lights to be on! (A first for me.) I wanted to see Phil's deep-blue eyes looking into mine while listening to music that fed my spirit. Not the music of our high school days, attached to unwanted memories, but soft instrumental praise and worship songs serenading our love.

I also wanted to invite *the* Artist, Designer, and Creator of this intoxicating gift into our experience. I wanted to sense God's presence as part of our togetherness. Sex without welcoming God's presence had been a duty, and I now wanted sex to be a delight. I banished "duty sex," convinced that God had something else in store for me. However, the thought of asking God to bless me, teach me, and lead me sexually seemed daunting. I had always associated sex with sin, which had created a noose of shame and condemnation. I didn't yet feel worthy of asking God to be part of something that still felt shameful. Then I discovered 1 Corinthians 10:13. "No temptation has overtaken you except something common to mankind."

Although Phil and I had discovered a few months earlier that our take-it-to-the-grave lists were similar, I still felt that my temptations were unusual and uncommon. But God showed me in His Word that *all* temptations were common. I then understood that many people carried those same feelings of shame, guilt, and condemnation about sexuality, believing what they had done or gone through was unusual, unique, perverted, or weird and God couldn't possibly forgive them.

When I realized that none of that was true and that God could heal every hurt and forgive every sin, I was freed from the shame of my past. I began to see that sex was an unblemished gift from God, not containing a hint of dirtiness, shame, or guilt. Marital sex was to be fully embraced and enjoyed. I asked God to help me delight in His magnificent gift to us as husband and wife—one with Him.

PHIL

Home from Spain, I further focused on building my spiritual and emotional connection with Priscilla. Although I let her know how much I enjoyed our final night in Barcelona, I said nothing about what might happen next. I leaned deeper into trusting God to restore us sexually, as He had restored us spiritually and emotionally.

I woke up early one morning as I felt Priscilla stirring. She asked in a sleepy voice, "Are you awake?"

"Yeah, sort of." I could feel the warmth of her body as she rolled next to mine.

"Good morning," she whispered.

We lay together for several minutes, resting in the moment, relishing the ease of being together without having to rush. She asked, "Do you want to turn on the oil diffuser and light the candles?" That was a new question for me. *Is Priscilla initiating an intimate time for us?*

"Sure, let me find a lighter." I stumbled around in the dark, eventually lighting our bedside candles, which, along with the oil diffuser, created a romantic, soft glow that illuminated and scented our bedroom.

I climbed back into bed and drew close to Priscilla. Lying there on my side with my arm wrapped around her, I sensed the same vulnerability she had shown only a few days earlier in Barcelona. My feelings toward her grew stronger as we became enveloped in the enchanting scent of lavender and shadows dancing in the soft glow of candlelight. *Is this the right time for us?* I sensed God's desire to be part of our healing and experience. I suggested, "Let's invite God into our time together."

"Yes, let's do that."

With over a hundred days for me to think about this moment, God had shown me that He had been in the Garden of Eden with Adam and Eve when they'd first tasted sexual pleasure. God had been pleased to see them enjoy what He had created, and they had been fully aware of

His presence. I had never sensed God's presence in our lovemaking, primarily because the images in my head made me feel too ashamed to invite Him into my union with Priscilla. Porn had always been my sexual tutor. I needed to shift my mindset to allow the Holy Spirit to teach me how to express physically to Priscilla what we were already experiencing spiritually and emotionally. We needed to go to the garden.

> I needed to shift my mindset to allow the Holy Spirit to teach me how to express physically to Priscilla what we were already experiencing spiritually and emotionally.

Even though I had never prayed prior to having sex in the past, my early-morning prayer seemed normal and entirely appropriate. "Father, we know You created sex as Your gift to us. We embrace Your presence. Please be our teacher and guide."

Our morning together was a precious union, not only of our bodies but of our souls. I had never engaged in sex as a complete spiritual, emotional, and physical expression. What I felt in that moment was completely different and indeed glorious.

What I had not anticipated was a spiritual attack in our intimacy, stemming primarily from my memories. At Priscilla's touch, my mind went to a past massage, and defeating thoughts rose to strangle me. *You are no different than before! You have not changed one iota! It's still all about you!* I recoiled from the shame pounding at the door of my heart. I didn't want to go back where I'd been before I'd come clean.

After lingering in our afterglow, I got out of bed, went into the bathroom, and sat on the tub step. Once again, I sensed the dark voices ringing threats and accusations, as if they were commanding me to forget that God had healed my mind. I knew I needed to be HOT with Priscilla about this battle, but as soon as I had that thought, the imaginary voices shouted louder. "Don't tell her anything! If you tell her what you were thinking—while you were in bed with her—you won't have sex for another hundred days. Maybe never!"

I was truly conflicted.

I knew I needed to be HOT, but I didn't want to destroy what God had created between Priscilla and me, and I certainly didn't want her to fear I was still a prisoner to my old way of life. *God, what should I do?* I heard His soothing, peaceful, nonurgent words: "Tell her everything. No hiding if you want to be truly free."

"Phil, are you okay?" Priscilla asked from the doorway. I was still sitting on the step, my head in my hands. Prior to checking on me, she must have thought this was the best day of my life. So seeing me sitting there, looking so downcast, was surely a surprise. "What's going on?" she asked sympathetically, concern in her voice.

This was decision time; I battled whether to go back to hiding my thoughts or to wholly embrace a HOT life, seeking to be fully known.

Again, the Holy Spirit prompted me, bringing a familiar verse to mind. "If we walk in the Light as He Himself is in the Light, we have fellowship with one another, and the blood of Jesus His son cleanses us from all sin" (1 John 1:7). The decision was clear. I would not take even one step back into darkness. I would walk in the light. "You know when you were caressing my back?"

"Yes, of course I remember."

"Well, my thoughts took me back to when I was getting a massage." I cringed, hating that I had to bring up something so disgusting. "I'm so sorry, Priscilla. We had such a wonderful time together, and I didn't want to tell you, but I can't go back to keeping secrets." My voice cracked with emotion as I dropped my head, unable to look at her. Shame was threatening to burst back into my life, still pounding at the door. It had been locked away for a hundred days and was now hungry for another piece of my soul.

Priscilla had listened from the doorway without showing emotion. Now she moved toward me. She put her hands on her hips and said, "So when I was caressing your back, it wasn't the first time you felt someone doing that, right?"

I couldn't bear to look up. "Yes, that's right." I felt defeat threatening to swallow me as I heard Priscilla take a step closer, and I tentatively lifted my head.

Looking squarely at me, she said like a warrior, "Well, that's just too bad because you are now *mine*, and the enemy has no right to you any longer!" With that declaration, she took her hands from her hips and struck the air as though wielding a sword, and she shouted a rebuke in Jesus's name to any tormenting spiritual forces seeking to affect my thoughts. She stood confidently, like she had power on her head—a savage marriage warrior taking authority over the enemy. I immediately felt a spiritual lifting, a freedom, and a united closeness with Priscilla.

I stood, and we embraced. Our tears of victory flowed. We had won a major battle by Priscilla standing up to the enemy as my battle partner and meeting him head-on with the truth. Many times, in future battles against the enemy, we would revisit this pivotal experience of freedom. The experience showed us that we were both on the path of freedom from our past thoughts.

PRISCILLA

Experiencing the birth of our sexuality was not the final key leading to reconciliation of our marriage, but it was rather like opening the door to a completely new journey of marital oneness. Phil and I began talking about our sexuality and praying that the Holy Spirit would lead us to understand God's intention for sexual intimacy.

One morning, Phil and I read about God's promise to Abraham and Sarah that they would bear a child in their old age. In Genesis 18:12, "Sarah laughed silently to herself and said, 'How could a worn-out woman like me enjoy such pleasure, especially when my master—my husband—is also so old?'" (NLT).

"Phil, do you ever feel like we missed the best years of our life for sex when we were young and sex should have been really amazing, out of this world?"

"Sometimes. But I believe God can restore all things, even the years we missed."

"Well, I do too," I said confidently. "Look at this verse in Genesis about Sarah. She was a really old woman, and Abraham was a really old man. It looks like she's wondering the same thing I wonder. Could she still experience pleasure at that point in her life? I realize she could just be referring to having a baby, but the Bible uses the word *pleasure*." Phil nodded, his eyes on the passage. He used to debate me on biblical terms and definitions, but he seemed to understand my point in this case. "Phil, I want to experience the pleasure of Sarah. I'm not sure what all that means, but whatever God has for me in this area of our marriage, I'm open to it."

Phil looked up and smiled. "I agree. He's done such amazing things. I'm willing to sacrifice whatever it takes to help you have a better sex life." He grinned, probably realizing he was taking a slight risk by making a sexual joke. But I grinned back, thinking that several months ago, this conversation would have never occurred.

On the first Saturday of each month, our church held a morning prayer service, and Phil and I decided to attend. At the end of the service, the prayer team stood up front, available to pray for anyone who came forward. I decided to put my pride aside and ask someone to pray for me to have the pleasure of Sarah. I didn't care how it might sound or that probably no one had ever asked for something like this. God had laid it on my heart, and I was going forward. I turned to Phil and asked, "Do you want to come with me?"

Although he appeared unsure why I needed prayer, he said, "Sure, I'll go up with you."

The background music started, and we stood and walked to the front, where a woman named Lisa approached me. She looked young and hip, and I felt like she would at least receive my request. Plus, she was a woman. I couldn't imagine talking to any man about this.

Lisa put her hand on my shoulder and asked, "What would you like prayer for?"

"God has done an amazing work in my marriage. I've been reading in Genesis about Sarah wondering whether she could experience pleasure again with Abraham, since they were both so old. I'd like for you to pray that I will experience with Phil the pleasure of Sarah."

Lisa had listened intently, and her eyes widened with surprise as she realized what I was asking. She tilted her head and nodded. "Our God can do anything, and He will do this for you."

She prayed with authority and belief that I would experience the pleasure of Sarah and that God would heal and restore my sexuality. Although I could have just prayed this on my own, I believed God wanted me to make a confession to someone else about what I needed. It was a step of humility that carried me further on a path of healing all my hurts, pains, and misconceptions I'd brought into our marriage.

PHIL

After Priscilla's prayer to have the "pleasure of Sarah," our lovemaking became more open as we listened to each other and the Holy Spirit about how to delight in His marvelous gift. It was hard to believe—there we were, married for over thirty years and just learning how to really enjoy making love. We prayed together before sex and asked the Holy Spirit to lead us, teach us, and free us to enjoy being with one another. We asked Him how to touch each other, the pace, the pressure . . . everything. Our lovemaking in the past had been very predictable, the same basic series of steps every time. We asked God to give us a new dance, a new pattern, and help us be creative together.

While many couples turn to books and magazines for sexual creativity, we decided to turn to God. We knew by His very nature—with all the wonders of life we could see, taste, smell, and feel—that He was the Master of creativity and the Father who wanted us to experience His best. We believed He would help us be creative in our lovemaking.

We also loved the change of atmosphere in our bedroom. We lit candles every night, used essential oil diffusers, and played soft instrumental praise music, just like the recent morning when we had truly made love for the first time in our marriage. We began using various body perfumes, even ordering special perfumes from Israel. The new atmosphere and creativity engaged all five senses and formed an idyllic way to end each day. Not that we made love each day, but we set the mood. We were so close spiritually and emotionally that whether or not we made love had very little effect on the way I felt toward Priscilla.

PRISCILLA

Our new sexual experience created something else special in our marriage that I had not anticipated: freedom to initiate nonsexual touching with Phil. In the past, I had been afraid that every physical move by me, even nonsexual, would be interpreted by Phil as a desire for sex. So I had seldom initiated a kiss or hug. Experiencing Phil's new sensitivity to my desires and his willingness to play, touch, and cuddle without leading to sex made me comfortable to be warmer with him physically. I could tell that Phil loved my new willingness to touch him nonsexually. We discovered that nonsexual touching created an environment to play and relax without sexual expectations from either of us. We even initiated what we called "non-genitalia nights," a time of touching, with or without clothes, with only two rules: no genital touching, and we had to wait until at least the next day to engage sexually.

Non-genitalia nights took all pressure of expectations off me and allowed me to relax into a delightful time with Phil. I have to admit, we occasionally broke a rule, but starting an evening as a non-genitalia night had brought ease to our physical closeness because there were no expectations of it turning sexual.

PHIL

As the months went by, I was amazed at how fulfilling our sexual life had become.

After coming clean, I had not looked at porn, masturbated, or done anything else sexual outside of my times with Priscilla. God had opened an entirely new sexual world for me, free from the bondages of my past.

Shutting the doors to the schoolroom of porn and its sexual tutoring allowed me to focus on God as my advocate, teacher, and guide to a divine sexual experience with my wife.

Going into marriage, I'd had warped sexual expectations, which was no surprise. I had thought Priscilla should act just like my imaginary lovers, who made me the center of their universe. When Priscilla had failed to act as I'd imagined, I'd demanded and pouted, leaving her emotionally naked and feeling used. Although I had sensed she wasn't being fulfilled, I'd chalked that up to her living a sheltered life. I had been so arrogant and self-centered I had failed to see I was causing Priscilla to further retreat from me and our marriage. All those years, I should have seen our sexuality as King Solomon had described his experiences—like preparing and living in a garden (Song of Sol. 5:1).

Priscilla and I had taken the long road to God's majestic garden, but He welcomed us in to enjoy its many pleasures.

Several years prior, we had decided to plant a garden with our kids. We'd picked an unused piece of our property that was completely overgrown with weeds. We knew it would take effort to create the transformation, but we all worked together to cut down the brush. We researched how to prepare the soil, and together we added new soil and tilled it into the newly broken earth. The process was painstaking and slow, but reading books about gardening grew our confidence, and we felt assured that if we put in time and labor, we'd enjoy some tasty produce.

We asked the kids what they would like to plant, and we went back and forth, knowing we couldn't plant everything. We wanted a mix of foods we had eaten before and some that were new to us. We settled on a variety of vegetables and fruits, each with different directions for planting, growing, and fertilizing, and we shopped for seeds.

The fruits and vegetables would ripen at different times and require work, but we had faith that what we planted would grow to look and taste delicious.

As the plants grew, we visited the garden often. We shared with excitement each new emergence and quickly pulled weeds that tried to choke out new growth. Within just a few months, we were enjoying beautiful organic vegetables and fruits. The harvest seemed even more tasty because we had been envisioning the results for months and appreciated the hard work it took to nurture the plants to full growth.

Until Priscilla and I intentionally created our intimacy garden, I had not seen our sex life like a garden that needed preparation, tilling, planting, and care. I had seen our sexual relationship more like a convenience store, available whenever I ran out of what I needed. Though I had settled for convenience, what I had really wanted (and didn't realize in those years) was a spiritual and emotional connection with my wife.

Entering our new door of sexuality was like preparing a garden at the back of our property—disregarded for too long and full of weeds. Our relationship had needed a lot of time, help, and preparation before we could expect to receive anything. We began the process by looking to the Master Gardener for direction, with faith that if we sowed seeds according to His plan, our garden would indeed produce an excellent, fully satisfying crop of lovely feelings, thoughts, and memories. And that was just what we gleaned.

Priscilla and I discarded old images that danced through our heads by creating radiant new memories that called out to us even when we weren't together, reminding us of what was in store when we reconnected. Our new memories were rich and filling, showing us how much more excellent is God's way. After all, He is the Artist, Designer, and Creator of the magnificent gift of sexual intimacy.

Like Adam and Eve, Priscilla and I then knew the beauty of the garden, and we rejoiced in God's presence during our romantic encounters, free to enjoy all that He had planned for us. We now gathered our myrrh and balsam, ate our honeycomb and honey, drank our wine and milk, and followed God's encouragement from Song of Solomon 5:1—"Eat, friends; Drink and drink deeply, lovers."

PRISCILLA

Opening the door of my sexuality removed significant insecurity from me. I had always seen myself as a wallflower, hanging back while Phil engaged with everyone around us. But unveiling who I was in Christ and letting Him into all facets of my life, including my sexuality, gave me a new boldness.

God began opening doors for us to share what He had done in our marriage. In a world obsessed with sharing every detail of life, there is one thing few people ever share—their marriage problems, real problems: adultery, pornography, prostitution, and the dysfunction that comes from hiding past trauma and wounds. Consequently, very few couples know how to solve such savage issues. If help is sought, the work toward healing and restoration is confined to a counselor's office and within the crumbling marriage walls. I discovered God was calling Phil and me to step out and publicly share what He had done privately in our lives. Yes, the freedom to share was right around the corner, and it would be the most exciting part of our story yet.

| Savage Questions for Reflection |

1. Who or what has been your sexual tutor? What impact has this had on your sexual intimacy with your spouse?

2. How do you and your spouse invite God into your sex life? What can be improved?

3. How does the atmosphere of your bedroom need to change to enhance your sexual experience?

4. Do you have any sexual shame and condemnation that need to be released for you to enjoy true sexual freedom with your spouse? What are they?

Chapter 12

RADICAL COURAGE AND VULNERABILITY

They overcame him because of the blood of the Lamb and because of the word of their testimony.

—Revelations 12:11

You know, sometimes all you need is twenty seconds of insane courage. Just literally twenty seconds of just embarrassing bravery. And I promise you, something great will come of it.

—Benjamin Mee, *We Bought a Zoo*

PHIL

Five months had passed since I'd come clean with Priscilla, and God was nudging me to be humble before the pastors and elders of our former church. I had projected so much arrogance and pride to that group of men, all the time trying to look like the perfect Christian leader while hiding a life of sin and shame. I needed to come clean with them and ask their forgiveness.

I reached out to a friend, Jim, to meet for breakfast. I had served as an elder with Jim at my former church, and he and his wife, Shirley, had been our good friends for over fifteen years. We'd shared many things in common—homeschooling, church work, and even family camping trips. But over the past couple of years, our times together had been few.

Stemming from Jim's training as a marine and his demanding schedule as a major airline pilot, he exuded a level of intensity I enjoyed. I'd always liked his bottom-line, get-it-done attitude. He wasn't shy about offering his opinions, and I felt good when he asked for mine. Jim was also a bit like me—somewhat arrogant—which had allowed me to project my pride without worrying what he may be thinking of me. Even though Jim and I had been out of touch for a while, I knew we would immediately pick up from where we'd left off.

I saw Jim walk through the restaurant door, and I jumped up to meet him. "Jim, how's it going!"

"Hey, Phil, good to see you!" He extended his hand and pulled me in for a hug.

As soon as we'd ordered breakfast, I got right to the point. "Jim, I want to tell you about something that God's been doing in my life."

"Okay," he said pensively, leaning forward and propping his elbows on the table.

I spilled the details of my secret life, my tears flowing as I reconnected with the pain I'd caused Priscilla. I was no longer a man trying to manage his image. I no longer cared what Jim may think of me; I just wanted him to know how God had healed my mind and transformed our marriage.

"Wow." Jim sat back in the booth and folded his arms tightly across his chest. I had caught him off guard with the bare truth and my vulnerability. He seemed at a loss for words. His eyes had widened, but he otherwise showed little emotion.

"Jim, will you forgive me for being such a hypocrite?" I didn't pause for an answer but went on to explain. "When I served with you as an elder, I'm sure my hypocrisy affected our church, affected relationships among us as elders, and maybe even some of our decisions. I'm so sorry I had such an arrogant, prideful attitude." My voice shook with remorse, making each word difficult to say. "Will you please forgive me?"

Jim shifted uncomfortably and leaned in again, his lips a tight line. "Sure, I forgive you. Can we pay and sit in the car for a bit?" I nodded. We quickly paid the bill and left.

When we were seated together in his SUV, Jim said, "I just don't know what to say . . ." He looked uneasy, and his eyes were moist. Men were usually taken aback when hearing my story, as the reality hit core issues present in most men. But Jim seemed lost in thought, not knowing what to say.

I broke the silence, easing back from the topic. "Jim, I'm just so happy you agreed to meet with me."

He nodded. "I'm glad we met too. Can we pray together?" I nodded, and he started praying. As elders, we had prayed together many times about church business and people's problems. But this time was different. This time was personal—about us, our families, and what God wanted to do in our lives.

We wrapped up after a few minutes, hugged, and agreed we would continue to pray for each other.

About a week later, I received a text from Jim asking if he could come by. A few minutes later, he arrived, and I ushered him in, glad to see him. He gave me a tight hug, and we moved into the family room. Jim chose the couch, where he perched on the edge, leaning forward. He looked official in his pilot's uniform, lending gravity and importance to our meeting.

"Phil," he began with a sense of urgency, "I need to share with you what happened after breakfast last week . . . with Shirley and me." His face was drawn like he hadn't been sleeping.

"Okay. What's going on?" I leaned in from the adjacent couch. I sensed Jim's struggle, and a prayer rose in me for God's wisdom.

"When I got home, I confessed to Shirley that I've been having an affair . . . for the past year. And it's not even the first time," he added, shaking his head in shame, regret, and loss.

Although he had listened to me at breakfast with very little emotion, his tone was now entirely different. He stammered, his sentences interrupted by his tears and weighted sighs. He was in a deep pit I recognized, and my heart ached for him.

He continued, "When Shirley found out about the previous situations, we decided to keep them secret from everyone because we were ashamed of what I'd done and too proud to let anyone see the real truth of our marriage. The first time was about five years ago, and I immediately felt like something died inside me and has been dead ever since. When you asked me to forgive you, my heart was burning, like it was a thousand degrees. I knew it all had to come out." Jim sobbed as he went on to describe his confession of everything to Shirley. He was a broken man. I could see the pain gripping his soul, exactly as I had experienced only five months earlier. I also felt Shirley's crushing pain through my experiences with Priscilla.

Right then, Priscilla called to say she was on the way home. I told her Jim was with me and briefly said what was going on with him and Shirley.

PRISCILLA

Jim's admission was a shock. Shirley and I had been good friends, able to share and talk with candor about our kids, homeschooling, and many other things. But we had not typically discussed deeper issues, such as problems in our marriages. Now, there I was, only five months out from my own hell, with an opportunity to help a friend in hers. Concerned, I began praying for her.

Learning that your husband is having an affair is devastating, and I wondered how Shirley was handling it. I dialed her number, and the call went to voice mail. "Shirley, this is Priscilla. Jim's with Phil, and I just heard what happened. I'm so sorry. I know you're hurting and in so much pain. I don't know if I can help, but I can listen. Can you call me?" I hung up, wondering whether she would call me back.

I remembered how I had felt in the wake of Phil's confession—shocked, humiliated, and thrown into disparaging grief. I hadn't wanted to talk because I hadn't thought anyone could understand—and I'd feared people might even believe Phil's wandering eyes were my fault.

PHIL

After Priscilla's call, Jim quickly stood, appearing anxious and ready to bolt. "Priscilla's on the way home, right?"

"Yes—I think so. I know she's going to try to reach out to Shirley, but she'll probably be here in a few minutes."

Jim looked toward the door. "I think I need to get out of here."

"Jim, I understand, but I think it would be good for you to share with Priscilla. I know it will be hard."

Still, Jim's face showed his worry as he looked back and forth from the family room to the front door. "I feel like running away."

"I understand."

Jim hung his head, glancing toward the floor with lingering hesitation while shouldering defeat.

After a moment, I asked, "What do you think you should do?"

Jim met my eyes with resignation. "I think I should stay." He sat back down on the couch, and we waited quietly together. All the while, my heart was praying for him and Shirley and for wisdom for Priscilla and me.

A few minutes later, we heard the garage door open and close, and then in walked Priscilla. The tension in the air was palpable as she made her way to the sectional and sat beside me. Her voice was sincere and nonjudgmental, as she sensed Jim's pain.

PRISCILLA

"Hi, Jim. It's good to see you," I said gently. His eyes were bloodshot, and his countenance was downcast. He didn't seem to want to talk to me, but I knew how important it was for him to share the wrongs he had done. I had come to understand that confessing sin was the beginning of healing, and I was determined to listen. Whatever he'd done, whatever temptations bound him, I wanted him to have a new heart and understanding, leave his old self and life behind, and be the husband God intended.

I gave Jim time to gather his thoughts, and then he explained what had brought him to our home. He was an emotional mess as he described how his choices had wrecked Shirley. My heart went out to them. I could see Jim's brokenness in God's pursuing presence. To be in that moment, seeing Jim's true repentance, was absolutely beautiful. I had seen such repentant sorrow only once before, in Phil.

PHIL

Although Jim's confession to me had been full of tears and remorse before Priscilla had arrived, his confession to her—a wife, mother, and friend—brought out an entirely new level of humility and brokenness. He was crying so hard he started hyperventilating, and it was difficult for him to get out consecutive words. The brokenness in Jim's soul took over his body, and he moved onto the floor, facedown, sobbing and confessing his poor choices. I joined him there, kneeling beside him and crying with him.

Jim's vivid brokenness starkly reminded me of what I had gone through. It was obvious God's grace was moving Jim's soul from darkness into light.

After several minutes, we returned to the couch, wiping tears from our eyes.

Jim turned to Priscilla and said, "I've been such a hypocrite, liar, and cheater . . ." He was trying to pull his emotions together but losing the battle, completely overcome. He finally managed a weak "Will you forgive me?"

Priscilla stood and walked over to Jim. She pointed at him and said, "Jim, I forgive you—and God has forgiven you too. My dear brother, I'm standing with you in prayer that God is going to rescue your marriage and heal your soul because you're worth it." Priscilla then prayed with authority for Jim and Shirley, asking God for His healing and restoration of their marriage. Jim wept so hard he could barely breathe.

After a moment, he managed to say through a heavy sigh, "Thank you, Priscilla." He appeared completely spent but relieved that the burden of his past was now in the open.

We all hugged, expressing our commitment to pray for each other and our desire for healing and restoration of Jim and Shirley's marriage.

Jim left our house a different man. After such a broken experience, he now seemed to have a new countenance of hope that his future was going to be profoundly different from his past.

PRISCILLA

Two days later, Shirley came over. She and I spent hours talking and crying as she shared her hurt, pain, and disappointment. I didn't have many answers for her, but what I did have were compassion and empathy. I shared my own story and encouraged her. "God can heal any hurt, no matter how deep."

When Shirley left, I texted her: *I'm so glad we got to talk today. I want you to know I'm standing with you in this fight. I love you, dear sister, and I'm praying for you. Be strong, brave, and courageous in our Lord Jesus.*

Shirley replied: *Thank you, dear sister! I feel so much better after meeting with you today. I would like to meet weekly or every other week if you can, and could you go over some things you learned from the conference, out of your workbook? I honestly don't feel ready to go this weekend, but I'm going to go next time it's offered. I'm clinging to God's promises, and I know He loves me. I'm going to look in the mirror daily and tell myself that. From no man on this earth will I derive my significance. Thank you for today.*

PHIL

After Jim's confession, we met for breakfast every week. He attended 4 Days 2 Freedom, and Shirley attended 4 Days 2 Hope. They had kept Jim's past infidelity quiet, but this time was different. They decided to put everything out in the open. Jim confessed to their kids and close friends, and we could see God rescuing their marriage, just like He had rescued ours.

Over the months ahead, Priscilla and I continued to share our story. Some people thought our radical vulnerability was crazy. They couldn't comprehend how we could tell our children something so private, and we could see that sharing our story sometimes made others uncomfortable. However, now and then, people responded as if our story was the rescuing hand of God for their marriages. That's how Jim and Shirley had responded, which proved that what God had done in our lives, He could do in the lives of others: rescue suffering marriages and make them whole, stronger . . . and savage.

The following year, Priscilla and I developed a Savage Marriage small-group curriculum, and Jim and Shirley attended our first group. Not only did they fearlessly contribute their testimonies, but they later began leading a Savage Marriage small group at their church. Shirley joined Jim in telling her story of forgiveness and healing. Jim even helped lead a men's conference, where he tearfully shared his testimony. No longer was it just *our* story creating freedom in other people's lives—*their* story was too. Jim frequently reminded me, "Phil, all I've got is a story." I thought of the feeding of the five thousand from Matthew 14. The masses were hungry, and all they had were a mere five loaves and two fishes. Jesus took the little they had and miraculously multiplied that into more food than the five thousand could eat. I also thought of the widow from 2 Kings 4. All she had was her last small jar of oil. God took that little and multiplied it, and through that miracle, the woman's life and her son's were restored.

The same was true with our savage marriages. God was taking our stories—the only thing we had to give—and He was multiplying those to feed, heal, and restore the hearts and lives of other couples through the power of the Holy Spirit.

Jim's and Shirley's willingness to share their story led to other couples becoming free from their pasts. Jim was right; all he had—all *they* had and all we had—was a story. But those radical, courageous, and vulnerable stories held savage power—God's power—to transform lives.

PRISCILLA

Sharing my story at the Whatever It Takes Couples Intensive was the first time I had ever felt God's peace and power when standing in front of a group. Afterward, I prayed, *Lord, if You create the opportunities, I will speak to whomever You want.*

Later that summer, Phil began attending a men's breakfast where they listened to each other give testimonies. I was sitting at the kitchen table when Phil returned from a morning meeting with a grin on his face.

"How'd your group go?" I asked, wondering why he was so happy.

"It went great! I gave my testimony, and the guys want to hear your side of our story!"

"You're joking, right?"

"No joke. Some of them couldn't believe you forgave me. They want to hear it directly from you!"

"No way!" I thought back to my prayer of commitment to speak to whomever God wanted. I had anticipated God would want me to share with a women's group. But no, rather than a small, friendly group of women, it looked like my first opportunity to share was going to be a men's breakfast group at a pub! God sure had a sense of humor. "Phil, did you create this opportunity yourself, or did God do it?" While Phil loved public speaking and would pursue every chance to get in front of a group, I was somewhat reserved.

"No, really, they want to hear from you. It was their idea."

"Okay," I said. "I'll do it." God was peeling back my layers of fears and insecurities, growing me to be stronger and truly open to sharing with anyone what He had done in our lives.

How strange that I was actually looking forward to speaking to a group of men about something so personal. Although I had shared with small groups in my home and at the couples intensive, being the only woman in a group of men made me feel really vulnerable.

As I stepped from the car, the cool air felt crisp and fresh on my face. The men were gathered around worn picnic tables and benches on the pub's outside patio. Some were in groups of two or three, while others sat alone. Brother Frank, who led the singing, was a kindhearted man, a gentle giant with a mighty baritone voice that could be heard across the parking lot. He sang with abandon, not caring who heard or what people may have been thinking. That was exactly how I wanted to testify of God's love through my personal story of healing, giving to God the only thing I had.

I spoke freely of the grace God had given me to forgive Phil and then told them about my own story of healing from apathy, pride, and self-righteousness. My tears cascaded as I told them how God had enabled me to experience His unbelievable love.

After I finished, several men asked questions, and one man said our story was the most powerful testimony he'd ever heard. Phil wrote in his prayer journal the names of the man and his wife. A few other men expressed their appreciation, saying they had never heard a woman share a testimony with a bunch of men. Thinking back to my historical fear of speaking, I was in awe that God would provide such encouragement. I was convinced He was going to continue to lead me into unconventional situations. I was on a wild, untamed, savage adventure with God.

Two years later, Phil received a call from the man whose name he'd written in his prayer journal. The man said his wife had just found out he had been committing adultery and doing many of the same things Phil had. When the man had heard our testimonies at the pub, he had been too ashamed to admit his sin and had continued in secret the next two years. The day after his call to Phil, he and his wife came to our house. They were shocked when Phil showed them their names in his journal from two years before. Later, the couple joined our Savage Marriage small group and experienced God's healing hand of rescue in their marriage.

Although Phil and I had been actively involved in church and many different ministries for over thirty years, those had been centered primarily on *knowledge about God*, but now we were sharing *encounters with God*. For the first time, we were seeing such amazing life changes.

All we had was a story and our willingness to share it with radical courage and vulnerability, and faith that God would multiply our offering through the power of the Holy Spirit. Just as God had rescued our lives through Paul's and Jenny's willingness to share their stories, He was using our transparency to rescue marriages.

PHIL

Priscilla and I were leading our third Savage Marriage small group and we invited Jim and Shirley to share their testimony. The group was to start at seven, and people began arriving at our house shortly before. Soon we were gathered in our family room. "Hey, guys, let's all find a seat. Our friends Jim and Shirley are going to be here shortly to share their story."

Everyone sat down, and I looked at my watch. It was a few minutes past seven. "It looks like Jim and Shirley are running late. Let's pray and begin reviewing the homework from last week. I'm sure they'll be here in a few minutes." I opened with prayer, and we jumped into the homework material.

After about fifteen minutes, the door opened, and in walked Jim. Alone. "Hi, Jim! Where's Shirley?"

"She's sitting in the car."

"Are you guys having a fight?" Jim was used to being HOT, so I didn't feel the question needed to be private.

"Well, yes, we are. We need a few minutes."

"No problem; take your time. We're just going through the homework. Join us whenever you're ready." Jim said thanks, quickly turned, and headed back out the door.

Everyone was looking around, a bit surprised that Jim would admit so freely that he and Shirley were in an argument. "Hey, guys, this is Savage Marriage," I reminded them. "If Priscilla and I have a conflict, we're going to share it with you and how we resolved it. And if not resolved, we'll let you know later when and how we resolved it." Thinking of my journey with Priscilla, I added, "Every marriage has conflicts, but no one wants to admit it. Let's give Jim and Shirley some time to work out their problem."

After about twenty minutes, the front door opened again, and Jim and Shirley walked in. Shirley was smiling and laughing. Jim still looked a little bit tight, but they were here nevertheless. "Did you guys work out your disagreement?" I asked.

"Yes," Shirley said, laughing. They shared with transparency and humility how their conflict had started, escalated, and then been resolved. They both took responsibility for their parts in the fight and didn't put the other down. They also acknowledged they would revisit the issue later to make sure everything was truly resolved and forgiven.

Seven weeks later was the last Savage Marriage session for that group. Priscilla and I were still refining our materials and seeking feedback. I asked the group, "What do you think you'll remember most from Savage Marriage?" Priscilla and I had thought some people might say the session on wounds or lies had been most impactful. We also thought some group members might even comment on our amazing story of redemption or our solid Bible teaching.

One person quickly spoke up. "The night Jim and Shirley had a fight!" Everyone laughed and nodded, voicing their hearty agreement. After hundreds of hours developing small-group materials and leading countless small-group meetings, Priscilla and I were amazed that the one thing readily remembered was the raw, vulnerable confession of an argument. Not one that happened twenty years ago but one that was still ringing in their ears. We understood why: It's rare for people to be authentic and allow God to open up their shadow life to those around them. Most people manage their life stories by allowing others to see only what they want to show versus showing who they really are. When someone becomes authentic and vulnerable, there's power in their story to transform everyone who hears.

> When someone becomes authentic and vulnerable, there's power in their story to transform everyone who hears.

We later told Jim and Shirley how much everyone had loved the confession of their fight. Shirley said, laughing, "Yes, someone in our group said that Savage Marriage is like reality television but in a good way."

PRISCILLA

The response to Jim and Shirley revealing their fight proved that people are searching for a place, a group, a circumstance where they can be *real*. When we're HOT with others about a problem we've had, that vulnerability shows irresistible authenticity. Realness is what people are seeking, both inside and outside the church. Jim was right. All we have is a story, and God will use it when we're free enough to share it. On the night that Jim had opened our front door and told us he and Shirley were fighting, twenty seconds of radical courage and vulnerability had made all the difference.

PHIL

It was Saturday morning, and I was getting ready to speak at a church conference. I was the first of several speakers, and I had been asked to share on pride (probably because they knew I had so much of it). My pastor had provided some scripted remarks but left the topic open to sharing my story. I had only about fifteen minutes, so I needed to select what would be most impactful.

After a time of worship, the pastor welcomed everyone and covered logistics for the day. I was praying, asking God to make clear to me what to share. I had already planned to say I had been addicted to pornography, but I heard a whisper from the Holy Spirit to reveal more. *Are you also going to say you were addicted to masturbation?*

Porn addiction was something many people were now acknowledging as a real problem, but I had never heard anyone say *masturbation* at church, and certainly not from the stage. I texted Priscilla: *I have about three minutes. I'm planning to use the P-word, but I'm wondering if I should also use the M-word. What do you think?* I hit Send and waited.

I kept looking at my phone, hoping she would provide a word, a smiley face—anything to let me know she was with me. There was no response, and I began a silent debate with God. *I haven't even cleared with the conference leadership what I'm going to say, and I don't want this first speaking opportunity to be my last.*

Again, I sensed the Holy Spirit's voice: "Is this your pride speaking? Don't let a spirit of hesitation get between you and your story."

"Phil, come on up!" Hearing my name over the speakers was a jolt. I rose to my feet, taking a final look at my phone—still no reply from Priscilla.

I stepped up to the podium and shared my prepared remarks on pride, segueing into the more difficult admission. "I was addicted to pornography." I looked up, hearing inside me again God's encouragement to not hesitate. I had a split second to decide. "And masturbation."

Silence.

I could immediately tell I had pushed through my imaginary wall of rejection. All eyes were on me as I stared wordlessly back at the crowd and then shattered the silence with, "There, I've said it! I used the M-word." A few chuckles among the group further eased the room's tension.

"I know it's a difficult word to hear, but it's a real word; it's in the dictionary, and everybody knows what it means. And how are we ever going to be free from something we can't even say aloud?" The room erupted in cheers, startling me. One guy in the back was swinging his jacket in the air and whooping it up. The anxiety I had felt earlier was all gone as I realized that being vulnerable would always create a great opportunity to connect with others and encourage them to acknowledge their deepest pain, sin, and shame.

After I spoke, several men asked me to pray for them, wanting freedom from their struggles with sexual immorality. Transparently sharing my weaknesses had encouraged them to put their pride aside, confess their struggles, and ask for healing.

Although I had hoped my fifteen minutes of prepared remarks on pride would be powerful, what impacted the men most were twenty seconds of radical courage and vulnerability.

PRISCILLA

You may think that God using our story in the lives of others is the real evidence of our restoration. However, the miracle in our marriage is not how we minister to others but how we minister to *each other*. Many people with successful ministries have marriages and families on a road toward destruction. Merely forgiving and stopping offensive behavior isn't the victory. The victory is in learning a new way to relate to one another that changes the trajectory of the marriage, the children, and the generations to come.

> Victory is in learning a new way to relate to one another that changes the trajectory of the marriage, the children, and the generations to come.

The most significant change Phil made was that he began treating me as an equal. This may surprise you, since Phil's sexual immorality was so offensive. However, if Phil had stopped all his sinful behavior without making this fundamental change in how he treated me, our marriage would not have been rescued. The significant transformation in Phil was that he frequently asked for my opinion and listened to my point of view on spiritual matters, financial decisions, and how we parented. This shift allowed a wound from my childhood to heal: the feeling that I didn't matter.

We were also now open to revealing our weaknesses and failures, not only to each other but also to our children. In the past, we'd hidden our thoughts and feelings from each other out of fear, thinking we couldn't handle knowing each other's deep, dark secrets. We also hadn't shared with our children out of fear they would be shackled with the same problems. But once we opened up the dungeon of our lives, we found that the opposite occurred. Our transparency created real emotional intimacy between Phil and me and freed our children to share with us their frailties and fears. Vulnerability has the power to break down the prison doors of shame and create intimate, cherished relationships.

Sexually, God brought us into a garden of delights that was fertilized and cultivated by Him. The Holy Spirit became our tutor, and we willingly embraced His presence during our times of intimacy. We learned how to pull out the weeds of our pasts that threatened to choke off our sexual intimacy, and we finally began learning what it means to make and share love with one another after almost three decades of marriage.

Finally, we also learned how to receive constructive criticism from each other without being offended. Once you realize your spouse isn't your enemy and they have more invested in your healing than anyone else, you see them as your battle partner. I now know that Phil wants the best for my life, and he's willing to do whatever it takes for our relationship to succeed, including denying himself and putting me, our marriage, and our family first. He has gotten off his high horse of pride and endeavors to walk in humility. And when he begins to saddle up that horse again, we both see it and name it, and he willingly takes a step down. He's no longer the proud, arrogant man I married.

PHIL

Our story is about much more than healing from betrayal and sexual addiction. It's about how God brought us to an entirely new level of spiritual, emotional, and sexual intimacy.

One of the most significant changes in our marriage is that we now prioritize spending time with one another each morning sharing God's Word and praying together. Even after we've had an argument, this daily time brings us to a place of humility, transparency, and forgiveness. In the past, offenses took days or even weeks to get over. But now they seldom take more than twenty-four hours. We've learned how to walk in mutual forgiveness and how to help one another spot the lies of the enemy that we can so easily believe. But none of this would have been possible without seeing that God wanted us to experience spiritual intimacy with each other just like we have with Him. Spiritual intimacy is truly the fuel of our marriage.

I've also learned that there's no other person who can help me experience spiritual victory more than Priscilla. Other than God, there's no one who loves me more, who knows me better, or who has more at stake in my healing than Priscilla. She's always looking out for my good, and I can trust her with my weaknesses and failures. I've seen more victory from sharing my problems with Priscilla than I've ever seen through sharing with an army of counselors, small groups, and accountability partners. She has truly become my battle partner.

I've been amazed at how God (and Priscilla) have pursued the healing of my mind and marriage. I've discovered that I not only have to be HOT—honest, open, and transparent—to be healed, but I have to be HOT *every day* to continue benefitting from my healing. Anytime temptation opens the door to my soul, secrecy isn't far behind, ready to turn the deadbolt so nothing can get out. Every time I've allowed God's light to shine on the shadows of my life, I've seen it result in true fellowship with Priscilla and a level of emotional intimacy that assures me that what God has done is real.

PRISCILLA

Phil and I frequently comment that we're now experiencing the best days of our marriage. God resurrected a beautiful new life from the ashes of our past. Even though our early steps of transparency were scary, we now see that God used every tearful confession—not only in our lives but in the lives of those around us.

Marriage is a journey of life or death. It can lead to joy and abundance or despair and ruin. Although most people start their marriage thinking they've found Camelot, the real journey is fraught with emotions that generate both joy and pain. Couples who have been married a long time know that marriage can be savage, requiring every ounce of strength you have, and even then, marriage will prove that your own strength simply isn't enough. In the middle of our despair and weakness is where we can see that God is our only strength and Jesus is the only rock we can stand on firmly. On the rock of our salvation is where Phil and I now stand. We invite you to join us in your own savage adventure.

| Savage Questions for Reflection |

1. When have you embraced twenty seconds of radical courage and vulnerability? If you haven't, why not?

2. What story in your life will you allow God to use in the lives of others? Are you willing to be HOT and let God use your story?

3. Have you accepted Phil and Priscilla's invitation to stand with them on the rock—Jesus Christ? If not, why not? What's holding you back from putting your full trust in Him?

EPILOGUE

Most of the events in this book occurred during the first couple of years after I (Phil) came clean. Since then, Priscilla and I have had many opportunities to share our story and help struggling marriages.

One question that frequently comes up is why we felt it was appropriate to share our story with our two youngest children, Anna Hope and Becca, who were respectively only eleven and nine at that time. This wasn't a decision we took lightly. We had prayed and asked for God's direction and ultimately felt we wanted a spirit of transparency in our home going forward—impossible if we hid everything we were doing from Anna Hope and Becca. So we brought them into our story during the same time we shared with our adult children, realizing that with Anna Hope and Becca, we needed to share only age-appropriate details.

When Anna Hope and Becca were fifteen and thirteen, we had the opportunity to go through our story with them again in more detail. We asked if they wanted to write how our story had affected them. To our surprise, they both enthusiastically said yes, and they wanted their thoughts included in our book. Their stories are shared below. We're so thankful for the maturity and wisdom God has given them to see His plan for our family.

BECCA (AGE 13)

When I first heard that my dad had caused my mom to cry, I was very sad and really hurt. I was very close to my mom because I was young and Dad had to go to work most days. So when I heard that my dad had hurt my mom, I was crushed and felt a little bit angry. I remember that my parents pulled me into their office, and my dad told me what he had done to Mommy. At first, I didn't really know how to react, but I knew that he had really hurt my mom. We talked for a long time, and there were a lot of tears and some confusion on my part. They were very patient and, in a simple way, told me what had happened.

I now understand their story a lot better and know why it hurt Mommy so much. Our family is now very HOT when we talk at dinner, in the car, and just in general. Ever since my parents started doing the Savage Marriage group, my relationship with God has really blossomed. I've become more open to what God has to say to me, and I pray for the couples in my parents' group, even though I don't really know them. I'm eager to pray for and help others in a way I wasn't before, and I believe it's because I see my parents helping these people who are a mess. But my parents don't give up on them, and they try their hardest to help. I love that they're willing to put so much time into helping others.

I've learned that when I get married, I need to be HOT and vulnerable with my husband and kids. I need to tell my husband all of my faults, even going back to my childhood. I need to know that my husband and I are one body and need to work together to keep a strong Christian marriage because if we don't, our marriage could fall apart.

Overall, I'm very happy about what's happened in my parents' marriage. It has made them better parents and made us open to talking about whatever we've done, no matter what it is.

ANNA HOPE (AGE 15)

I was eleven years old when Daddy first came clean. I was so young and didn't completely understand the full picture. When Daddy explained what adultery was, in kids' terms, and how he'd hurt Mommy, I tried to make sense of it but really didn't know what was happening.

While he was talking, his tone was very gentle, and Mommy seemed sad. I could obviously tell that something was wrong. The whole conversation was awkward for me because I didn't know what to do or really what to say; I just sat there and listened. The only thing I knew for sure was that Daddy had done something bad, and it had really hurt Mommy. After a while, I began crying and asked, "Wait, are you guys getting divorced?" It then hit me. I thought, *This is real, and what if we're not together anymore?* Life would be so different.

Mommy responded quickly, "No, we are definitely not getting a divorce. We're just working through some stuff, and it's hard." I was reassured and grateful that they weren't getting a divorce. It might take some time, but our family wouldn't be ripped apart.

Daddy then asked me to forgive him. Right away, I said, "Yes, I forgive you." I had learned in church that we should forgive others because God first forgave us. Daddy was relieved, and his face lightened up. Daddy said, "Thank you," and all three of us hugged.

After Daddy confessed to the whole family, there were seasons when I thought Daddy was the bad guy because he had brought dishonor to our family. But I still knew he was my father and that he cared for me. Mommy had become less talkative and not as joyful. She was in pain and needed time to heal. I stayed strong and tried to comfort her even though I still didn't fully understand what was happening.

Time passed, and Mommy became herself again, and our life somewhat went back to normal.

Daddy went to 4 Days 2 Freedom, and Mommy went to 4 Days 2 Hope. At these weekend retreats, miracles took place, and marriages were restored. One of the key things taught at Whatever It Takes Ministries is being open, broken, and free. The teaching affected me personally because Daddy and Mommy became HOT with our family.

As an example, we had a thing called the "feelings wheel," which had many different feeling words sorted into categories—like *sad, happy, mad*, etc. If they asked me, "How was your day," instead of saying *good* or *fine*, I was encouraged to use other words to describe my feelings such as *exciting, boring, exquisite*, etc. The feelings wheel helped me understand my feelings better and become more open.

Another example was the "three bottles," which Daddy and Mommy learned from Whatever It Takes Ministries. Basically, three bottles were filled with different-colored water: red, blue, and green. The red bottle meant *actions*, the blue meant *feelings*, and the green meant *thoughts*. For example, if you punched someone in the face, your action was *punching*, your feeling was *anger*, and your thought was that they had done something you didn't like, which caused you to do what you did.

In short, we do what we do because we feel what we feel because we think what we think.

At first, I thought the three bottles were awkward to use and a bit unusual, but over time, I got used to it and became better at describing why I had done whatever I'd done.

Our family has become a lot more open with one another (which is good), and we now know what's going on in each other's lives, including why we think, feel, and act the way we do.

When I was fifteen and Becca was thirteen, four years after Daddy told us that he had hurt Mommy, they decided it was time to give us more details about what had happened to them. Since we were older, we could understand more, and they wanted to answer any questions we had. Instead of talking separately, we all talked together at the dinner table. We already knew what had happened to them, and we had forgiven Daddy and moved on; but this time, their conversation with us was more detailed, and they answered all our questions. So we had a better idea of what had happened. I got the whole picture instead of parts of it. I was glad they shared more because if they hadn't, I would have had to rely on only what I'd heard when I was eleven and what I'd gathered from hearing my parents talk about their ministry.

I realize now that when Daddy first came clean about the things he was hiding, he was walking in humility. He swallowed his pride and became vulnerable. I'm very proud of him for doing that because everybody has sinned and done things they are ashamed of. Most of the time, we never mention them and don't want anybody to know what we've done because we're prideful. We care too much about what others may say and think about us. But pride comes before the fall, and you can hide for only so long before you get caught. It's just better to be straight-up honest than wait for your sin to be exposed.

Yes, I know it's hard to be HOT, but trust me—it's worth it. It might take time, but that's okay. In fact, bravely sharing what you've done wrong causes people to have respect for you. Remember, no one is perfect. We all make mistakes. Thank God for His new mercies every morning and His never-ending and unfailing love.

Now Mommy and Daddy are leading a marriage small group at church, working on a book (the one you're reading right now), and making podcasts. My parents are now busier than before, but they're changing lives and making a difference.

At first, I was a bit selfish and thought they cared more about the people in their group than Becca and me. But I now realize that was the enemy speaking lies to me and that Daddy and Mommy do care for us. They hang out with us, do fun things with us, and take us on vacations.

I've prayed for many people in my parents' small group who are struggling in their marriages. Although I don't even know them, I've heard and seen so many miracles take place. The miracles build my faith in God and make me happy that we're making a difference in the kingdom of God.

INVITATION

It's amazing that some people who've attained tremendous worldly success have been unable to attain this one elusive goal: maintaining a lifelong, vibrant relationship with their spouse.

Being married isn't something you learn how to do; it's something that's revealed by God to couples who search for a sacred relationship with all their heart. With this in mind, we've designed small-group materials, podcasts, and other resources to provide hope and healing in your most challenging marital problems. We're confident God can use these materials to reveal how His presence, purpose, and passion can be reflected in your marriage. We invite you to take a step toward hope and freedom by joining our Savage Marriage community at SavageMarriageMinistries.com, where you can access these resources.

Also, please follow us on Facebook at Savage Marriage Ministries and Instagram (@savagemarriageministries) to stay connected with us, interact, ask questions, and be encouraged through the testimonies we share of couples who have overcome adversity in marriage.

If your marriage story has connected with our story, you may be interested in learning how you can lead a Savage Marriage small group for your church or community. We've seen many marriages changed through our curriculum, developed through our savage-marriage journey.

We'd also love to speak at your church or conference! And we enjoy spending ministry time with couples who need prayer and encouragement, either online or in person. If you're interested in learning more, please reach out to us at info@savagemarriageministries.com.

Thank you for investing in your marriage by reading our story. We pray the seeds planted through this book will germinate in your hearts and lives and help your marriage experience all the fullness God has to offer: your own savage adventure.

www.ingramcontent.com/pod-product-compliance
Lightning Source LLC
Chambersburg PA
CBHW022048020426
42335CB00012B/592